OUTDOOR
RECREATION
POLICY

Outdoor Recreation Policy

Pleasure and Preservation

EDITED BY
John D. Hutcheson, Jr.,
Francis P. Noe, AND
Robert E. Snow

Foreword by James Carroll

PREPARED UNDER THE AUSPICES OF THE POLICY STUDIES
ORGANIZATION
Stuart S. Nagel, Publications Coordinator

CONTRIBUTIONS IN POLITICAL SCIENCE, NUMBER 263

Greenwood Press
New York • Westport, Connecticut • London

790
094

Library of Congress Cataloging-in-Publication Data

Outdoor recreation policy : pleasure and preservation / edited by John
    D. Hutcheson, Jr., Francis P. Noe, and Robert E. Snow ; foreword by
    James Carroll.
        p. cm.—(Contributions in political science, ISSN 0147–1066 ;
        no. 263)
        "Prepared under the auspices of the Policy Studies Organization."
        Includes bibliographical references (p.   ) and index.
        ISBN 0–313–27522–X (lib. bdg. : alk. paper)
        1. Outdoor recreation—Government policy—United States.
    I. Hutcheson, John D.   II. Noe, Francis P.   III. Snow,
    Robert E. (Robert Ellis)   IV. Series.
    GV191.4.0868   1990
    790'.0973—dc20   90–36580

British Library Cataloguing in Publication Data is available.

Library of Congress Catalog Card Number: 90–36580
ISBN: 0–313–27522–X
ISSN: 0147–1066

First published in 1990

Greenwood Press, 88 Post Road West, Westport, CT 06881
An imprint of Greenwood Publishing Group, Inc.

Printed in the United States of America

The paper used in this book complies with the
Permanent Paper Standard issued by the National
Information Standards Organization (Z39.48–1984).

10 9 8 7 6 5 4 3 2 1

CONTENTS

FIGURES AND TABLES

FIGURES

TABLES

FOREWORD

As a political scientist in the National Park Service, I know what it feels like to be isolated. That is why it is encouraging to see this volume produced under the aegis of the Policy Studies Organization and observe it addressing many of the topics that political scientists examine: sociology, history, economics, public administration, and philosophy.

The relationship of outdoor recreation policy and political science should not come as a surprise in a world of depleted ozone, befouled beaches, and increasingly limited natural resources. If Harold Lasswell's dictum is correct—that political science is the study of who gets what, when, and how—then it is obvious that outdoor recreationists, those who make decisions affecting them, and those who study the body politic will be found on the same phone indexes for some time to come.

The cogency of political philosophy is examined in Craig W. Allin's "Agency Values and Wilderness Management" and J. Douglas Wellman's "Forestry and Outdoor Recreation Policy: The Origins and Impacts of Professional Core Values," in which they trace the antecedents of current recreation policies to fundamental philosophies.

Under Gifford Pinchot, Wellman reminds us, progressive and utilitarian core values were institutionally embedded in American forestry. Foresters believed that the application of their technical skills was producing economic benefits essential to the sustenance of American democracy. The profession came to have a limited interest in recreation and related amenities.

The rise of the environmental movement, therefore, has caused problems for foresters as they have struggled against the desire to allocate forest lands to economically nonproductive uses. Wellman attributes the Wilderness Act of 1964 largely to a distrust of the Forest Service and believes that if foresters fail to manage their areas with an understanding of American society's evolving desires, "unfavorable public opinion will relieve them of their responsibilities."

Allin ascribes the wilderness management techniques of the Forest Service and National Park Service (NPS) to their core values and historical origins. The Forest Service wedded Prussian and progressive ideals and became utilitarian rather than ecological. Early national park areas, such as Yellowstone and Yosemite, were administered by military calvary and engineers. Hence the author finds NPS a relatively eager wilderness manager, aggressively using law enforcement and engineering strategies. Recreationists on parklands may encounter a welter of regulations as NPS strives to balance the conflicting mandates of preservation versus use, given official sanction when Congress created the agency in 1916.

This fundamental conflict has weakened NPS politically—it generally being conceded that the Forest Service is more influential on Capitol Hill—and the predicament may become even more acute for NPS in a nation growing more populous and industrial. "As is typical with an expanding economy, the prospect for amiable mediation between production and recreational consumption of limited resources appears disquieting," says Michael Heiman in "Recreation Policy and the Ideology of Nature in California's Coastal Zone."

The flexibility of the Corps of Engineers, described by William J. Hansen in "The Changing Federal Role in the Provision of Outdoor Recreation Opportunities: A Perspective from the U.S. Army Corps of Engineers," is one form of accommodation. In response to rising demand, the corps began providing highly developed recreation areas, but it has since reverted to a policy of reduced involvement in a climate of budgetary constraints.

If some bureaucracies are adroit at flowing with the political winds, others take a more ostrich-like approach and attempt to avoid issues. As Dale J. Blahna and Susan Yonts-Shepard point out in "Preservation or Use? Confronting Public Issues in Forest Planning and Decision Making," administrators resist having certain problems highlighted, but other issues may be neglected because of poor public input collection.

Blahna and Yonts-Shepard present a convincing analysis of the pitfalls an agency can encounter, in this case the Forest Service, even when issues are not being ignored. They caution against a vote-counting approach to decision making because some interested publics may not have been represented or comments may be grouped into categories of management concerns that are too broad. Furthermore, they lament the tendency for issues to become sanitized as they move through echelons.

Dennis L. Soden's discussion ("Developmental Pressures on Recreation Areas: Public Decision Making as a 'Galvanizing' Effect Among Local Citizenry") of public choice theory—that actors pursue strategies to maximize their interests—is apropos here because he reminds us that some actors carry more weight than others and, after all, self-interest often is difficult to determine, especially where the results of action cannot be measured in monetary terms.

Self-interest, in fact, is so basic a tenet that it is surprising that recreation policy makers and even Office of Management and Budget (OMB) directors (see Lloyd G. Nigro and William D. Richardson's "Founding Principles and Contemporary Public Policy: The Case of the Office of Management and Budget and the Sport Fishing Restoration Program") often appear to overlook it. The rational calculation of benefits and costs is a human trait taken for granted by economists, who assume that the task of the administrator is to tap and channel it. Constituency support for programs, Nigro and Richardson remind us, depends on the perception that funds collected will not be made available to noncontributors (free riders) or other programs.

In "The Economic Value of Wilderness: A Critical Assessment," Jerry W. Calvert and Patrick Jobes emphasize that cost-benefit analyses have a hypnotic effect on policy makers, but the authors believe these calculations are limited by the inability to anticipate the variables that will be important for the future. Needed are data sensitive to the economic values associated with wilderness preservation. Calvert and Jobes rule out the possibility that an economic measure can be assigned to the aesthetic value of wilderness, but they believe any planning model should incorporate economic as well as cultural, scientific, and aesthetic merits. They envision a continuing role for government because "private enterprise cannot be trusted to protect and preserve what is precious."

In "Private Management of Public Recreation: Is It Cost-Effective?" Steven E. Daniels tests the hypothesis that private management of public campgrounds is more cost effective than traditional management by public employees and declares his advocacy of private management of developed camping.

Robert H. Patrick and Stephen B. Lovejoy in "Rationing the Congested Recreational Facility: Market Versus Political Instruments" promote the use of the market, in particular time-of-use congestion fees, rather than political instruments, in rationing scarce recreation resources. "Societal welfare can be improved by allowing access to those who value the amenity more highly," they write.

On the other hand, V. Kerry Smith in "Benefit Analysis and Recreation Policy" believes that determining recreation policy on an individual's perceived willingness to pay to participate is inadequate because personal valuations can be composites reflecting use, prospects for future use, and an appreciation for the continued existence of certain resources regardless of any pattern of use. William R. Mangun and John B. Loomis in "Financing Outdoor Recreation in the United States" also note that some nonusers derive satisfaction from knowing that wilderness, parks, and recreation areas exist, and they stress that a mixture of funding sources is needed to optimize efficiency and equity.

In "Wild Land Recreation and Resource Impacts: A Pleasure–Policy Dilemma," William E. Hammitt states that the best policy ultimately will maximize effectiveness and minimize costs, but he decries the tendency of agencies to select management techniques that are familiar or administratively expedient but not ideally suited to the situation at hand. The challenge is to reach a balance, for the ecologist must protect an area while the recreationist must use it.

The outdoor recreation resources matrix described by Barbara A. Knuth in "Balancing Competing Interests to Achieve Policy Goals: A Conceptual Framework" and the goal programming model advocated by James L. Regens and Jackie Sellers in "Goal Programming Applications for Outdoor Recreation Policy" offer potentially helpful policy-making methodologies. Without a conceptualization of the diverse interests encompassed by different recreation philosophies, Knuth reminds us, outdoor recreation providers cannot be pure brokers and cannot ensure an explicit consideration of all important interests and consequences of alternative management policies. Regens and Sellers believe that goal programming can be useful in dealing with multiple objectives in outdoor recreation administration and enhancing awareness of the possibilities and limitations of policies.

In "Resources Policy and Outdoor Recreation," Hobson Bryan and Nicholas Taylor stress that policy development should be sensitive to the costs of "foregone futures." They recognize that the anticipatory approach implies agreement on what is good and what is bad. Further, they lament the lack of policy frameworks and decry the vagueness of values and ad hoc reactions to crises that generally prevail in regulatory agencies.

Bryan and Taylor point out that biological and thermodynamic boundaries determine resource availability, but social factors determine in what way, shape, or form a resource is delivered—if it is delivered. They cite attempts to locate hazardous waste repositories as examples of "good science" often unaccompanied by social acceptance. Hence they favor an integrated perspective and participatory approach in seeking solutions to resource problems.

Like Knuth, who believes that her matrix enables managers to be sure that all relevant concerns and interactions are considered, Zachary A. Smith focuses on the need for interaction in "Coping with Cutbacks in Park and Recreation Administration: Priorities, Innovation, and Mobilizing Interest Groups." Smith emphasizes the importance of cultivating public and outside organizations for their political and budgetary support, especially in a period of economic constraints. He finds, however, that outside groups are not directly involved in budgetary decisions for the overwhelming majority of state park directors he studied. "The development of relationships with interest groups has not been seen by many public managers to be as crucial to agency health as has development of relations with legislators," he writes.

Knuth points out that her matrix is useful for research purposes also, enabling the researcher to look for knowledge gaps in any of the sixteen cells. Political scientist Aaron Wildavsky reminds us that data and information are not knowledge without analysis, and in some cases action.

Joseph T. O'Leary, Francis A. McGuire, and F. D. Dottavio, authors of

"Recreation Policy and Planning Options with Nationwide Recreation Survey Data," remark that a significant problem with most government agencies is the lack of time to study data in detail. There are "never agendas outlined for more condensed or detailed reports, subtopic exploration, specific policy issues or questions, or more sophisticated analysis to test hypotheses and answer questions in a more comprehensive and succinct manner," they write. They believe that secondary analysis possibly by academics must be explored if policy and planning problems are to be addressed in the short run.

Francis P. Noe, Robert E. Snow, and Gary Hampe present a model they describe as a first attempt to overtly include values in the evaluation of outdoor recreation policy in their "Deriving National Outdoor Recreation Policy from a Limiting Demand Participation Model." While they admit that outdoor recreation has received little attention by policy analysts because it "obviously lacks the harsh sting of pressing social problems associated with crime, health care, aging, and other issues which are more disruptive to institutions and individuals," they make a case for outdoor recreations significance by showing that it reinforces the social values of society.

This introduction can provide only the briefest description of the contents of a work of this nature, and some of the authors may be surprised that I have highlighted some of their findings and remarks and omitted others. My apologies.

Since the book contains nineteen chapters drawn from disparate scholars located throughout campuses and in several public and private institutions, this was an inevitable dilemma for a summarizer and synthesizer. I hope that the multidisciplinary character of the contents will be recognized by the reader, and that he or she gains in the appreciation and understanding of the growing need to address issues and seek solutions from a broad perspective.

Outdoor recreation issues may be relatively neglected in our national political discourse, but they are not trivial and never will be on our shrunken planet.

The questions of who plays and who pays are fundamental ones—it would be nice to have Plato and Aristotle around to address them—but short of being able to recall the ancient philosophers to help us, I think this collection provides a good start for the scholar, student, or interested citizen who wants to see these environmental and recreational concerns addressed in a refreshingly new and undelimited approach.

James Carroll
Chief Social Scientist
National Park Service

PREFACE

This book organizes different and sometimes conflicting views on outdoor recreation. The authors' diverse training brings fresh insight into some of the most fundamental policy issues that have captured the attention of public decision makers and politicians about outdoor recreation. The issues are real but the subject is benign. The subject of outdoor recreation falls low on the list of public priorities that is understandably preoccupied with more malign topics. These problems so often threaten the very fabric of society that we often fool ourselves into accepting any opportunities for recreation as free of controversy. While we may try to shield ourselves from the serious side of recreation, there are issues confronting the public sector charged with delivering these services. The views organized in this volume focus on the serious questions of dealing with policies on how to balance pleasure and preservation.

How we physically relate to the natural environment results in unmistakable consequences. When we act in the context of social and cultural beliefs, man-made impacts are left behind. Many of these impacts are serious and degrade the environment, while others detract from the quality of an experience. We also derive social benefits from outdoor recreation. Many of these activities provide reinforcement for serious values learned in society. Competition, risk taking, and seeking out personal challenges, for example, result in recreation that is not all "fun" and escapism. The methods used to finance outdoor recreation have left in their wake some sobering and serious debates about who plays and who pays. If one were to accept simply the demands of the public and fulfill their preferences, one would again find serious concern about how these expressed needs are measured. Finally, the complex bureaucracies and management techniques available and invented by man periodically come under serious reconsideration and the viability of institutions in the service of outdoor recreation is not immune from being called into question. These are all issues and concerns evaluated by the contributing authors who have endeavored to bring their collective expertise to bear on these issues in today's changing world.

This book includes chapters by some of the leading analysts in outdoor recreation research. Experts in the fields of natural resource management, geography, economics, political science, forestry, and leisure sociology address current issues in outdoor recreation policy. The underlying themes of all chapters are the preservation/use dilemma inherent in outdoor recreation policy and the management of natural resources. Extremely comprehensive and current, the volume focuses on the economic, social, attitudinal, and demographic considerations pertinent in today's outdoor recreation policy formulation.

The nineteen chapters included in this book are divided into six parts. The authors of Part I, "Social and Physical Issues in Outdoor Recreation Policy," define some of the most salient public policy issues in the field of outdoor recreation. Part I defines the dimensions of the preservation/use dilemma as well as key concepts in outdoor recreation research. The next two parts focus on the measurement of the benefits of recreational resources and the financing of maintenance and management of natural resource areas. Part IV includes chapters on the assessment of public preferences and the outdoor recreation demands/needs of various constituencies. The fifth section of the book includes chapters on federal agencies' approaches to the implementation of recreation resource policies. The final section includes chapters describing management techniques that may be utilized in attempting to balance the demands of preservation and use. Accessible to a wide audience, the book makes valuable reading for policy makers, administrators, and scholars in the areas of recreation and natural resources.

The editors of this volume are indebted to the authors of each chapter for their insights and expertise, as well as their patience. Additionally, we appreciate the editorial assistance of Regina Brandt and the cooperation and sponsorship of the National Park Service, the Policies Studies Organization, and the Center for Public and Urban Research at Georgia State University. However, statements contained herein do not constitute Park Service policy or any official position of any of the sponsoring or cooperating agencies.

Francis P. Noe
John D. Hutcheson, Jr.
Robert E. Snow

Part I

Social and Physical Issues in Outdoor Recreation Policy

1.

RESOURCE POLICY AND OUTDOOR RECREATION

Hobson Bryan and Nicholas Taylor

Management decisions for the allocation of outdoor recreation and other resources are seldom guided by policy frameworks. Decisions are typically made in a reactive, ad hoc manner in reaction to various pressures from groups competing for the same resource or lobbying for different management of a particular resource. Decisions may result from the hue and cry of various groups saying "do something" in response to a controversial issue—"We are losing our river to that dam!" They may result from protracted power struggles over allocations among competing interests—"The timber beasts have won, now they will cut everything in sight." Or they may be the result of implicit or hidden value stances adopted long before—"I never have been able to understand why those environmentalists want to lock this land up for a few people to play in the wilderness when the oil and gas potential is so high here!" Such decisions often serve as cornerstones for an array of other positions and take the form of an umbrella of policy—"On numerous occasions this administration has reaffirmed our commitment to the full development of our energy potential!"

What is needed is a broad level resource policy, an explicit statement of resource priorities concerning who uses the resources, what form the use takes, and how conflicts over allocation should be resolved. This policy would encompass outdoor recreation issues, as well as energy and other development options.

There are many examples illustrating the ill consequences of not having an explicit recreation resource policy. Issues frequently transcend the recreation arena but apply to the broader need for a natural resource policy in general. Wilderness protection is a classic issue. Different governmental agencies, and even segments within these agencies, have various agendas. On one side, an agency vigorously advocates timber and minerals extraction to supply the country's building and energy needs. On the other side, another agency advocates with equal vigor to set aside lands in question for wilderness protection. Each administrative unit has a policy governed by its particular mandate. A national resource policy, one that is subject to political party platform debate, should be part of the nation's agenda to determine priorities and decide how conflicts will be resolved before they occur. For example, "The country will give priority to preserving unique and significant natural areas, while maintaining the option of mineral and other commodity exploration and extraction in a manner of minimum adverse impact."

FROM REACTION TO ANTICIPATION

A number of broad assumptions guide the approach to formulation of an outdoor recreation resource policy. These assumptions and the more explicit statement of concepts to follow apply to natural resource/environmental issues in general with specific applications to the outdoor recreation arena.

Anticipating the Future

The first assumption underlying the need-for-a-policy call is that effective planning for and utilization of natural resources requires a clear visualization of values and goals. This visualization might insure, for example, that, all other things being equal, the widest possible array of resource options is maintained. In other words, the development of resource-based policy should be sensitive to the costs of foregone futures. Because use of the resource as it once was is usually impossible once major resource development decisions have been made, explicit recognition of foregone futures should be a part of the decision process.

One of the best illustrations of foregone futures is dam construction for hydroelectric, flood control, and other water storage purposes. Stream or river-based activities such as those of anadromous and other types of recreational fisheries have been lost, as have canoeing, kayaking, and rafting. Large tracts of agriculturally rich land, wildlife-abundant bottomlands, and other valuable real estate have also been inundated. While the loss of these options is compensated for in varying degrees by new uses (electric power generation, lake recreational activities), a return to other uses is virtually impossible. Ironically, the beauty and uniqueness of free stream and river resources in the face of decreasing supply around the world has reached the point that the direct economic benefits accrued from such resources now usually exceed the value of impoundment. In New Zealand and in Tasmania, its Australian island neighbor, dam construction continues to the extent that these countries must shop for uses for excess electricity production. Meanwhile, a large number of overseas tourists go there looking for stream and river recreational opportunities.

Another illustration of the foregone futures issue is the failure to anticipate the rise in land values on which outdoor recreation opportunities may be based. Twenty years ago fishermen in Montana were enjoying fly fishing on abundant spring-fed streams dotting the vast agricultural valleys. Most of the water resources were on private land (while land at higher elevations is publicly owned, the water-based recreational opportunities are located in the valleys). Fly fishermen enjoyed fishing for large trout in small, clear waters. Angling specialists from as far away as Great Britain, famed for its chalk streams and big fish, made annual pilgrimages to the spring-fed streams of Montana and other western states because they considered those streams superior to their own.

Sportsmen began to recognize the value of these resources as the access to private lands necessary to fish these waters became increasingly more difficult to obtain. Land owners began responding negatively to the nuisance of increased requests to cross their land. Ranchers sometimes resented the outcry of some sportsmen who pointed accusing fingers at ranchers whose cattle eroded stream banks and whose irrigation demands reduced the water flow, resulting in other stream degradation problems. State officials in the West, however, were slow to respond to the conflict and slow to recognize the value of the spring-fed stream as a resource. A number of years later, when states finally began to purchase easements to such water, much of the water had already been amassed by wealthy individuals and sportsmen's groups for their private use, or land values had become so high that it was impractical to purchase easements. Lack of recognition and anticipation of the worth of these resources created another foregone future.

A review of the history of wilderness and parkland values around the world would reveal a constant tendency to undervalue or fail to anticipate future values of wilderness and park areas. The St. John's National Park near St. Thomas, U.S. Virgin Islands, is an example of partial recognition; yet, again there was insufficient vision to purchase the entire island. This was during a time that most thought of these islands as tropic wastelands, however beautiful they may have been. Some feel that the numerous private enterprises that have surrounded the park and even dotted its interior are obtrusive encroachments on what could have been an island national park paradise.

A proactive stance with regard to recreation resources implies the recognition and use of data bases chronicling past experiences to derive a model of why different futures develop. For example, if it can be shown that the social and eventual economic value of wilderness preservation will soon exceed resource extraction values, then that case should be made. There should be an advocacy of wilderness preservation before the costs of acquisition are too high.

Application of Present Value to Future Design

A second assumption is that recreation resource policy should take into account what was desired in the past and is desired in present experience, and incorporate these into future plans. The design of dams and what happens to their tail waters is an apt illustration. In some rivers in the western part of the United States, water will not support a trout fishery due to high temperatures, siltation, and irregular flows. (A good case can be made that such rivers should be among the first to be dammed for hydroelectric and other purposes, not streams already containing thriving cold water fisheries.) The social and economic benefits of cold water fisheries recreation are possible by applying present value to future design. A dam or series of dams can be designed to create tail-water fisheries, streams with relatively constant and cool temperatures, low gradient, and turbidity. The secondary dam on the Big Horn River in Montana created just such conditions (and an outstanding fishery). At a different level, if it is known that different groups of sportsmen value different attributes of the outdoor experience depending on their degree of involvement in this sport (see the specialization discussion to follow), then planners should incorporate elements of these preferences in their management and design of different resources. In fact, this principle is recognized quite explicitly in some sports. Operators of ski resorts have color coded ski slopes labeled according to their level of difficulty, alerting skiers to the type of conditions they will face.

Fish and game managers are incorporating present and past value into future design when managing fish and game stocks. There is increasing recognition of the importance of incorporating the value of trophy fishing and hunting into management plans, whether preference is for lakes that require all but the largest fish be returned to the water or to hunting areas managed to produce large animals and big racks. It is important to apply the principles underlying what is valued to future situations rather than simply reacting to lost opportunities or resources.

Development of Decision Criteria

An anticipatory approach to resource management implies above all that there is some agreed upon standard or set of criteria governing judgments about what is good and what is bad. Policy should be predicated on clearly stated assumptions of value, and these assumptions should be guided by specific human and ecological principles. Yet value vagueness typically prevails. Such vagueness may be the result of intentional disguise (a developer passing on the hidden costs to a community), unexplored assumptions (belief that bigger is always better or that development is always preferable to nondevelopment), or lack of consensus over goals (recreation resources geared to the greatest number versus resources tailored to meet the needs of certain constituencies). The best illustration of the value vagueness of decision criteria is in large-scale dam construction. Some dam opponents assert that just as a mountain climber when asked why he would climb a difficult and dangerous peak would say "because it is there," an engineer would say that he builds a dam "because he can." Beyond the value of practicing technology for technology's sake, construction businesses prosper, agricultural interests benefit (if the water is to be used for irrigation) or lose (if their farms are to be flooded), and politicians link their rise (or fall) to high energy use technology.

The development and review of decision criteria explicates the values and premises of decision makers. The process need not put the formulators in jeopardy if the criteria are made available for public debate and possible modification. But the public must be assumed to be good faith bargainers in the decision-making process. Avoiding the public arena and the development of explicit criteria puts the decision process at risk. Unanticipated results of actions are more likely to occur when specific values and assumptions are not scrutinized, and without such public scrutiny, those entities with the most political power are more likely to prevail, sometimes to the detriment of the public welfare.

Not only must values or decision criteria be specific, they must be incorporated into a natural resource policy for outdoor recreation. This policy would clearly state assumptions of value, and these assumptions would be guided by specific human and ecological principles. The recent adoptions of national fishery policy statements in New Zealand, Canada, and the United States are examples of such activities.

An Integrated Approach

An outdoor recreation resource policy must be formulated using an integrated approach. The human-ecological perspective can be used as a guide to develop such a policy. That dynamic interactions exist between physical, biological, and social systems is not new to many cultural anthropologists, geographers, environmental sociologists, or some recreation researchers. It has not been elaborated very well, however, as an overall perspective for natural resource policy and management. As Rambo and Sajise (1984) suggest:

This perspective is distinguished from other conceptual frameworks by a number of major features: (1) it employs a systems viewpoint on both human society and nature, and (2) it describes both the internal behavior of ecosystems and social systems and their interactions with each other in terms of flows or transfers of energy, materials, and information. It is, moreover, concerned with understanding (3) the organization of systems into networks and hierarchies, and (4) the dynamics of systems change. (p. 2)

The most important qualifier of an integrated framework for natural resource policy is that any management scheme must operate within the bounds of the resources available. Thus, the concepts of resource sustainability and renewability and thermal efficiency are excellent criteria on the biological/physical side of the resource equation. Abundant literature is available to make this point; yet the essence is well captured by the analogy of the lack of wisdom in burning one's furniture (and ultimately, one's house) to keep warm. People who have to do this obviously are guilty of poor planning (they did not cut enough wood for the winter fires) and/or poor resource management practices (they cut all the wood the winter before and did not plant any trees for replacement). The poor planning analogy can be carried further: they realized that they were going to run out of wood (and that replanting would not solve their problems, because the trees would not grow back fast enough) and would need some kind of alternative energy source, but they were going to rely on market forces for incentives to develop new energy technology. The problem is that these forces did not come into play until the scarcity level (no more wood to burn) had been reached.

It is ironic that it is precisely during times of scarce resources—and usually under difficult economic conditions—that such arguments (burning one's furniture) prevail, but in the guise of "not locking up the resources," "people have to have jobs," "what is all this social bunk," "let's look at the economics of the situation," etc. During such times, and posed as conservative philosophies, one hears many laments about the costs of pollution control, and the bureaucratic and paper work burden of undertaking those long, costly environmental impact assessments. One also hears about the sanctity of market forces and the marketplace. It is equally ironic that it is during these times that the most careful, integrated analyses of long-term social/biological consequences need to be undertaken.

During periods of resource scarcity and economic difficulty, the more intangible and difficult to quantify elements in the human arena tend to be left out of analyses. A detailed and long-term view needs to be taken of land-use change, technological change, and institutional change. The key to natural resource policy and the management of that policy lies in the conceptualizing of resource priorities so that the physical or biological dimensions are integrated with the social dimensions. The biological and thermodynamic boundaries determine resource availability, but the social factors determine in what way, shape, or form the resource is delivered—and if it is delivered.

An integrated perspective should apply to all resource management—whether to water, minerals, forests, soils, or the often conflicting uses of these resources for recreational and other purposes (fishing and irrigation, mining and agriculture, timber and agriculture, etc.). Resources should be maximized within a context that recognizes and accommodates the wishes and needs of different public and private constituencies.

A Participatory Process

Perhaps one of the more controversial assumptions underlying the call for a recreation resource policy is that scientists involved in natural resource management must serve in advocacy roles. If they are to work with people to visualize and create futures as a basis for resource policy, then choices must be made about what is desirable and undesirable. Natural resource managers must openly determine values and adopt stances based on resource development consequences determined during prior research.

It is probably unwise and perhaps impossible to go much beyond general statements of value because as the level of specificity increases, so does the probability of disagreement and unresolvable conflict. One may be able to advocate and defend such value stances in resource use and development as participatory democracy, equality of opportunity, community stability and values, open information, or the value of preserving wilderness resources. But it is not so easy for involved parties to agree on the extent of participation in decisions, the issue of how to implement the equality of opportunity, which community values come before others, and whether certain areas hold wilderness attributes. These decisions are usually made through the political process.

A participatory, proactive approach for formulating resource policy emphasizes consultation and resolution of potential conflicts in the early stages of planning and decision making. The process helps to mobilize communities and interest groups to participate in change, usually through techniques of information exchange and issue-oriented research methods. This technique is usually very cost effective for it brings all participants in the decision together early in the process to deal with the resolution of distributions of costs and benefits. This type of process is now being promoted in New Zealand as the preferable basis for planning and assessing cases of rapid social change (Conland, 1985).

An important corollary of the participatory approach is that scientists must be prepared to deal with various entities involved in resource decisions on an equal footing. Just as officials in the policy arena cannot effectively implement decisions from a top-down perspective that ignores public preferences and concerns, scientists cannot afford to adopt the attitude that their findings and interpretations can automatically dictate public policy. This view of the decision-making process is predicated on the assumption that all constituencies have vital information and perspectives to offer in resource decisions and that they actually seek resolution of conflicting issues.

At the most general level of resource policy, the issue of hazardous waste repository siting is an example of good science being pursued with little citizen consultation. The rapid polarization of views bearing on this issue has prevented participatory decision making. So while geologists may have done painstaking work to determine areas that are geologically the safest for burying hazardous waste, the public is now extremely negative about siting such repositories anywhere, and public officials have had to use political clout on siting issues. The result is that not only has the best science not been followed, but people remain unconvinced of the wisdom of having repositories anywhere in their proximity.

Similar examples are found in the outdoor recreation area. Reactive policy has occurred during the heat of battle between recreational and commercial fishers of red fish on the Gulf Coast. Timber interests battle wilderness advocates in Alabama over the issue of the expansion of the Sipsey Wilderness Area. Cross-country skiers battle snowmobilers. Homeowners who value the peace and tranquility of their lake-side settings battle with tournament bass fishermen who enjoy the challenge and competition of their sport as they race around in their high-powered bass boats. Development of policies to accommodate people with different perspectives and interests will rely on all parties negotiating to determine a way to meet most people's needs, or providing a clear rationale if some people's wishes cannot be accorded.

On a cautionary note, an informed and involved public is a vital part of any natural resource policy, but the literal counting (i.e., polling) of public opinion to formulate policy is a misconception about both policy and the democratic process. Policy should be formulated on the basis of clearly enunciated values and principles and subjected to public comment and discussion. Policy, in fact, should be a matter of debate in the political arena. However, the values and principles underlying the policy must be stated broadly enough to exceed local or parochial interests; they should be universal in nature. In fact, the test of a strong policy is being able to implement it when it conflicts with public opinion for the good of the principle. Thus, if a nation has a recreation resource policy that places high priority on the uniqueness of wilderness and its preservation, this priority can be weighed against demands for mining coal reserves for energy development.

PRINCIPLES OF A NATURAL RESOURCE POLICY FOR OUTDOOR RECREATION

A natural resource policy for outdoor recreation could be built around a number of principles firmly established in the outdoor recreation literature during the past fifteen years. These principles should be linked to build a conceptual framework of policy. While the following illustrations are socially driven, it is possible to envisage their use by all participants in an integrated approach, regardless of disciplinary background, in the same way that the useful principles of thermodynamics or sustainability are derived from other sciences. These principles do not exclude the use of more traditional social science concepts as part of the approach. Of course, a natural resource policy cannot be considered as separate from either social or economic policy. The principles outlined are at an early stage in conceptualization; there is room to improve or refine them, and to add further ones. In fact, this is a highly productive area for further work.

Carrying Capacity

The term *carrying capacity* has its origins in the physical/biological literature. In fact, concern was expressed as early as 1929 about the effects of higher visitor use·on vegetation in national parks (Verberg, 1975). "Carrying capacity·can be expressed quantitatively as the number of us, living in a given manner, which a given environment can support indefinitely" (Catton, 1982, p. 4). The term *social carrying capacity* "introduces a human perceptual component; it denotes the level of use at which individual user satisfaction begins to decline due to the presence of others" (Bryan, 1983, p. 17). The latter term was developed to

apply to the effect of encountering others on people's satisfaction during recreational experiences. Both concepts lay the groundwork for the first principle:
*resource development should not exceed a point whereby the biological or social
carrying capacities of that resource (or the area affected by the development)
are exceeded.*

Thus, this principle points to dual concerns. First the amount and type of use
given a resource must not impair the environment's future suitability for accommodating that use over time (Catton, 1982, pp. 272–273). Of course, the concept
of sustainability as it refers to the resource itself dictates that the exploitation of
a given resource should not deplete that resource, or if the resource is not
renewable, then alternative resource policies must be in place. Second, human
perceptions and expectations are important components in the equation. In other
words, the physical carrying capacity of a resource sets the limits as far as
sustainable use is concerned, but the social carrying capacity sets the limits for
human satisfaction. These are independent concepts—physical carrying capacity
may exceed social carrying capacity and vice versa. An integrated approach to
natural resource would start with physical carrying capacity as the basic limit
set to sustain a resource and then place further limitations on resource use to
meet human expectations and satisfactions.

For example, in wilderness backcountry use concerns about the physical environment might include limiting trail use to reduce erosion or limiting off-trail
use to minimize damage to flora and fauna. With these limits, people's satisfactions with or perceptions of the wilderness experience might further restrict
trail use. Shelby and Nielson's (1975) findings regarding perceptions of crowding
on Colorado River float trips illustrate the importance of human perception in
this regard. Managers generally recognize these principles and employ a variety
of techniques to limit use of outdoor recreation resources, such as using reser-
vation systems for visiting national parks, limiting the number of wilderness
camping permits, and employing size restrictions on fish not only to enhance
the fishery resource, but to discourage certain segments of the public from
overusing some waters.

Multiple Satisfaction

The notion of social carrying capacity denotes people's expectations and perceptions of resource use that often differ from the availability or sustainability
of a resource. Studies of social carrying capacity have revealed, however, that
the relationship between perceptions of scarcity (or crowding when reference is
to use of recreation resources) is not always a direct and simple one. Further
exploration revealed that expectations regarding resource use vary across different
individuals (Bryan, 1982).

Thus, there are different needs and motivations for resource use, and resources
can be used for a variety of purposes (Hendee, 1974). The use of one resource
may completely preclude the use of another, as in the case of large-scale strip

mining for coal in an area of agriculturally rich land or, pertaining to recreation, the damming of a river for hydroelectric power precluding the river's use for its free-flowing characteristics. The use of a resource in a certain way may hinder or reduce the same resource's use in another way, as the case of single-crop timber production to the detriment of a biologically diverse base for game production (for hunting). Varying degrees of use for a single resource may also affect the quality of the usage for other purposes, as in the case of dewatering a river for irrigation to the detriment of its fishery. Thus, different resources have different attributes for different uses and users.

These conclusions lead to the second principle: *a system of resource-use priorities should be developed that reflects that different groups of people derive multiple satisfactions from the same resource or from different resources having conflicting uses.*

The concepts of carrying capacity, multiple satisfaction, and conflicting resource demands are obvious, lie at the core of resource conflicts and, of course, provide an intellectual impetus for developing a natural resource policy.

Specialization

The specialization concept was first developed to apply specifically to outdoor recreation management from the point of view of the user (Bryan, 1977; 1979) but finds ready application to understanding and managing conflicts within any resource context (Bryan, 1982). The key premise is that a continuum of use preferences and orientations is derived for any resource ranging from the general to the specific. As use becomes more specialized, it becomes more closely linked to the specific properties of the resource.

The specialization concept is particularly well grounded in social and behavioral science theory and has been explored in a number of research settings. But what is most significant for purposes here are the implications of the concept as part of a recreation resource policy. First, recreational and sport categories cannot be considered homogeneous. Rather, sportsmen's groups represent a variety of preferences and orientations to the activity. This variety of orientations and preferences needs to be recognized in any sound management framework. Second, once recreationists have been divided into specialization subgroups, it should be recognized that at the lower ends of the continuum it is likely that these activities can be more substitutable than for those individuals who fall at the higher end of the continuum. The preferences and orientations of those in the high specialization end are very specific and usually strongly held. They require rather exact settings and conditions for fulfillment in their sport and are not likely to be satisfied in the attempted substitution of other activities that do not hold the same characteristics.

The specialization concept can be inverted from its recreational and behavioral context and applied to resource use in general. For example, a valley can be flooded to serve the uses of a dam, used to grow crops, used for recreation, or used as space for sidewalks, parking lots, airports, and towns. In fact, some of the more classic clashes of usage occur over land. The application of the specialization dimension implies recognition not only that the same land area may be put to a variety of usages but that motivations for these uses as well can be arranged on a continuum from the general to the more specialized.

At the general end of usage would be land for space, simply that there is sufficient room in which to locate some kind of human activity. A bit more specialized use would be that this space is located proximate to some feature or activity that makes the use of the space more convenient than other spaces (e.g., the land lies along a large river that can serve as a transportation corridor). Still more specialized use would be that the land has some kind of attribute or function that is not found in abundance nearby (the land along the river is especially fertile). There may be other attributes as well that point the way toward specialized use (the area is characterized by a warm, dry, sunny, climate).

The third principle is that *first priorities of resource development and usage should go to people requiring the most specialized attributes of a resource and wanting to use it in the most specialized manner*. Resources should be used first and foremost for attributes not found elsewhere (or not found in abundance elsewhere). Other uses can be shifted to resources having more generalized characteristics. For example, use fertile land for farming; build housing developments on infertile land and use fertile stream resources for fishing, canoeing, and kayaking; use less fertile stream resources for hydroelectric impoundments and lake-based recreation activities.

Substitutability

A corollary to the specialization principle is that potential resource users may satisfy their needs (or wants) by being offered alternative resources, depending upon how specific their requirements are. In other words, those who have less specialized demands can be sent elsewhere to fulfill those requirements. Wilderness hikers may have very specialized requirements for the enjoyment of their sport—desiring a demanding trail with few amenities and seeing few others along the way (a low social carrying capacity attribute). There must be the peace and solitude of a wilderness-like setting. The likely resource for such pursuits is the high country of mountains and alpine meadows. Conflicts between different types of uses often occur when individuals with more general motivations have sought out these same high country areas—perhaps for picnics and other family or social outings or because of the attractions of fishing well-stocked lakes in these meadows. Managers have realized that less specialized recreationists could be offered substitute experiences and still be satisfied. Picnic areas and well-stocked lakes could be offered in nonwilderness settings, leaving the solitude and undisturbed beauty of the wilderness to the trampers.

The fourth principle is that *those who have less specific motivations for the use of a particular resource should be the first candidates offered substitute resource opportunities*. This principle has a number of implications for land use and is closely linked to the foregone futures concept. Resources should be managed primarily for people with the most specific motivations for using a particular resource. Motivational specificity is the guiding principle for substitutability. People with more general motivations for using a resource are sent elsewhere. With regard to land use, the idea of specificity translates into the concept of uniqueness, with a slight shift in emphasis.

The fifth principle is, *all other things being equal, that resources should be managed to protect unique qualities*. The many possible examples all involve some assessment of value and stem from human perceptions that differ from person to person. They all have some contextual basis in terms of extent of similar resources available in a given geographic region. Examples include priority of preservation of free-flowing streams and rivers over impoundments, wilderness areas and ecological diversity over single-use forests, areas of exceptional geological significance and areas of great natural beauty over management practices that would alter these qualities. In practice, such areas tend to be preserved if they are particularly exceptional—our national parks and monuments and numerous wilderness areas. Where this fifth principle becomes especially important is in reference to resources that at present do not seem to possess these exceptional characteristics. These are the marginally unique areas that will stand out more in the future in the context of increasing population pressure on available areas. Battles over these kinds of resources are already being fought in the East over the proposed Sipsey Wilderness expansion, the ill-fated proposal of the Cahaba River for inclusion in the National Scenic Rivers system, and over preservation of coastal lands. These areas have become more unique over time as increasing population pressures and increasing use have reduced or heavily strained existing resources.

This points to a sixth principle of a proposed resource policy: *assessments of resource values for outdoor recreation should be made in terms of future value rather than present value*. This is particularly true when considering land with such basic attributes as very low population density, mountainous terrain, streams, rivers, lakes, seashores, unusual geologic/biologic characteristics (scenic canyons, redwood trees), or unusual fish and game populations. Value becomes even more escalated if these areas happen to be relatively close to population centers. As these resources become more scarce in the face of increasing pressure and competition for other uses, such remote wilderness areas as in Alaska will have even more meaning and value as well.

CONCLUSION

Natural resources of energy, land, and water are becoming increasingly difficult to manage, preserve, or allocate. As stock resources are diminished and sustainable resources are competed for with increased vigor, the stakes involved become greater. As people in society become increasingly concerned with the allocation and use of natural resources, it will be necessary for both scientists and managers to turn from a reactive to a more proactive mode.

The proactive approach involves planning, where the existing data base is used to develop and test models of how and why particular futures develop. To do this work, social scientists need to be more explicit about the values that they are promoting and applying in their futures designs and provide a more specific basis for establishing decision criteria. Furthermore, social scientists need to learn to work more effectively with a variety of social groups in order to help them to participate in the process of formulating resource policy. Consultation and information exchange may even entail direct statements of advocacy based on explicit value stances.

Thus, an integrated framework for the development of a natural resource policy is advocated. The framework needs to be based on sets of principles that should reflect that every resource has both biological and social carrying capacities and that the biological carrying capacity sets the outside limits of use, while the social carrying capacity may legitimately pose even more restrictions (but never less than the biological). The complementary notion of multiple satisfaction denotes that a variety of satisfactions can be derived from the same resource. The specialization concept recognizes that among the variety of satisfactions (uses) some are more narrowly focused and resource dependent than others. The concepts of usage specificity and substitutability provide a rationale for allocating alternate resources to some users and establishing first priorities of use to others. The dimensions of uniqueness and future value provide justification for acquiring and preserving resources whose greatest value will be in the future. These principles are proposed as a starting point for a conceptual framework that effectively integrates the social dimension into resource management.

REFERENCES

Bryan, H. (1977). Leisure value systems and recreational specialization: The case of trout fishermen. *Journal of Leisure Research, 9* (3), 174–187.

Bryan, H. (1979). *Conflict in the great outdoors: Toward understanding and managing for diverse sportsmen's preferences.* Tuscaloosa: University of Alabama Press.

Bryan, H. (1982). A social science perspective for managing recreational conflict. In R. H. Stroud (Ed.), *Marine recreational fisheries* (pp. 15–22). Washington, DC: Sport Fishing Institute.

Catton, W. R., Jr. (1982). *Overshoot: The Ecological Basis of Revolutionary Change.* Urbana: University of Illinois Press.

Conland, J. (1985). *Social impact assessment in New Zealand—A practical approach.* Wellington, New Zealand: Ministry of Works and Development, Town and Country Planning Directorate.

Hendee, J. C. (1974). A multiple-satisfaction approach to game management. *Wildlife Society Bulletin, 2*, 104–113.

Rambo, A. T., & Sajise, P. E. (1984). *An introduction to human ecology: Research on agricultural systems in Southeast Asia.* Los Banos: University of the Philippines.

Shelby, B. B., & Nielsen, J. M. (1975). *Use levels and user satisfaction in the Grand Canyon*. Boulder, CO: Human Ecological Research, Inc.

Verberg, K. (1975). *The carrying capacity of recreational lands: A review* (Occ. Paper No. 1). Ottawa: Parks Canada Planning Division (Prairie Regional Office).

2.

WILD LAND RECREATION AND RESOURCE IMPACTS: A PLEASURE-POLICY DILEMMA

William E. Hammitt

Recreational use of wild land areas causes the natural conditions of these areas to be altered. Hiking trails are quickly worn bare and soon erode to varying depths. Backcountry camping commonly leads to trampled campsites that are void of vegetative ground cover, resulting in a bare core area of compacted soil. Such impacts are common to most designated wilderness areas and the backcountry of most national parks. However, the Wilderness Act of 1964 and the National Park Service Act of 1916 both require that these wild land areas be protected and preserved for future generations. Public policy requires that these areas be managed in as natural a state as possible. However, the same policies that call for protection also call for use and enjoyment; policy has made these natural areas available for recreation and associated uses.

The balancing act of providing recreational use, yet resource protection, requires that policy be established for the proper use and management of wild land recreation areas. Before establishing policies, it is necessary to identify the major issues, people, and tools for shaping policy.

ROLE OF POLICY AND MANAGEMENT

A major issue in dealing with recreation resource impacts is the proper role of management. Should management emphasize resource protection at the expense of recreation use or are there situations in which recreation should be emphasized at the expense of resource protection? If so, what are the major factors defining each of these situations.

When considering the importance of recreational resource impacts in wild land areas, it is easy for policy makers and managers to develop an anti-user bias. Would our wildland areas not be better off if recreational use did not occur on them? Perhaps our national parks and official wilderness areas should be only viewed and appreciated from a distance, perhaps only on film and in pictures. Parks without people are natural forever from the perspective of recreational impacts.

This philosophical policy position is unrealistic and certainly is not the position proposed in this chapter. Society and public policy have made most wild land areas available for recreational use, and the propriety of using these resources for recreational purposes must be accepted. Humans, as recreationists, are to be a part of these wild land ecosystems. Because man is a part of all ecosystems, wild land management is an effort to maintain a natural site environment in which human impact and influence are minimized as much as possible, while still allowing recreational use. That recreational use will occur in parks and wilderness should be accepted, and that no matter how small, use will produce an impact of some type. Policy and management's role, in general, is not to halt change within wild land recreation areas but to manage for acceptable levels of environmental change. The philosophical role of policy cannot realistically be to eliminate recreational use any more than it can be to eliminate recreation impact. The challenge of recreation policy and management is to find the proper balance between satisfying public demand for recreational experiences without creating substantial irreversible degradation of wild land resource conditions.

Given that both recreational use and natural resource conditions are to be preserved when formulating resource impact policy, how are each of these perspectives to be weighted in balancing use and preservation? Whose perspective is given the most emphasis—the ecologist who must protect the area, the recreationist who must use the area, or the resource manager who must provide for a balance between the two?

WHOSE PERSPECTIVE IS MOST IMPORTANT?

All types of resource impacts occur as a result of recreational use. Who determines the reaction to these impacts? The ecologist or park scientist can measure most recreational resource impacts, determining the magnitude of environmental change. It is a very different matter, however, to assess the importance or significance of these impacts. It might be agreed that 95 percent of the spiders on the forest floor of a campsite have been eliminated by recreational use; it is unlikely individuals could agree on the importance of this change or whether this is a positive or negative change (Hammitt & Cole, 1987). In a recreational context, impacts only become good or bad, important or insignificant, when humans make value judgments about them. Those judgments are primarily determined by the type(s) of recreation an area offers, the objectives of various user groups, and the objectives of resource management.

Recreation areas differ in their resource conditions, provide for different types of recreation and, accordingly, offer different perspectives for evaluating the importance of resource impacts. For example, some wilderness areas and state parks have experienced a conversion from native vegetation to a turf of Kentucky bluegrass. In wilderness areas this creates a problem because loss of natural conditions is undesirable in wilderness. The importance of this change is probably related to how large an area is affected and the uniqueness of the vegetation replaced. In the state park the conversion may be both important and beneficial because it greatly improves the quality of picnicking and ball playing.

Even within an area people vary in their opinions about the meaning of recreation-related impacts. Recreationists have diverse perspectives and ideas. Confronted with erosion of a hill used by motorcyclists, a hiker is more likely to react negatively than the motorcyclists. Conflict, resulting from different perspectives on ecological impact, commonly occurs between motorized and nonmotorized recreationists whether the activity occurs on land, water, or snow. Similar conflicts and viewpoints separate many hikers from users of horses and pack animals. These conflicting perspectives on the appropriate recreational use of wilderness influence the development of appropriate policy.

When determining policy for the management of visitor use and resource impacts, the three big players are the ecologist/scientist, the recreationist, and the park manager. Each views resource impacts from a different perspective and makes different value judgments concerning the importance and need for management.

The ecologist is more likely to be concerned about impacts that impair the function of ecosystems or destroy unique features. Ecologists are also likely to evaluate the importance of a change in terms of how long it takes for recovery to occur. Using this criterion, trail erosion is extremely serious because it will take centuries to regenerate eroded soils.

Recreationists are generally more concerned with the impacts that interfere with their use of an area or the area's resources. For example, a study in Yosemite National Park found facilities (toilets, tables, etc) and litter detracted more from users' enjoyment of backcountry campsites than other impacts (Lee, 1975). To the ecologist such impacts are likely to be relatively unimportant because they are easily reversible and do not greatly harm the function of natural ecosystems.

Resource managers are usually caught somewhere in between, due to their dual role of promoting use and preservation. Impacts that affect visitor enjoyment, particularly those that impair the functionality or desirability of sites, are of particular concern. Legislative mandates and agency guidelines provide additional constraints. Wilderness designation, for example, places some limits on the types and levels of impact that can be tolerated. Different agencies also have differing perspectives. Even in designated wilderness, presumably subject to the same mandates, each managing agency has a different style. For example, the U.S. Fish and Wildlife Service has a particular concern with wildlife. The National Park Service (NPS) is much more likely to restrict recreational activities to avoid resource impact than the Forest Service (Washburne & Cole, 1983). In dealing with recreational impacts and policies, managers must balance the concerns of ecologists, recreationists, and other user groups with the constraints of legislation and agency directives and tailor all these to the particular impact situation.

When balancing the concerns of the ecologist, recreationist, and other user groups in the formulation of policy for managing recreational impacts, there are many alternative management strategies and actions available to mitigate any particular impact. Selecting the most appropriate actions, however, depends on many factors.

WHICH MANAGEMENT STRATEGY TO IMPLEMENT

Land management policies are abstract until implemented by management. They provide the strategy underlying the action in the field. Given the many alternative management actions available for managing resource impacts, it is imperative that the strategic purpose of actions be considered.

Too often there is a tendency to select management techniques that are familiar or administratively expedient but not ideally suited to the situation at hand. Among the factors to consider when choosing a course of action are effectiveness, costs to administer, costs to the visitor, and likely side effects, particularly those affecting environmental naturalness. Ultimately, the best policy and management programs consist of carefully selected sets of actions that maximize effectiveness and minimize cost.

When considering the strategic purpose of impact policy and management actions, it is logical to focus on the major factors that influence recreational impacts—the amount of use, type of use, and environmental conditions. Focusing on each of these variables offers a unique strategic approach to controlling impact. The most obvious—but seldom the most desirable—approach to reducing impact is to reduce use. Everything else being equal, less use should cause less of an impact. However, one party that builds a campfire or that travels with horses can have a greater impact than several parties of backpackers using a portable stove. Thus, policies concerning the mode of travel and campfire use are common in most wilderness areas. Another approach to reducing impact is to leave the amount of use constant but modify the behavior of use to reduce the amount of impact caused by each visitor. This can be accomplished in several ways.

Use dispersal. Use can be spread out, so that areas of concentrated use and impact are avoided.

Use concentration. Conversely, use can be concentrated in space so that only a small portion of the resource is altered.

Type of use. Type of use can be managed in such a way that particularly destructive uses are minimized.

Table 2.1
Strategies and Actions for Reducing Impact on Campsites

Strategy	Possible Actions
Reduce amount of use	Limit number of parties entering the area
Reduce per capita impact	
Use dispersal	Persuade parties to avoid camping on highly impacted campsites
Use concentration	Prohibit camping anywhere except on designated sites
Type of use	Teach low impact camping techniques
Site location	Teach parties to choose resistant sites for camping
Site hardening/shielding	Build wooden tent pads on campsites
Rehabilitation	Close and revegetate damaged campsites

Site location. Use can be directed to particularly durable places that are able to tolerate heavy use.

Site hardening or shielding. A site's capacity to tolerate use can be increased by either hardening it or shielding it from impact.

Examples of how each of these strategic policies might be implemented to reduce impact on backcountry campsites are provided in Table 2.1.

All of these strategies attack the cause of impact problems. Another strategy is to attack the symptoms through site maintenance and rehabilitation. Generally, this approach is costly and never ending and should be complemented with attacks on the causes. There are situations, however, where treating symptoms must be the core of management policy. A good example is dealing with human waste in areas of concentrated use. Ecologically harmful waste can be concentrated, and the resource can be shielded by building outhouses and requiring visitors to use them. However, there is little alternative to establishing a flushing system, a composting system, or hauling the waste out.

A final important point about these strategies is that they often simultaneously impact a number of different problems. This is a reflection of the interrelatedness of man and nature. Some of the effects of implementing any course of action may be undesirable, however. In the end, the impact of park and management policy should be explicitly evaluated before implementation to gain multiple benefits where possible and avoid potential unwanted side effects (Manning, 1979).

SOME EXAMPLES OF IMPACT POLICY PROBLEMS

User versus Manager Perceptions

Because their role is to protect the resource base, resource managers are often quick to formulate policy. Given their training and orientation toward resource protection, they often perceive resource problems much sooner and more often than the general public. Managers have been accused of generating a problem when in the eyes of the public there is none. Recreational resource impacts certainly fall into this category. Campers are commonly observed camping on some of the most severely impacted sites. While a denuded and compacted campsite is a resource concern of resource management, it is commonly a preferred campsite of the public. Thus, the common policy of closing these severely impacted sites for restoration purposes is in direct conflict with the public's desire to use these sites.

While the manager is quick to perceive resource impacts and the need for control, most recreationists do not even recognize resource impacts. Knudson and Curry (1981) asked campers in three Indiana state park campgrounds for their opinions about ground cover condition. Then they compared these judgments to actual conditions. Most campers felt conditions were satisfactory or good on the less devegetated sites; however, even at the most severely impacted campground where 99 percent of the sites were over 75 percent denuded, most campers found conditions satisfactory. Over two-thirds of the campers saw no tree or shrub damage, despite the fact virtually every tree was damaged. Finally, a majority of those that did notice tree, shrub, and ground cover damage also said degeneration did not adversely affect their enjoyment and recreational experience.

The perspectives of the resource manager and the recreationist are quite different when justifying particular policies. Managers are most likely to be concerned about impacts that impair the function of ecosystems. They view resource impact policy as a long-term phenomenon. The recreationist, on the other hand,

Figure 2.1
Rate of Soil and Vegetation Impacts

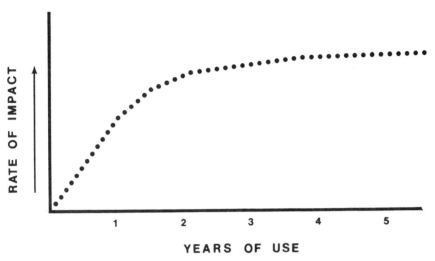

Note: The majority of impact to soil and ground cover vegetation in wild land recreation use areas occurs during the initial years of use, often the first two to three years.

seems more concerned with short-run impacts that decrease the functionality of a site or with "unnatural objects left by other parties." A good example involves the removal of dead woody debris to burn in campfires. Wild land recreationists frequently enjoy campfires and are unlikely to notice or appreciate the harm caused by collecting firewood. However, managers have found it an important enough impact to implement policies prohibiting campfires in about 50 percent of national park wilderness areas (Washburne & Cole, 1983).

Because the perceptions of users and managers of resource impacts may vary considerably, policy makers expect conflict over acceptance of those policies where the differences in perceptions are the greatest.

Rest and Rotate Areas

One of the most common policies concerning campsite impacts is the resting and rotating of impacted sites. The logic behind this policy is to stop recreational use of severely impacted areas while they recover and simultaneously directing use to new or recovered sites. While this policy appears rational, the ecological resistance and resilience of sites are not balanced. That is, sites do not typically recover from impacts in the same amount of time that created the impact—man destroys faster than nature creates. For example, field studies show that the majority of vegetation trampling and soil compaction occurs during the first couple of years of a site's recreational use (Figure 2.1), yet an average of eight to thirteen years is typically required for these sites to recover when they are closed and permitted to recover naturally (Hammitt & Cole, 1987). Sites in many western states require much longer to recover. Because of the imbalance between impact resistance and resilience, the policy of resting and rotating campsites is not very practical (Merriam et al., 1973). For example, four to five sites would have to be sequentially opened to use for each one rested. In an area like Sequoia-Kings National Park where there are 4,000 backcountry campsites, a rest-rotation policy would require a large portion of the park's resources devoted to campsites. Such policies also cause recreational impacts to be relocated to new areas of the park. Thus, while the policy of resting and rotating severely impacted recreation sites at first seems logical, ecological factors do not support its practice in most situations.

Setting Use Capacities

Since recreational resource impacts result from use, it naturally follows that policies are necessary to control the amount and types of visitor use. Use levels should be set in accordance with the capacity of the resource base to tolerate resource degradation. The U.S. Forest Service, in applying the National Forest Management Act, specifies that wilderness plans will "provide for limiting and distributing visitor use of specific portions in accord with periodic estimates of the maximum levels of use that allow natural processes to operate freely and that do not impair the values for which wilderness areas were created" (Rules, 1979). Though this mandate applies only to Forest Service wilderness, other agencies also face pressure to resolve the question of how much use is appropriate. As of 1980 the NPS had made the most progress; 21 percent of its areas had established carrying capacity limits in all travel zones (Washburne & Cole, 1983).

Policies concerning carrying capacities are based on the assumption that recreational impacts are directly related to the amount and type of recreational use. However, ecological and human behavior factors do not allow for such a simple and direct relationship between amount of impact and use. Research shows that the importance of the amount of use on recreational impacts varies between environments, between activities, with impact parameters, and with the range of use levels being examined. Also, the relationship between the amount of use and its impacts is asymptomatic curvilinear rather than linear (Figure 2.2). Because even light levels of some uses (i.e., less than thirty nights of camping use per season) commonly cause serious levels of impact, reducing frequency will not necessarily reduce impact substantially. Even low levels of some uses cause considerable impact, while further increases in use may have less and less additional effect on the resource. Thus, can use be legitimately limited to the low levels required to prohibit evidence of resource impact and still allow adequate recreational use of wild land recreation areas?

Figure 2.2
Soil and Ground Cover Vegetation Impacts under Light (0–30 days use/year) to Moderate (31–60 days use/year) Levels of Recreational Use

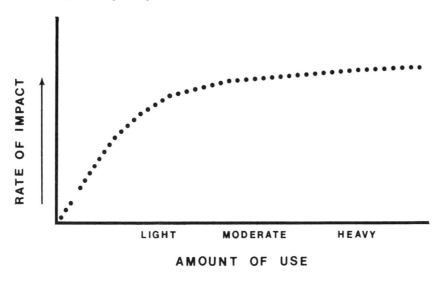

Redistributed versus Concentrated Use

Visitors of wild land recreation areas often concentrate use in a few popular places, campsites, and trails. Such use patterns result in the overuse of some areas while other areas are seldom used. In one of the most heavily used wild land areas, the Boundary Waters Canoe Area of Minnesota, nearly 70 percent of the user groups entered using only seven of the area's seventy entry points in 1974. Impacts are not only concentrated on these few entry points but also on the few portages and campsites near these entry locations. In the Mission Mountains in Montana over 90 percent of users entered at only two of the area's nineteen trail heads (Lucas, Schreuder, & James, 1971). When one considers that backcountry trips average only three to four days, there is little chance for these heavy concentrations of users to disperse. As a last example, use patterns in the Desolation Wilderness (California) show that 50 percent of all camping occurred on only 16 percent of the campsites. Thus, both visitor preference and their resulting impacts are policy issues influencing how we should manage patterns of spatial and concentrated use.

Because distribution of use is related to resource impacts, use distribution policies are a major concern for recreation resource managers. When Washburne and Cole (1983) asked wilderness managers to name their most significant problem, the most frequent response was "local resource degradation and lack of solitude as a result of concentrated use." The management technique most

Figure 2.3
Model of Acceptable Ecological Change in Wild Lands

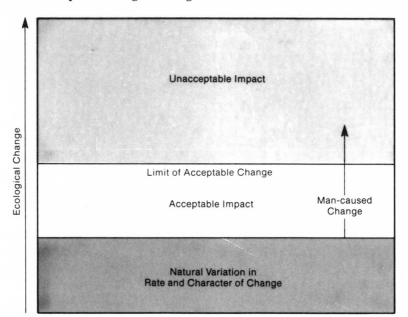

frequently mentioned as most efficient for dealing with this problem was increased use dispersal.

Use dispersal policies need not be related to use level restrictions. One can disperse use and not restrict use levels. Dispersal can also mean different things to different people. Using backcountry camping as an example, use dispersal could involve spreading people out on the same number of campsites but with greater distance between parties (Figure 2.3), spreading people out on more sites with or without increasing the distance between parties, or spreading people out in time (increasing off-season use) with or without spatial distribution. The appropriateness of each alternative for reducing ecological impacts may also be very different from its utility as a means for reducing crowding (Hammitt & Cole, 1987).

While many wild land recreation areas have policies concerning the dispersal of use, few have considered concentrating use as a policy alternative. Because resource impacts occur predominantly during the first years of use, and even under light levels of use, one could argue strongly that dispersing use only serves to disperse resource impacts. In certain situations policy makers might better concentrate use. For example, resource managers may want to encourage existing patterns of use if visitors are concentrating use on impact resistant trails and campsites. Also, use occurring on already heavily impacted sites does less damage than on new sites. However, in fragile areas or low use areas, resource managers may want to disperse users from areas of concentrated use.

Tolerance Limits

Given that public policy has made wild land areas available for recreational use, and given that even light amounts of recreational use will impact the natural conditions of these areas, the ultimate policy question for management becomes ''How much impact can be tolerated in these wild land areas?'' Tolerance limits refer to what percentage of a wild land recreation area is allowed to be impacted as well as what degree of resource impact will be tolerated at individual sites.

Although recreational impacts can be quite pronounced at the local site level, they are usually concentrated and restricted to a small percentage of a wilderness area's total acreage. For example, Wagar (1975) estimated that one European park, by restricting use to developed trails, has confined the direct impacts of use to only 0.1 percent of the park's 42,000 acres. In the Eagle Cap Wilderness, where users are free to travel where they will, Cole (1981) estimated that no more than about 0.5 percent of two popular drainage basins had been substantially disturbed by use of campsites or trails. Even around two very popular subalpine lakes in the same wilderness, the proportion of the area that had been substantially disturbed was less than 2 percent (Cole, 1982). Thus, recreational use directly impacts only a very small portion of total wild land acreage. When policy is made to eliminate or very severely restrict use of wild land recreation area, the policy will need to be justified on grounds other than the amount of acreage impacted.

Degree of impact at the local site level, however, can be quite severe, and how much change in site conditions that policy tolerates is an important decision. Is there a point or threshold where impact exceeds an acceptable limit (Figure 2.4)? While this decision now is largely a value judgment, the U.S. Forest Service is testing a procedure for determining limits of acceptable change (Stankey, et al., 1985). This concept calls for identifying sensitive indicators (ecological and social parameters), measuring recreational impact, setting tolerance limits for acceptable change in the indicator parameter, and monitoring the indicators to determine whether they are approaching (or have exceeded) the tolerance limits set for impact. If the limits of acceptable change procedure proves successful, it is likely to be adopted as a policy implementation tool in many wild land recreation areas.

IMPACT SIGNIFICANCE: ECOLOGICAL VERSUS RECREATIONAL

Recreational impacts on wild land environments are complex and interrelated, as are the policies concerning recreational use and resource impacts. Policy that optimizes wild land recreation use will damage natural condi-

Figure 2.4
Recreation Use Dispersal

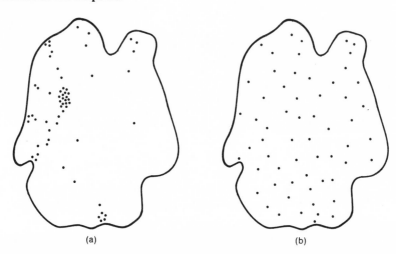

(a)   (b)

Note: In (a) use is concentrated in a small part of the recreation area. Each dot represents a camped
party. In (b) use dispersal has increased the distance between sites without changing
the number of sites (Cole, 1982).

tions. The significance of these impacts is of concern when formulating wild
land recreation policy. Are bare ground campsites, eroded trails, and the
number of fire rings truly significant, and if so, to what degree? Alternatively, can these recreation activities take place in less wild and natural
areas? The question of significance has to be addressed, and significance at
what level—the ecosystem or the recreation level.

Recreation-caused impacts are usually categorized as ecological (resource related) and sociological (experience related). Resource protection concerns ecological impacts. In answering the significance question one must ask: what
significant changes at the ecosystem level are recreational impacts causing to
our national parks, wilderness, and other wild land areas? It is generally agreed
that parks and wilderness should be managed on an ecosystem basis. If this
assumption is made, then do user impacts affect the conditions of these wild
land areas on an ecosystem basis? Are campsite impacts and firewood removal
significantly affecting the biological processes and quality of wild land ecosystems? The answer is probably no for most impacts. For example, campsite
trampling, firewood gathering, fire ring construction, and so on affect a minimal
portion of the total acreage of wild land ecosystems—they are microsite impacts
and not ecosystem-wide impacts. However, while they are not significant as
ecological impacts at the ecosystem level, they are significant as recreational
impacts at the wild land level. Public policy has defined the desired state of
wild land recreation areas (i.e., natural parks and wilderness) as natural.
However, natural is not restricted to an ecosystem level—it also refers to the

microsite level. Campsite impacts and eroded trails are perceived as significant changes to the natural conditions of wild land areas, regardless of their influence on ecosystems. Camping litter is not a significant factor affecting ecosystems; yet it is one of the most significant factors affecting the natural conditions of wild land campsites and trails.

While most recreational impacts do not have ecosystem-wide implications, some do. Horse grazing on high elevation meadows, by retarding the growth of indigenous plants, has introduced many exotic species to these habitats, altering them significantly. Aquatic ecosystems, particularly small streams and alpine lakes, can be influenced substantially by fishing pressure and inputs related to soil erosion (Hammitt & Cole, 1987). Recreationally caused impacts to wildlife behavior and breeding success are little known but may also have ecosystem-wide significance. Thus, recreationally caused impacts to wild land areas must be evaluated for their significance at both the recreational and ecological levels. While it is true that parks and wilderness are commonly managed on an ecosystem-wide basis, the majority of recreation-related impacts seem to have more significance as recreational impacts than as ecological impacts. In the eyes of the recreationists and the recreation manager, campsite and trail impacts are significant in that they alter the natural conditions of microsites, regardless of their ecosystem-wide significance.

In terms of policy for monitoring impact conditions and management of recreation use, both the recreation and ecosystem levels of significance must be considered. Policy to direct, restrict, and even eliminate certain recreational practices (e.g., campfires) in wild land areas to preserve the ecosystem have little justification. However, they might have considerable validity on the basis of preserving wild land recreation. Ecologists, scientists, and policy makers must learn to appreciate the principles governing wild land recreation as well as those governing the preservation of ecosystems.

CONCLUSION

To a large degree policy-making decisions are value judgments. When these value judgments are made, they are more rational if all major influencing factors are considered. This chapter has described some key factors that need to be considered when making policy concerning recreational use impacts in wild land areas. These factors should play a major role in policy decisions that aim to allow wild land recreation areas to be used for public pleasures yet preserved in an acceptable natural state for future generations. A preservation ethic for wild land recreation should supplement the preservation ethic for ecosystems that commonly underlies the policy and management of our wild land recreation areas. These areas can be preserved in an acceptable natural state while concomitantly hosting recreational activities.

REFERENCES

Cole, D. N. (1981). Vegetational changes associated with recreational use and fire suppression in the Eagle Cap Wilderness, Oregon: Some management implications. *Biological Conservation, 20,* 247–270.

Cole, D. N. (1982). Controlling the spread of campsites at popular wilderness destinations. *Journal of Soil and Water Conservation, 37,* 291–295.

Hammitt, W. E., & Cole, D. N. (1987). *Wildland recreation: Ecology and management.* New York: John Wiley.

Knudson, D. M., & Curry, E. B. (1981). Camper's perceptions of site deterioration and crowding. *Journal of Forestry, 79,* 92–94.

Lee, R. G. (1975). *The management of human components in the Yosemite National Park ecosystem.* Yosemite National Park, CA: Yosemite Institute.

Lucas, R. C., Schreuder, H. T., & James, G. A. (1971). *Wilderness use estimation: A pilot test of sampling procedures on the Mission Mountains Primitive Area* (Research Paper INT–109). Washington, DC: U.S. Department of Agriculture, Forest Service.

Manning, R. E. (1979). Strategies for managing recreational use of national parks. *Parks, 4,* 13–15.

Merriam, L. C., Smith, C. K., Miller, D. E., Huang, C. T., Tappeiner II, J. C., Goeckerman, K., Bloemendal, J. A., & Costello, T. M. (1973). *Newly developed campsites in the Boundary Waters Canoe Area: A study of five years' use* (Bulletin 511). St. Paul: University of Minnesota Agricultural Experiment Station.

Rules and regulations: National Forest System and resource management planning. (1979). *Federal Register, 44* (181).

Stankey, G. H., Cole, D. N., Lucas, R. C., Petersen, M. E., & Frissell, S. S. (1985). *The limits of acceptable change (LAC) system for wilderness planning* (Research Paper INT–176). Washington, DC: U.S. Department of Agriculture, Forest Service.

Wagar, J. A. (1975). Recreation insights from Europe. *Journal of Forestry, 73,* 353–357.

Washburne, R. F., & Cole, D. N. (1983). *Problems and practices in wilderness management: A survey of managers* (Research Paper INT–304). Washington, DC: U.S. Forest Service.

3.

RECREATION POLICY AND THE IDEOLOGY OF NATURE IN CALIFORNIA'S COASTAL ZONE

Michael K. Heiman

Most conceptions of nature within the natural and social science fields recognize the complex of biotic, physical, and climatic forces affecting an individual or a community. A more insightful interpretation acknowledges that our concept of nature, as well as our modification of that which is accepted as nature, articulates with a particular mode of production and with the social relations defining that mode of production. To illustrate, in our industrialized urban society, nature is commonly thought of as a residual spared from commodity production, perhaps protected in wilderness preserves, suburban greenbelts, and even in residential backyards. While not exclusive to capitalism, this interpretation of nature as a refuge from the forces of industry and production is common in advanced capitalist societies. Here, in the protected natural space, estranged individuals, be they workers or business managers and owners, can escape from the rigors of the workplace, to consume through residence and leisure the hard-earned fruits of their endeavors.

How does this particular view of nature as a refuge, to be found outside of the workplace and outside of production zones, articulate with capitalism and with the social relations engendered? In brief, the drive to expand economic development is one of the fundamental characteristics rising out of a class-stratified production system in which individual investment and production decisions are made by private entrepreneurs operating in a competitive market. Among other benefits, a growing economy helps secure social harmony among unequal social strata and, as such, is a concern for the state. The actual motor behind growth lies with individual entrepreneurs, or firms, each acting in its own self-interest, as they search for new and expanded markets while lowering production costs. In a growing and dynamic economy the portioning of space into production or workplace zones, and nature as leisure and residential consumption zones, is widely accepted. The separation, both conceptually and in practice, permits the development of production areas and of the resources contained within, as inputs into commodity production, while, on the other hand, those areas set apart from commodity production and from attending environmental degradation and social conflict are reserved and protected as nature for the biological and psychological rejuvenation essential for social reproduction.

The division of space between workplace or production areas and nature as leisure and residential consumption areas is heuristic, indeed contingent, because the division is not necessary for the existence of capitalism. Moreover, as every act of production is also an act of consumption, and vice versa, the same locale simultaneously serves both purposes. Nonetheless, the actual demarcation, while heuristic, is an important distinction because it permits a credible accounting for individual, group, and state positions on land use regulation.

This perceptual partitioning of the environment into production areas and consumption refuges, while useful, also generates crisis anew. Such is to be anticipated given that production and consumption constitute a dialectic relation, with the realization of one both contributing to and presenting barriers for the generation of the other. As a result, in a growing economy the physical and psychological integrity of previously sanctified refuges tends to be compromised, while the defense of nature as residential and recreation space presents serious problems for further capital expansion (Heiman, 1988, pp. 7–15).

In a system in which growing productive forces generate negative social and environmental externalities, the public sector, or state, is under dual pressures. The state is pressured to protect the investment climate and assist with economic expansion, particularly as growth is perceived as contributing to social welfare. In addition, the state is petitioned by citizens to address the problems generated by growth, and especially where growth compromises leisure and residential districts. Using the California coast as a geographic setting, and examining attempts to provide for three important coast-dependent production activities— port development, offshore oil production, and commercial fishing—as examples, the conflict between production and recreational consumptive use of nature as mediated through public policy and state intervention is reviewed.

THE SIGNIFICANCE OF COASTAL RECREATION

With 85 percent of the state's population living within thirty miles of the ocean, the coast is California's most important recreation resource. Recreation is one of the fastest growing uses of the coast. It is fueled by population growth, increased disposable income and personal mobility, advances in equipment design, and by a host of other variables. Moreover, coastal recreation is encouraged through the rising popularity of physical fitness and environmental awareness, as well as by recent state and national policies favoring the provision of coastal access. Coastal recreation is also the mainstay of many local economies. To illustrate, in California alone ocean- and bay-based boating is a $2 billion industry (Center for Continuing Study of the California Economy, 1982).

The remarkable expansion in recreational use of the coast is likely to intensify conflict over the use of a scarce and limited resource base. In addition to the demand for residence, recreation, and for other consumption amenities, California's narrow coastal region, hemmed in by the coastal mountain range for most of its length, supports a majority of the state's production activities, including office, industrial, and energy development. With free-market forces threatening to preclude many low-revenue uses, regulation is necessary to protect a broader public interest in recreational access to the shore.

PROTECTING THE PUBLIC'S RIGHT TO RECREATIONAL ACCESS

Proposition 20, the 1972 ballot initiative, was passed in response to widespread public dissatisfaction with local land use decisions favoring coastal development over resource protection and provision for public access. Bitterly opposed by developers, industry, and energy concerns, the initiative established a temporary state coastal commission to regulate land use decisions in the (average) 1,000-yard coastal zone, while simultaneously preparing a plan for the coast. The permit process required that, where feasible, all new development along the coast provide for access to intertidal and submerged coastal lands to which the public has a constitutional right of access (California Constitution Article X, Sec. 4). Following four years of interim state control and completion of the coastal plan, the California Coastal Act (Division 20, Sec. 3000 ff. of the California Public Resources Code) was passed in 1976 formalizing the state commission and the permit process. Through companion legislation the California State Coastal Conservancy was established to assist local communities with planning and development in accord with objectives of the Coastal Act.

Under the 1976 legislation, the basic land use regulation of the coastal zone is returning to the local governments as they prepare commission-approved local coastal programs. The major consideration of local and state planning and permit programs is to determine and attain a proper balance between competing coastal-dependent uses of the coast. Nondependent uses, such as office, residence, and industrial development, are encouraged to locate further inland.

The Coastal Act provides officials with only a rough guide to ranking coastal development proposals: "The use of private lands suitable for visitor-serving commercial recreational facilities designated to enhance public opportunities for coastal recreation shall have priority over private residential, general industrial or commercial development, but not over agriculture or coastal-dependent industry" (Sec. 30222). Not surprisingly, balancing coastal-dependent production and consumption concerns, while protecting as much of the fragile coastal environment as possible, presents coastal administrators with a multitude of problems.

PORT DEVELOPMENT

In the days before adequate rail and road transit, almost every cove and bay, however sheltered from the rugged Pacific surf, served as anchorage for ships plying the coastal timber and agriculture trade. With improved inland transportation and the requirement for more substantial facilities to accommodate larger vessels, cargo handling concentrated at a few principal ports such as in the Humboldt, San Francisco, San Pedro, and San Diego bays. Although the majority of former anchorages were abandoned, some were successfully converted to commercial and recreational fishing use, with waterfront structures recycled as restaurants, hotels, and other visitor-serving amenities (e.g., at Crescent City, Fort Bragg, Bodega Bay, Moss Landing, Monterey, Morro Bay, and Santa Barbara). Here the principal production-consumption conflict surfaced over the allocation of berthing space and support facilities between commercial fishing and recreational boating. For the few remaining cargo ports, the issues were more complex as port and state administrators attempted to accommodate a wide range of coastal-dependent uses.

The situation at the adjoining ports of Long Beach and Los Angeles in San Pedro Bay is instructive, both for the economic significance of the largest harbor complex on the West Coast, and for the pioneering attempt by port officials to include public access and provision for recreation with port expansion. In Long Beach the port's recreation facilities are a recent addition to the sprawling complex, constructed in accord with the state policies favoring public access to accommodate new development. The recreation district is isolated along the eastern portion of the port. Here a pedestrian promenade links several restaurants, the Queensway Hilton Hotel, a small craft mooring area, and the port's two star attractions, the Queen Mary and Howard Hughes's Spruce Goose, respectively the largest passenger ship and the largest airplane ever built. Although not yet competitive with the more lucrative port leases for cargo handling, the recreation facilities are partially subsidized through the port's oil well revenues.

The West Channel/Cabrillo Beach area of the Los Angeles Harbor contains that port's largest recreation complex. Several million visitors a year are drawn to the port's harbor and oceanside swimming facilities, a nature sanctuary, public fishing facilities, and a commercial district modeled after a nineteenth-century California whaling village. While the port's sixteen small craft marinas can accommodate 3,500 pleasure craft, this is less than half of expressed demand (California Department of Commerce, 1986, p. 89; Heiman, 1986, p. 50).

Although always tense and requiring careful management, the balance between shipping, coastal-dependent cargo and oil storage facilities, dredging for channel enlargement, fish processing, shipworks, and other hazardous production activities on the one hand, and public access, recreation, and nature preservation on the other, is now threatened by the very success of the ports in attracting both production and consumption activities. With booming Pacific Rim trade about to overtake trade across the Atlantic, the ports, once fierce competitors, have embarked upon a joint planning and development program designed to more than double their cargo capacity by the year 2000. Most of the expansion is occurring through a 2,600-acre landfill between the existing docks (already comprising the largest artificially created harbor in the world) and their outer breakwater. This seriously compromises recreational use of the outer harbor area where over half of all pleasure boating and allied activities—such as water skiing, scuba diving, and wind surfing—occur within the ports' calm waters (Queenan, 1986, pp. 159–161; U.S. Army Corps of Engineers, 1985, pp. 146–150, 302). In addition, a major portion of the harbor's sensitive shallow-water habitat will be lost due to filling and dredging, thereby destroying much of the biological resource base attracting recreationists to the area in the first place.

As is typical with an expanding economy, the prospect for amiable mediation between the production and recreational consumption of limited resources appears disquieting. This is indicated by the coastal commission's recent approval of a pipeline terminal in the Port of Los Angeles. Here the required mitigation for a 110-acre landfill in the crowded harbor was assigned to habitat restoration at Batiquitos Lagoon, some seventy-five miles to the south in San Diego County. While the latter is essential to protect what remains of southern California's dwindling coastal wetlands, the controversial off-site mitigation process contributes little to recreational resources where demand may be greatest.

OFFSHORE OIL DEVELOPMENT

The proposed pipeline terminal is just the beginning of what threatens to be a flood of oil-related development along the California coast. The battle lines between production and recreational consumptive use of coastal resources are quite visible, particularly following the spectacular 1969 Santa Barbara Channel well blowout, which blanketed twenty miles of the coast with oil. In the wake of that disaster, coastal communities and the state's federal delegation eventually prevailed and secured a congressional moratorium on further exploratory lease sales in federal waters beyond the three-mile state zone of jurisdiction.

The federal Coastal Zone Management Act of 1972 (PL 92–583) is another ambiguous expression of public support both for productive development and for protection of coastal resources. According to Section 303 (e) ''it is national policy . . . to preserve, protect, develop, and where possible, to restore or enhance, the resources of the nation's coastal zone for this and succeeding generations.'' Furthermore, Washington ''to the maximum extent practical'' must have policies consistent with California's federally approved state management program, while California, in turn, must provide for ''adequate consideration

of the national interest involved in siting of facilities necessary to meet requirements which are other than local in nature'' (Sections 307 [c] and 305 [c] [8]).

In 1981 Secretary of the Interior James Watt proposed that most of the nation's
outer continental shelf be available for federal lease sale. California's share,
approximately 60 million acres, would be greater than the entire federal acreage
offered nationally for bid since the beginning of the federal offshore lease program. Here as elsewhere, coastal communities united in bipartisan opposition
to the proposed policy change. Often dependent upon the recreation and tourist
trade, the threat to local economies from unsightly offshore drilling platforms,
increased air pollution, loss of fishing grounds, the release of toxic drilling muds,
and accidental as well as routine oil spills accompanying exploration and drilling,
figured at the top of their objections. With the ocean floor too rugged to allow
for pipelines to shore, the oil would have to be loaded and unloaded by barge,
a risky procedure along a rough coast exposed to the full fury of Pacific storms.
Environmentalists and local officials cited the Department of the Interior's own
worst-case scenario that a thirty-day beach closure due to a major oil spill in
Santa Monica Bay would result in over $132 million lost in recreation services
and over $362 million lost, through multipliers, to the local economy (Heiman,
1986, p. 82).

Following years of legal and political wrangling, the congressional moratorium
had been lifted by 1987. Citing national security interests, then Secretary William
Hodel was pressing on with a scaled down, but still substantial, lease sale, while
the local and state governments, also referring to the 1972 federal act, were
threatening to block necessary onshore support development within their jurisdiction. In coastal ballot initiatives voters were siding three to one against the
offshore lease program. Most of the opposition was actually based upon the
visual aesthetics of offshore platforms and on the threat to the image of nature,
even as the oil industry and government argued over the potential for and possible
impact of oil spills (California Coastal Commission, 1986; Travis, 1985).

With the courts caught in a political tug-of-war between the state and the
federal positions, the immediate future of the leasing program is still undecided.
Although California Governor Duekmejian and even the Democrat-controlled
state assembly have, in the past, sided with development and appointed members
to the coastal commission willing to compromise in favor of the offshore lease
program, the tide of opposition remains strong (Cicin-Sain, 1986; Taylor, 1988).
What is clear is that pressure from offshore oil development on the multibillion-
dollar recreation industry and on other coastal-dependent activities, such as
commercial fishing, appears ominous as California, with an estimated quarter
of all remaining federal offshore oil reserves, seems destined to play a much
larger role as a supplier of the nation's energy.

COMMERCIAL FISHING AND RECREATIONAL BOATING

Unlike outer continental shelf development, the provision and allocation for
berthing facilities remains primarily a state and local deliberation. While some

major harbors are built in natural bays, such as San Diego, San Francisco, and Eureka, the majority are artificially excavated from low-lying coastal lands. With further dredging discouraged under the Coastal Act, new marina development has been slowing, even as the phenomenal postwar boom in recreational boating continues unabated.

Point Conception in Santa Barbara County is a natural division between the typically warmer, sunnier, and calmer coastal waters of southern California, and the foggy, cooler waters of the central and northern coasts. Accordingly, most pleasure yachting occurs in the south, with its great complex of service and destination ports. An estimated 1 million boaters reside there. Despite the extensive infrastructure, the wait for wet moorage can run to several years, with recreationists willing to drive 100 miles and more to reach their berth.

In the face of this overwhelming demand, the state's commercial fishing industry stands little chance in the free market. Recreational boaters usually outbid the fishermen for berthing space and are favored by marina operators as more stable year-round tenants, with far fewer dockside support requirements. In Orange County's Dana Point Harbor, once an important fishing port, there are now no slips set aside for commercial fishermen among the 2,500 berths (California State Coastal Conservancy, 1984, p. 43; Heiman, 1986, pp. 26–31, 55–56).

The commercial fleet, of course, can point to the significant contribution it makes to the state economy—a $300 million to $400 million catch responsible for thousands of jobs—and to public health in a cholesterol conscious society (California State Coastal Conservancy, 1984). In response to these benefits, and in recognition that maintenance of a viable commercial fleet is a productive use of the coast that actually enhances recreation where tourists come to view and sample the catch, Section 30703 of the Coastal Act mandates provision for commercial requirements to accompany harbor and marina development.

In San Francisco, Santa Cruz, Monterey, Santa Barbara, San Diego, and at a few other major tourist destinations, the commercial fleet is a mainstay of the waterfront. Here the fleet is threatened by the very success of its tourist appeal as commercial development and hoards of sightseers overwhelm the production zone. By and large, the fleet can no longer afford to berth at the congested waterfronts and the fishermen's wharves are only used to unload the catch. With assistance from the California State Coastal Conservancy, harbor officials have endeavored to protect the handling areas from commercial intrusion, while providing viewing platforms and other nonobtrusive access for the tourists.

Outside of the major tourist centers, the conflict between the commercial fleet and recreation is of a different nature. Here boaters compete both for berthing space and for fish resources. At Channel Islands Harbor in Ventura County the coastal commission required additional fish-cleaning and berthing facilities for the small commercial fleet as a requirement for harbor expansion. This came despite objections from nearby yachters who did not care for the sight and smell of fish processing. As it complains, the southern commercial fleet has difficulty maneuvering ships and gear around legions of weekend sailors, while fishermen along the central and north coasts are particularly worried about the major expansion of a sports fishery directly competing for choice catch such as king salmon and tuna.

As late as the 1970s, Moss Landing on Monterey Bay was less than 30 percent recreation in use. Today, despite major expansion for sport use, the pressure on the commercial fleet is still growing and the state, through the auspices of the coastal conservancy and commission, has to actively intervene on the fleet's behalf. To the south, at Morro Bay in San Luis Obispo County, and to the north at Bodega Bay in Sonoma County, the commission and the conservancy are also working with local governments on major marina expansions designed to protect and service the important commercial fleets still berthed there, while controlling the commercial tourist development that threatens to totally engulf the working waterfront. In all of these projects state agencies have endeavored to minimize further habitat destruction yet provide public access so as not to preclude recreational benefits from production zones.

The pioneering provisions of the Coastal Act and the efforts of the conservancy and commission notwithstanding, development pressure on the commercial fleet is likely to increase. With full implementation of the federal offshore oil lease program capable of generating a forty-fold increase over current levels of onshore processing facilities, many miles of the coast could be taken over by oil-related industrial development (Cicin-Sain, 1986, p. 4). Furthermore, a major portion of the fisheries could be closed to use because offshore platforms and underwater support structures foul and tangle fishing lines and nets. Pressure will be most intense at the existing harbors capable of serving the offshore platforms. Here energy companies readily outbid commercial fishing as well as recreational uses for limited dock space and for other requirements, such as the facilities for fuel and boat repair. Although state and local governments may yield to the enormous financial pressure and tax revenues associated with energy development, attempts will be made to comply with those provisions of the Coastal Act that support the commercial fleet and provide for public recreational access to, or at least mitigation of, coastal energy development.

CONCLUSION

In the past recreation management tended to focus on the resource base to the relative neglect of the needs and desires of particular users and user groups. Today more attention is directed to the recreationists themselves and to the social and economic contexts affecting their experience. It appears that the tension between production and recreational consumptive use of the coast is largely in the eye of the beholder, as influenced by experience and through economic and social privilege. To illustrate, one finds affluent communities along the central and south coasts virtually unanimous in opposition to coastal industrial and offshore oil development as a threat to aesthetic sensibilities. On the other hand, ethnic minorities continue to catch and consume fish in polluted Santa Monica Bay despite posted warnings, and unemployed north coast residents enjoy beach side camping and surf casting directly across the road from the massive timber and pulp mills of Humboldt Bay.

Coastal resource managers must be sensitive to this wide range of individual experience when providing for recreational access. Although access must be restricted with energy, petrochemical, shipping, and other more hazardous production projects, it should not be excluded as even passive observation and interpretation can educate an inquisitive public.

California has been at the national forefront on the effort to harmonize production and recreational consumption of nature, with access, or compensation, required for new coastal development. Moreover, the state has committed the most resources to the planning and design of projects blending public amenities with private development. Nonetheless, despite the impressive accomplishments to date, harmony between production and recreational consumptive use of nature in the intensely utilized coastal zone is, at best, transitory. In such a dynamic economy, new forms of production continue to intrude upon recreation zones, while sensitive industries, such as commercial fishing, are threatened by burgeoning recreation demands. In this situation, and short of structural change in our mode of production whereby material expansion is no longer favored or necessary, state and local governments can only mediate in an intensifying battle between economic growth and the protection of nature as a sanctuary from the negative externalities of that growth. This is anticipated as long as there is a social system that encourages leisure and residential consumption of nature as a refuge from the problems of an environmentally degrading production system, while simultaneously requiring ever greater inroads into nature for commodity production.

REFERENCES

California Coastal Commission. (1986). Voters tackle offshore oil, approve control measures. *Coastal News, 1* (November), 3–4.

California Department of Commerce. (1986). *California's major commercial ports.* Sacramento: Author.

California State Coastal Conservancy. (1984). *Commercial fishing facilities in California.* Oakland: Author.

Center for Continuing Study of the California Economy. (1982). *Recreation activity in California: 1980 with projections to 2000.* Palo Alto: Author.

Cicin-Sain, B. (1986). Offshore oil development in California: Challenges to governments and to the public interest [Special issue]. *Public Affairs Report, 27* (2).

Heiman, M. (1986). *Coastal recreation in California: Policy, management, access.* Berkeley: University of California, Institute of Governmental Studies.

Heiman, M. (1988). *The quiet evolution: Power, planning, and profits.* New York: Praeger.

Queenan, C. (1986). *Long Beach and Los Angeles: A tale of two ports*. Northridge, CA: Windsor.

Taylor, R. (1988, February 24). Panel approves final O.K. of 3 offshore Exxon rigs. *Los Angeles Times,*, Section I, pp. 3, 18.

Travis, W. (1985). Must oil development be ugly? *California Waterfront Age, 1* (Winter), 25–37.

U.S. Army Corps of Engineers. (1985). *Final programmatic environmental impact report/ environmental impact statement for landfill development and channel improvements Los Angeles–Long Beach harbors* (Vol. 1). Los Angeles: Author.

Part II

Measuring Recreational Benefits

4.

BENEFIT ANALYSIS AND RECREATION POLICY

V. Kerry Smith

Applied welfare economics maintains that policy choices should be made based on how individuals value the resources under study and on how much the changes implied by those policies cost (i.e., the aggregate net benefits). The focus of this chapter is on measuring the benefits from providing or improving the natural resources that support outdoor recreation. It assumes that this information is to be used as part of a larger benefit-cost analysis of an investment decision or in the design of a management policy for existing environmental resources.[1]

While the conceptual rationale for using the aggregate net benefits realized from alternative allocations of recreation resources in the decision-making process is usually argued to be one of efficiency, this does not mean that efficiency must be the exclusive basis for these judgments. Rather, a net benefits measure provides a convenient standard for evaluating the implications of responding to other objectives. It offers one means to express the trade-offs involved.

This is hardly news to most policy analysts. What are new, however, are the innovations in methods for measuring consumers' values for environmental and natural resources and, with them, the increased attention given to using benefit estimates for policy decisions. Thus, there is every reason to believe that they will play an increasingly important role in the design and evaluation of recreation policies.

ON THE DEFINITION OF RECREATION BENEFITS

Traditional definitions of the economic benefits provided to an individual by a resource would equate them to the individual's willingness to pay for that resource's services. Recently, there has been increasing recognition that this definition, even when adapted to conform with consistent Hicksian benefit measures (i.e., dollar measures defined to hold an individual's utility or well-being constant), is an inadequate description of the values an individual can derive from the resources supporting recreational activities. An individual's valuation for a resource can, in principle, be a composite reflecting use, the prospect for future uses, and appreciation (with associated valuation) for the continued existence of certain resources regardless of any pattern of use. Recognition of the potential for all three motives has fundamentally changed the issues that must be addressed in a benefit analysis, and even the conceptual basis used to define what monetary measures of benefits attempt to represent.

A Taxonomy for Benefits

In order to specify a consistent taxonomy for the benefits arising from recreational resources, one must first decide whether the consumer's decision process involves sufficient uncertainty that it must be explicitly reflected in any description of his behavior. Clearly such an appraisal is a judgment on the part of the analyst. In the real world no decisions are free of uncertainty. What is at issue in distinguishing the conventional description of individual behavior under certainty from one adjusted to incorporate uncertainty is whether that uncertainty can be expected to be important enough to affect an individual's behavior. If this is the case, then a framework reflecting how individuals can be expected to respond to the uncertain conditions must be used to define the benefit measures.[2]

As a rule, economic models have assumed that the individual seeks to maximize the expected value of his utility (calculated over the potential outcomes, given a subjective probability distribution for those outcomes). Within this description the relevant measure for defining individual well-being is the value for the expected utility (EU) (i.e., well-being is held constant on average, with the average defined over the possible states of the world). Use and nonuse values for resources are then defined using this standard (Smith, 1987). Use related benefits would correspond to the maximum amount an individual would pay for specified conditions of access over the situation where there is no access (but the resource supporting the recreation continued to exist).[3] This can differ from the conventional *ex post* definition because it is the expected utility and not the level of utility that is used to define individual well-being and is held constant. In this context an *ex ante* version of existence values could also be defined to hold *EU* constant. It involves a comparison between conditions where a resource supporting recreational activities exists but is not available to the individual in comparison to complete elimination of the resource.

Basically, this description of the valuation concepts requires considering a particular counterfactual situation. Suppose the recreation site becomes too expensive for the individual to use (i.e., the entrance fee raises the total cost of use above the maximum amount an individual would be willing to pay for a trip to it). How much additional income must he have to realize the same level of well-being as his current situation with an entrance fee that is consistent with being able to use the site? This is our conception of the use value. When well-being is measured by his utility, this level is known to the individual when his use value is calculated; therefore, the benefit measure does not reflect uncertainty. By contrast, when well-being is measured by the expected utility, the actual satisfaction that will be realized once the actions are taken is unknown. It will not be known until the events that are uncertain are resolved. Thus, values measured before this resolution reflect the importance of the uncertainty to the individual. Existence values could also be translated into these terms as monetary values for the presence of a resource even though it is never anticipated to be used, with the standard for determining well-being defined as actual utility for *ex post* values and expected utility for the *ex ante* values.

Finally, a third concept—option value—is often argued to be a distinct component of the nonuse value experienced by individuals. This argument is incorrect. Option value reflects the importance of specifying the conceptual standard (constant expected utility or constant utility) before defining monetary benefit taxonomies.

Thus, in defining use and nonuse value one must specify whether uncertainty is important to the individual's circumstances; therefore, the observed behavior (and valuations of resources) must be assumed to reflect some response to that uncertainty. If it does, then the definitions of use and nonuse value must recognize both the motives for valuing the resources involved and the opportunities available to the individual for adjusting to risk. If uncertainty is not an important factor in individual behavior, then use values correspond to the conventional Hicksian consumer surplus, and nonuse would be the conventional definition for the existence values (see McConnell, 1983; Freeman, 1985; Smith, 1987).

Investment versus Management: The Benefit Questions are Different

There are two primary areas of public sector decision making in which benefit measurements contribute to evaluating the efficiency of policy decisions. The first, and most widely discussed, involves public investment decisions. In the case of recreation benefit analysis, several types of measurements taken to analyze these decisions can be distinguished. For the most part, they seek to value the services provided by a recreation resource with a defined set of characteristics. The benefit estimation task might, for example, also be one of valuing the services of a lake created by a dam constructed to improve control over periodic flooding, to produce hydroelectric power, or to benefit all three simultaneously. Alternatively, it might involve valuing the recreation afforded by a free-flowing river as part of a decision on whether to modify the river (i.e., to build the dam in the first place).

The common element in these examples is that the valuation is focused on a resource and its services under a specified set of conditions.[4] Thus, as a rule, changes in the attributes of the resource or the quality of the recreation services it provides are not attempted.

Tasks involving the valuation of site characteristics are generally encountered as part of management decisions for existing resources. How much hunting (e.g., length of season, number of hunters, etc.) should be permitted? Should access to beaches be restricted over weekends? What restrictions should be placed on the emissions of effluents into specified rivers? To use economic information in making such decisions, requires the valuation of changes in one or more characteristics of a recreation resource—the importance of catch or hunting success rates to hunting recreation; the detrimental effects of congestion on recreation activities at a specific beach; or the value of water quality changes at a specific river. This distinction is important because the process of estimating these values requires different levels of resolution or understanding of the factors that influence household behavior.

Consider the example given in Figure 4.1. DD' represents an individual's demand for the use of a recreational resource (e.g., a park, beach, or free-flowing river). To estimate his valuation of the resource, the terms of access need to be defined (usually an implicit price—the entrance fee plus the travel and time costs per trip to reach the site). ACD is the measure of the consumer surplus. While this may not be an easy task if there are no records of use, or in the case of a new recreation facility, it requires less detail on the individual's choice process than valuing a change in one or more characteristics of the resource.

For valuing changes in the characteristics of a resource, how the demand function would change with alterations in the site characteristics needs to be estimated. Improvements in water quality could be expected to shift an individual's demand to the right, say to $\overline{DD}'$. The valuation task is to measure the area $\overline{DD}EC$. To accomplish this one must observe, isolate, and measure, changes in the resource's characteristics that individuals recognize as important to the recreational activities they undertake using that resource. The full implications of this process will clearly differ from one recreational resource to the next.

Measuring nonuse values is even more difficult for both the resources and their attributes because there is no observable behavior that can be linked to the presence of nonuse values. Indeed, their definition precludes any form of direct use (McConnell, 1983).

MEASURING RECREATION BENEFITS

It is now common practice to classify the methods for measuring individuals' values for recreation (as well as other nonmarketed commodities) into the indirect and the direct approaches. The first relies on observed behavior plus a set of maintained assumptions to recover from those observations an individual's demand or marginal valuation of the resource involved. The travel cost recreation demand framework is the most common approach for recreation. It has had a

Figure 4.1
Demand for Recreational Resources

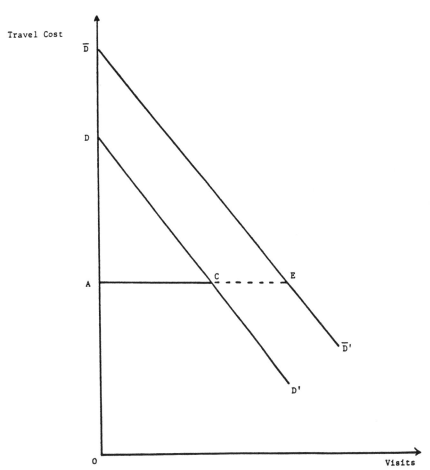

long and quite successful history over a wide range of applications. This method relies on travel costs (including both the vehicle-related and time costs of travel) playing the role of the implicit price an individual incurs by using a particular recreation site. While the basic idea underlying the model was simple, the insight it provided and the success of the framework in practice has been impressive over more than forty years, since Harold Hotelling first described it in a letter to the director of the National Park Service.

Today the method is usually interpreted as providing an estimate of the demand for the particular recreation site that the analyst observes individual recreationists using. Two basic sources of data have been used in these models—aggregate (or zonal) information surveys of individuals' patterns of use and micro surveys.

The former usually consist of the aggregate rates of use (visits per capita) for the towns (or counties) surrounding the site of interest, while the latter generally consist of on-site surveys of users.

Both sources are imperfect. Typically neither provides sufficient information to fully implement and evaluate a detailed theoretical model of recreationists' behavior. For example, with the aggregate data the model must be treated as a representative individual framework, wherein the influence of individual characteristics for demand are assumed to be adequately reflected by the averages or percentage-based summary statistics for the population in each county (origin zone). As a rule, the data do not identify the length of stay, the patterns of use (during each trip), or the vehicle-related travel costs and opportunity costs of time of the individuals involved. These are generally estimated (or, in some cases, assumed constant across the individuals involved) and are attached to aggregate visit rate data. There is usually no basis for defining the extent of the market for any particular site within the aggregate area (Smith & Kopp, 1980).

Micro survey data are also not free of problems, two of which are especially important. First, they usually result from surveys conducted at the sites involved. This implies that information about individuals who did not come to the site during the particular time span of the sample is unavailable. Second, and equally important, the surveys usually do not indicate other site(s) the surveyed individuals consider as substitutes.

Attempts to deal with these problems have appeared in recent literature (Smith & Desvousges, 1986a; Ward & Loomis, 1986). It is fair to conclude that based on the evidence to date micro data are preferred to the aggregate or zonal data. The treatment of the opportunity costs of time, role of substitutes, truncation effects, length of stay per trip versus more trips, as well as site characteristics remain important areas of current research with these models.

A second indirect approach with fewer applications to valuing recreation, but with the potential for providing estimates of those values, involves using the markets for housing. In this case, the sale prices of homes adjusted for the homes' characteristics, local public goods, and site-specific costs (e.g., tax rates), as well as site amenities, can be used to infer a household's marginal valuation of proximity to recreational resources—therefore, indirectly, the value of the resources themselves. (See Brown & Pollakowski, 1977, for an example involving the valuation of shoreline.) The process of inferring these values from estimated marginal values required a further array of assumptions to attempt to separate the role of the implied access to the recreational resource as a contributing factor to the individual's demand for the home. One of the most important of these arises from the assumed nature of the equilibrium. This equilibrium concept, on the one hand, provides the mechanism that allows hedonic price functions to signal an individual's marginal valuations for housing and site characteristics, and yet, it also impedes the use of these marginal values in estimating demands.

The issue is simply described, but not as simply solved. The price function defines a condition that assures an equilibrium matching of diverse demanders with diverse suppliers. The factors underlying demand diversity can often be expected to be correlated with factors leading to the supply diversity (Bartik, 1987). Both will be related to individuals' valuations of attributes, as well as to the presence of specific mixes of those attributes. This correlation implies that the separation of demand and supply motives in explaining the determinants of the equilibrium price function (as an outcome of the equilibrium matching) will be exceptionally difficult. In other words, the hedonic price function describes the interactions of both buyers and sellers. To value an improvement in one characteristic, one must distinguish what the equilibrium condition implies about how the price needs to change (across houses) in response to changes in these houses' characteristics from the change in an individual's marginal valuations of a characteristic. This process requires more information than simply the equilibrium hedonic price function.

Fortunately, for small changes it is often possible to use the method to approximate the values. Bartik (1988) has argued that the slope of the price function times the change in the characteristic provides an approximate upper limit for the values.

A third indirect approach can be developed from the same types of data used for the first two, but it relies on a reinterpretation of the choice processes involved. Both the travel cost demand models and the hedonic property value model assume that the individual can make marginal changes in site usage or housing characteristics. For the demand model these small changes are possible because the time horizon assumed to be involved in planning consumption is implicitly treated as long enough that any discrete change in usage patterns (e.g., an additional weekend trip) approximates a small change in the total use for a season. Within the hedonic framework the implicit assumption permitting the continuous, marginal changes underlying the price function is a diversity of housing choices, with all possible variations in characteristics represented.

An alternative approach with the same basic information entails assuming each decision that is not affected by trips taken before or after the specific occasion. In this context a random utility model (McFadden, 1974) can be used to describe the selections. It describes infra-marginal decisions (and not marginal decisions) and relies on them to be made based on a comparison of the total utility realized when the trip is taken versus when it is not.

Application of the framework to housing decisions is analogous to the framework emphasizing the limited nature of the housing choices available. An important issue in such applications is the question of defining what the nature of the discrete alternatives will be. This last class is important because it has provided one of the most frequently used new models in recreation for evaluating the values households place on changes in site characteristics. In addition to its use in benefit estimation, this model can be used to describe site usage or housing selections, depending on the available information and the analyst's view of how these decisions are made.

Three of the refinements to the indirect methods for modeling recreation decisions should be discussed further. While each offers the prospect for improved estimates of the values for specific recreational resources, often their principal objective was to provide estimates of the value of changes in one or more site attributes. The first of these is the varying parameter model (Smith & Desvousges, 1985; 1986a; Vaughan & Russell, 1982). This framework relies on the ability to observe demands for an array of recreation sites, each following approximately comparable recreational activities. Variations in the estimated parameters for these site demands are then hypothesized to arise from differences in these sites' characteristics.

A second approach introduced by Brown and Mendelsohn (1984) is the hedonic travel cost model. Unfortunately, the name is a bit misleading. In this case a price function is used to summarize the opportunities available to individuals. Moreover, these opportunities are assumed to be best characterized by the recreation sites' characteristics. However, this is not the result of an equilibrium process. The price function in this case is a convenient statistical summary of the available sources of attributes and the prices the model assumes each individual perceived for them (Smith & Kaoru, 1987).

Application of the hedonic travel cost model is a two-step process: (1) estimating cost models for an array of residential zones and calculating from them the implied prices of the sites' characteristics that are assumed to be relevant to the decisions in each zone; (2) using these prices together with the actual levels of characteristics to estimate demand functions for characteristics. Both stages should be considered approximations. None of the applications of this method has fully developed the theoretical restrictions required for the model to describe consistently consumers' valuations. Nonetheless, convenience and ability to deal with the task of valuing site attributions has certainly contributed to its use (see Mendelsohn, 1987, for a more spirited defense).

The last indirect framework is the one described above and is actually a multitude of approaches that use the random utility structure to describe different types of choices, depending on available data and problems involved. Here the analysis begins with the specification of an indirect utility function and derives from it a set of estimating equations that can involve shares of the total trips to specific recreation sites (Morey, 1981), multi-nomial logit models of the site selection decisions (Bockstael, Hanemann, & Strand, 1986), or probit models of each decision to visit a single site (Smith & Kaoru, 1986). The principal difference between these approaches and conventional demand models (or even those involved in the varying parameter approach) is in the assumptions that must be maintained for the model to be valid. Each also makes specific assumptions about corner solutions (i.e., situations in which the individual chooses not to use some of the available set of recreation sites).

Direct methods for valuation substitute questions involving hypothetical situations for the assumptions on behavioral functions to obtain the required information for estimating how individuals value nonmarketed resources. Inevitably, comparisons between direct and indirect methods means judging whether individuals can accurately respond to questions involving hypothetical conditions or changes in them, or whether analysts can impose appropriate restrictions on observed actions to indirectly recover the desired information. This issue is an essential element in the assumptions used by those who argue that the survey (or direct) methods can be expected to yield more reliable values than those inferred from an indirect model with extensive (and often untestable) maintained assumptions.

The use of direct approaches has grown as interest in valuing a wide range of environmental resources (and their attributes) has increased. The most well-known approach, referred to as contingent valuation, attempts to elicit individuals' values for the resources. There are different questioning styles, but all ultimately elicit a dollar valuation (Mitchell & Carson, 1989; Smith & Desvousges, 1986a).

With a decade and a half of applications,[5] contingent valuation is now recognized as an acceptable method for estimating consumers' values for nonmarketed resources. While initial reservations about the feasibility of using this approach focused on the likelihood of strategic responses to valuation questions, these concerns have proved to be largely unfounded.[6] The hypothetical nature of what is asked is currently regarded as among the most important concerns. Along with questions as to what each respondent is assuming will be his or her income and the terms of availability of other private goods and of public goods, these two issues offer the reasons why Mitchell and Carson (1987) place the development of these methods at a relatively early stage of the learning curve.[7]

An alternative approach to the direct format for deriving valuation information has involved questions that are referred to under a variety of headings—closed-ended contingent valuation (CV), contingent behavior, purchase intentions, voting, or contingent quantity surveys. These efforts elicit respondents' reactions to an issue with a specified price inherent in the question. It can involve a vote in a referendum, a one-time purchase, or a specific decision for stated price and quality conditions. Some examples in which these methods have been used to elicit intended quantities for specified price and quality conditions include McConnell (1986), Ribaudo and Epp (1984), and Smith and Desvousges (1986b).

More recently, discrete CV and contingent ranking have been considered as alternative approaches for benefit estimation. Initial experience with them has provided some indications that they may not be as difficult for individuals to understand and may therefore be easier to implement.

The discrete CV simply asks whether an action would be taken under a specified set of conditions. The yes/no answers to these questions are then used to infer what an individual's preferences must have been in order to realize these decisions (Hanemann, 1984). Clearly, to recover sufficient information to estimate an individual's valuation of a resource, more structure must be added. In this case, this structure takes the form of a functional specification for the deterministic portion of the random (indirect) utility function, along with an assumed distribution (and interpretation of the source) for the errors.

By contrast, the contingent ranking method asks respondents to rank different hypothetical situations that are posed as potential outcomes of a decision process. These situations involve different values for the prices and site conditions. The method then uses the reported ranks in a fashion somewhat comparable to the discrete CV methods to estimate the parameters of an indirect utility function. Once the parameters of these functions are estimated, it is possible to also estimate individuals' values for changes in the access conditions or quality of the recreational resource involved.

Overall, the survey approach enhances control over the situations and associated recreational resources that are to be valued, reduces the number and types of maintained assumptions, but requires one to assume that the respondents' stated values, actions, or ranks mimic what their actual behavior would be. Because the work to date has emphasized the influence of the framing of valuation questions for the values elicited, there remains a need for careful checking and pretesting to be sure wording has not induced a particular pattern of responses that arises solely from the description and not as a reflection of actual behavior.

Where Do We Stand with Indirect and Direct Methods?

After nearly a decade of extensive experience with the contingent valuation method (CVM), a 1984 conference to take stock of its performance (Cummings, Brookshire, & Schulze, 1986), and several comparisons between the benefit estimates derived from indirect and contingent valuation methods, there has been a growing acceptance of CVM. At the same time, however, the potential for substantial random variation inherent in CVM based estimates is clearly recognized. Because of the high level of noise (i.e., stochastic error) in these responses, Cummings, Brookshire, and Schulze (1986) proposed, as part of their state-of-the-art assessment, some guidelines for use of this general class of methods. Familiarity, choice experience, little uncertainty, and the use of "a willingness to pay" valuation questions are the attributes of the valuation tasks where CVM is likely to perform best.[8] It is important to recognize that these conclusions are based primarily on comparisons of estimates of the benefits from improving specific environmental resources using different methods (usually an indirect and a direct approach).[9] As such, the comparisons do not validate either approach. Both are estimates of consumers' actual values. Equally important, the comparisons have clearly highlighted the importance of the judgments made in both classes of methods.

Today valuation methods have progressed from Eckstein's (1958) pessimistic appraisal of prospects for estimating the value of the recreation outputs of water projects. Thirty years ago recreation benefits were considered to be some of the intangible benefits associated with water projects. He observed that the benefits which defy valuation at market prices are usually in the value of by-products; they are never the primary justification [for a water resource project]. To assure proper consideration of such immeasurable outputs, an analysis of intangibles should be a part of every project report. Verbal discussion of the intangible benefits and costs will communicate the facts to Congress more clearly than invalid benefit estimates. (p. 41)

Today recreation is no longer an intangible. Indeed, this summary has suggested that society is rapidly moving to the point where characteristics of environmental resources will be routinely evaluated using reasonably standardized criteria. Two sets of research support this optimism. First, Loomis and Sorg's (1982) critical summary of the available estimates of wildlife, wilderness, and general recreation relevant to the National Forest Regions was able to identify at least one study (and often more) from one of the two approaches to provide valuation estimates for seventeen activities[10] and to relate them to the Forest Service Regions.

Second, Smith and Kaoru (1990) have recently completed a comprehensive review of all published and unpublished travel cost demand models. Using these studies it is possible to construct statistical summaries for over 300 benefit estimates in a metanalysis of the factors influencing the estimated consumer surplus measures. The findings were quite encouraging. They clearly support the fact that benefit estimates (using indirect methods) exhibit consistent relationships to the resource valuation and estimation decisions. Variations in the characteristics of the resources, methods used in modeling, and maintained assumptions were of assistance in explaining variations in the valuation estimates across studies. This finding leaves little doubt that recreation resources can be consistently valued.

However, it does not mean the research is completed. Based on this review it is possible to identify areas where valuation estimates are particularly limited. These would include marine recreational fishing and boating; beach recreation activities using developed or high-density recreation facilities; and winter-based recreation activities (skiing, etc.). The emphasis given to these activities should not be misconstrued. The available information is not sufficient to permit a ready transfer of benefit estimates based on the off-the-shelf results for other types of sites or activities in most policy applications. Rather, by highlighting these examples, areas that appear to have the greatest deficiencies are indicated. Moreover, when one attempts to identify benefit estimates for changes in site characteristics, the record is even more limited. Finally, virtually all of the estimates discussed above have focused on what are best interpreted as *ex post* use values.

When the studies have attempted to measure nonuse benefits, the framework has not consistently distinguished the effects of individuals' motivations from the effects of uncertainty. Thus, it is difficult to know, in general, how to interpret most of the past estimates of nonuse values. Indeed, because of these questions, the use of the available estimates of nonuse values for evaluating decisions involving new recreation sites or in the recreation activities identified above, would seem to introduce the prospect for large variance in the valuation estimates.

IMPLICATIONS

During the past eight years increased attention has been given to the use of benefit analysis in evaluating a wide range of policies, including environmental and resource policy. The results from this increased attention have led to several important outcomes, including:

1. refinements and extensions of the conceptual framework used to define and classify components of the benefits provided by environmental resources;
2. advances in the development of models to describe individuals' behavior in their patterns of use of recreational resources with particular focus on the role of the characteristics of the resource for the decisions involved;
3. expansion in the econometric methods for recovering estimates of the behavioral relationships in these models and the associated benefits derived from use of the recreation resources;
4. greater recognition and acceptance of the potential for survey methods to directly elicit valuation information;
5. enhanced experience in applying the models to actual resources supporting outdoor recreation.

At the same time, however, this process has served to expose the limitations in our ability to provide practical valuation information that can be used to support policy decisions involving either different resources (than those studied) or changes in attributes (for specific resources) that are outside the range of recent experience.

It is probably fair to say that those analysts involved in doing research on valuing recreation resources are unlikely to admit that we do not need more research. This natural inclination is not the source of these conclusions. Rather, they follow from consideration of the task that routinely confronts the policy analysts seeking to calculate the net benefits from a particular set of activities.

The analysis must be done quickly and with resources that are usually insufficient to permit new valuation estimates. Thus, since there will rarely be time or monetary resources to permit a new specific study, our preliminary evaluation of the adequacy of available research is encouraging in that it suggests there appears to be a clear pattern linking features of the recreation resource and methods used in demand modeling to the observed variation in the benefit estimates. This is a potentially important first step in developing a logical process for adjusting the existing benefit estimates to fit the requirements that must be addressed in the policy analyses. This process is necessary for a reasonable benefits transfer (i.e., use of the benefit estimates derived from existing studies to estimate benefits in the new situation).

When interpreted in these terms the research record is certainly not complete. The understanding of the reasons for the diversity in benefit estimates is only at an early stage, too early in fact to permit benefits transfer as a routine exercise. Nonetheless, continued research to evaluate the consistency of implementing benefit analysis for policy must involve the development of transferrable models and estimates, as well as methods to evaluate their performance.

NOTES

1. A complete general discussion of benefit measurement is available in Freeman (1985) and one specific to valuing recreation resources in Smith and Desvousges (1986a).

2. For a more detailed discussion of these issues, see Chapter 2 of Smith and Desvousges (1986a) and Smith (1987).

3. Basically when uncertainty was judged unimportant, the willingness to pay would be defined with Hicksian expenditure functions (E [.]) as the difference in the minimum expenditures necessary to realize a given level of utility (u) with the price of the resource (P_R) at the choke price (i.e., where zero quantity would be demanded) versus the expenditures at the existing price, and all else held constant.

> Use Value $= E(P_R^C, \bar{P}, u) - E(P_R, \bar{P}, u)$, wherein P_R^C = choke price for the resource, P_R = existing price for the resource, and $\bar{P}$ = vector of prices for everything else.

This is an *ex post* value.

4. Of course, ideally the decision process would involve selecting, as part of the project design, a mix of attributes for the recreational resource that was expected to provide the greatest aggregate value for its service life. In practice the design of projects that are subjected to a benefit-cost analysis does not follow this ideal. Generally, political and legal factors are important influences in project design. While ideal conditions would require the optimization as part of the selection, changes in the characteristics are often not considered as part of project value.

5. The first application of the method is usually attributed to Davis (1963), and Ciriacy-Wantrup (1947) is credited with the first suggestion for doing it.

6. Of course, it may be, as Alan Randall has suggested, that if the issue were immediate, where individuals felt their responses would influence outcomes, then strategic responses might be observed.

7. There is some evidence that this performance may vary with the cultural context of application. MacRae and Whittington (1988) find as much in their paper and report the results for contingent valuation study to appraise clean water demand in Haiti.

8. These conditions are referred to as the reference operating conditions. The authors clearly recognized that the comparisons of benefit estimation methods in which the true values for consumer benefits are unknown do not validate either method. They simply apply a standard in terms of what might be described as established practices.

9. This is important because CVM may not be needed in cases where the alternative methods are not available. In these cases it cannot be said how they are likely to perform until there is a model of how individuals respond to contingent valuation questions.

10. The specific activities were anadromous fishing, big game hunting, camping, downhill skiing, cold water fishing, warm water fishing, salt water fishing, hiking, mo-

torized boating, motorized travel, nonmotorized boating, picnicking, small game hunting, upland game hunting, waterfowl hunting, water sports, and wilderness.

REFERENCES

Anderson, J. E. (1979). On the measurement of welfare cost under uncertainty. *Southern Economic Journal, 45* (April), 1160–1171.

Bartik, T. J. (1987). The estimation of demand parameters in hedonic price functions. *Journal of Political Economy, 95* (February), 81–88.

Bartik, T. J. (1988). Measuring the benefits of amenity improvements in hedonic price models. *Land Economics, 64*, 172–183.

Bockstael, N. E. Hanemann, W. M., & Kling, C. L. (1987). Modeling recreational demand in a multiple site framework. *Water Resources Research, 23* (May), 951–960.

Bockstael, N. E., Hanemann, W. M., & Strand, I. E., Jr. (1986). *Measuring the benefits of water quality improvements using recreation demand models.* Unpublished manuscript.

Brown, G. M., & Mendelsohn, R. (1984). The hedonic travel cost method. *Review of Economics and Statistics, 59* (August), 272–278.

Brown, G. M., & Pollakowski, H. O. (1977). Economic valuation of shoreline. *Review of Economics and Statistics, 59* (August), 272–278.

Cameron, T. A., & James, M. D. (1987). Efficient estimation methods for "closed-ended" contingent valuation surveys. *Review of Economics and Statistics, 69* (May), 269–276.

Carson, R. T., Hanemann, W. M., & Mitchell, R. C. (1986). *The use of simulated political markets to value public goods.* Unpublished manuscript.

Ciriacy-Wantrup, S. V. (1947). Capital returns from soil conservation practices. *Journal of Farm Economics, 29* (November), 1181–1196.

Cummings, R. G., Brookshire, D., & Schulze, W. D. (1986). *Valuing environmental goods.* Totowa, NJ: Rowman and Allanheld.

Davis, R. K. (1963). *The value of outdoor recreation: An economic study of the Maine woods.* Unpublished doctoral dissertation, Harvard University.

Eckstein, O. (1958). *Water resource development: The economics of project evaluation.* Cambridge: Harvard University Press.

Freeman, A. M. (1985). Methods for assessing the benefits of environmental programs. In A. V. Kneese and J. L. Sweeney (Eds.), *Handbook of natural resource and energy economics* (pp. 223–270). Amsterdam: North Holland.

Hanemann, W. M. (1984). Welfare evaluations in contingent valuation experiments with discrete responses. *American Journal of Agricultural Economics, 66* (August), 332–341.

Loomis, J., & Sorg, C. (1982). *A critical summary of empirical estimates of the value of wildlife, wilderness, and general recreation related to National Forest Regions.* Unpublished manuscript.

MacRae, D., Jr., & Whittington, D. (1988). Assessing preferences in cost-benefit analysis: Reflections on rural water supply. *Journal of Policy Analysis and Management, 7*, 234–238.

McConnell, K. E. (1983). Existence and bequest values. In R. D. Rowe and L. G.

Chestnut (Eds.), *Managing air quality and scenic resources at national parks and wilderness areas* (pp. 254–264). Boulder, CO: Westview Press.

McConnell, K. E. (1986). *The damages to recreational activities from PCBs in the New Bedford Harbor*. Unpublished manuscript.

McFadden, D. (1974). Conditional logit analysis of qualitative choice behavior. In P. Zarembka (Ed.), *Frontiers in econometrics* (pp. 172–187). New York: Academic Press.

Mendelsohn, R. (1987). Modeling the demand for outdoor recreation. *Water Resources Research, 23*, 961–967.

Mitchell, R. C., & Carson, R. T. (1987). *How far along the learning curve is the contingent valuation method?* (Quality of Environment Division, Resources for the Future Paper 87–07). Unpublished manuscript.

Mitchell, R. C. & Carson, R. T. (1989). *Using surveys to value public goods: The contingent valuation method*. Washington, DC: Resources for the Future.

Morey, E. R. (1981). The demand for site-specific recreational activities: A characteristics approach. *Journal of Environmental Economics and Management, 8* (December), 345–361.

President's Commission on Americans Outdoors[PCAO]. (October 24, 1986). *Americans outdoors: A call to action*. Unpublished manuscript.

Ribaudo, M. O., & Epp, D. J. (1984). The importance of sample discrimination in using the travel cost method to estimate the benefits of improved water quality. *Land Economics, 60* (November), 397–403.

Smith, V. K. (1987). Nonuse values in benefit cost analysis. *Southern Economic Journal, 54* (July), 19–26.

Smith, V. K., & Desvousges, W. H. (1985). The generalized travel cost model and water quality benefits: A reconsideration. *Southern Economic Journal, 52* (October), 371–381.

Smith, V. K., & Desvousges, W. H. (1986a). *Measuring water quality benefits*. Boston: Kluwer-Nijhoff.

Smith, V. K., & Desvousges, W. H. (1986b). The value of avoiding a LULU: Hazardous waste disposal sites. *Review of Economics and Statistics, 68* (May), 293–299.

Smith, V. K., & Kaoru, Y. (1986). Modeling recreation demand within a random utility framework. *Economic Letters, 22* (December), 395–399.

Smith, V. K., & Kaoru, Y. (1987). The hedonic travel cost model: A view from the trenches. *Land Economics, 63* (May), 179–192.

Smith, V. K., & Kaoru, Y. (1990). "Signals or noise? Explaining the variation in recreation benefit estimates." *American Journal of Agricultural Economics, 72* (May), 419–433.

Smith, V. K., & Kopp, R. J. (1980). The spatial limits of the travel cost recreation demand model. *Land Economics, 56*, 64–72.

Vaughan, W. J., & Russell, C. S. (1982). Valuing a fishing day: An application of a systematic varying parameter model. *Land Economics, 58* (November), 450–463.

Ward, F., & Loomis, J. (1986). *The travel cost demand model as an environmental policy assessment tool: A review of the literature*. Unpublished manuscript, New Mexico State University.

5.

THE ECONOMIC VALUE OF WILDERNESS: A CRITICAL ASSESSMENT

Jerry W. Calvert and Patrick Jobes

This chapter demonstrates that economics is inadequate as the sole or even the primary basis for making decisions regarding the future of America's wild land. The inadequacies of the economic model are demonstrated in the context of contemporary natural resource decision making. Data drawn primarily from Montana demonstrate the difficulty in long-term wilderness planning based on an economic perspective alone. An argument is then presented to demonstrate the impossibility of validly converting the value of wilderness to economic terms. It is argued that government decision makers have been accommodating to privateers (advocates of privatization) and have favored traditional exploitive development of natural areas, even when such decisions make no economic sense. It is further argued that when economic values are examined, preservationist orientations make more sense in dollars gained than do traditional exploitation orientations. In spite of the economic value demonstrated for preservation of natural areas, it is maintained that any economic model is inadequate as a basis for decision making concerned with wild lands.

THE CONTEMPORARY CONTEXT OF NATURAL RESOURCE DECISION MAKING

Privatization

During the 1970s a national debate waged regarding where the proper authority for managing natural resources should rest. The issue was whether public lands and other resources should be managed as part of the public trust or be converted to private ownership and made subject to free enterprise. The general conclusion by social scientists is that the argument was one sided, and benefited a few politically conservative advocates of free enterprise (Buttel, Geisler, & Wiswall, 1984).

The call for privatization was justified on the basis of economic utility. Private ownership was presented as morally and politically superior to public ownership on the grounds of economic efficiency (Friedman, 1980). Schnaiberg (1980) maintains that privatization masks what are fundamentally unscientific issues with the guise of economic science. This follows the intellectual heritage of the preservation of natural resources that are too precious and essential for humanity to be cast into the single-minded perspective of economic efficiency (Leopold, 1949). As currently used, economic efficiency cannot be adequately measured or projected for a long enough period to provide a sufficiently inclusive perspective for allocating natural resources.

Privatization also assumes that the value of land and all natural resources on it, including animals, is best measured through profit (Friedman & Friedman, 1962). The call for privatization tries to make profit the goal by which the administration of public lands should be measured (Baden & Stroup, 1981). In response, government officials have been shaken by the emergence of charges of economic inefficiency raised by privateers (Schnaiberg, 1980). Many accept the premise that profit should be the goal of public administrators. They are, after all, socialized into a society that makes that simplistic and rigid assumption (Scitovsky, 1978).

Several negative results followed the recent call for privatization. The most direct effects have been through the selling of public lands to private interests (Gamache, 1984). Selling of small plots of land that are long distances from wilderness has some advantages, particularly if their administrative costs were high. If land exchanges or the direct purchase of new lands adjacent to wilderness occurred as a result of privatization, then some benefit might result. However, the principal is dangerous (Krutilla & Fisher, 1975). Once initiated, the risk of expanded selling off of large tracts of land becomes possible. Short-term economic gains may result in the loss of the long-range values of the properties, which once sold are no longer available for public use.

The privatization of wildlife, particularly for hunting, is an associated problem. Rocky Mountain states stand to lose control of a public resource as well as the enormous revenues generated by that resource. The public would lose hunting privileges, part of their heritage, as well as face higher taxes while a few land owners and elite sportsmen would gain (Wyoming Game and Fish Department, 1987).

Even more abusive than the selling of tracts of land has been the increased leasing of public lands for private resource exploitation at prices less than the return and certainly less than the value for recreation or wildlife (Clawson, 1976). The sale of fossil fuel reserves frequently has effectively amounted to giving public resources away to provide income for a few recipients (Schmidt & Boyer, 1983). Similarly, timber sales on public lands in the northern Rocky Mountains frequently have generated less money than the costs of administering the sales (Irland, 1979).

Finally, privatization can be criticized on the basis of the observable inequities that have been associated with it. A relatively small number of persons have actively advocated it. Found among that number are the few who directly benefited from it. Privatization provides an argument based on the welfare of the majority that actually benefits a tiny minority of advocates of free-market economics-based decision making (Held, 1980). By leading the argument, they have distinct advantages over all other potential users of resources. They are able to specify unknown uses, which generally work for their short-term profit, when other perhaps more valued uses remain unarticulated or unknown. They impose premature closure of the discussion of valid uses by imposing the artificial limitation of economics as the determining factor for settling the fate of resources that once used can never be returned to their natural state.

Cost-Benefit Analysis

Cost-benefit analysis is frequently touted by advocates of development or by policy makers as a rational tool for decision making (Mishan, 1976). The attractiveness for privateers of a simplified summary seems to be its hypnotic effect on the policy makers who lack expertise or varied perspectives regarding proposed developments yet must make decisions.

Literally thousands of cost-benefit analyses of various uses of natural resources have been conducted (Peterson & Randall, 1984). Estimates of costs and benefits are based on a plethora of measures, variables, and assumptions. Many have been conducted to articulate the value of minimal development uses, particularly recreation. While such studies generally document some economic value for amenity uses of the natural environment, they vary greatly due to the characteristics of the models employed. Walsh, Gillman, and Loomis (1982), for example, document the values of several specific wilderness uses in Colorado. They assign current wilderness a value of $1.9 billion. However meritorious their exercise, the value assigned could vary by a magnitude of six or eight, depending on the number of acres and the assumed dollars per day people would be willing to allocate.

The great limitation of economic analysis is its inability to anticipate what variables will be important for the future (Schelling, 1968). This weakness goes beyond the inability to achieve a valid operationalization of the potential effects of development. It certainly goes beyond the deliberate selection and rejection of concepts and measures that typify advocacy and adversarial procedures for influencing how a development decision will be made. It is impossible to know what future uses may exist for wilderness in an area. If wilderness has been converted to some other use, however, many potential uses will clearly no longer exist.

The ability to suggest future uses is no less limited. Some uses seem to promise increasing concern for the future, and for some of these it is effectively impossible to assign any meaningful dollar value. The pivotal point of our analysis is whether the natural environment is sufficiently precious to exempt it from the whims of the market and the measures of cost-benefit analysts. Allowing the free market to decide the fate of resources is extremely attractive. It appears intrinsically democratic. It prevents the confusion caused by poorly enacted or administered regulations. It seems to be historically and culturally consistent with social beliefs and policies.

The Role of Government

This nation has never really believed in or operated as a free marketplace. Some behaviors have been deemed too precious or too endangering to allow the free market to determine them (Kelman, 1981). The precedent of protecting the long-term good of all over the short-run preferences of individuals has been repeatedly affirmed. Protection of the environment for the collective good is an extension of the same principles as legislation controlling vice, vehicle safety, insurance regulation, and most other civil regulations (Burch & DeLuca, 1984). The right to control it is well established. The issue of whether it is precious enough to protect is vital.

The consequences of development rest in the future. Expectations of what will happen if enormous tracts of land are set aside in perpetuity or opened to the free market are largely a matter of faith. They cannot be accurately measured and projected, though general trends indicate preservationist values will increase relative to those favoring materials conversions (Krutilla & Fisher, 1975). The free-market system lacks the goal of preserving anything. If anything is preserved it will only be deemed so by the temporary values of consumers. If at any time the public temporarily agreed to develop natural areas or to sell them to private developers, their protected status would be violated. Once lost, they may be lost forever. They cannot be remanufactured from an old blueprint. They continue to exist only if they are left alone.

Thus government, despite its weaknesses, has continued to play a major regulative role because private enterprise cannot be trusted to protect and preserve what is precious. The costs of inefficiency and corruption of government are more acceptable than the unmitigated exploitation by business when the essentials of survival are concerned. Land, air, and water existing in their natural state are such essentials (Dumas, 1986).

RESOURCE DEVELOPMENT OR RECREATION—THE CASE OF MONTANA

Natural ecosystems rarely coincide with legislative boundaries (Athern, 1986). This is no less true in the northern Rockies than elsewhere. The issues that are discussed in this chapter are particularly pertinent to this region as it contains some of the largest unexploited tracts of preservable natural resource lands. A relatively high proportion of income comes from the tourist and recreational uses of these lands, uses that could be diminished by any massive exploitation of the area's oil, gas, minerals, and timber. In addition, the area has many sections where natural resources are contributing minimal returns to the economy or to people when exploited in their traditional manners. The focus of this analysis is Montana, which encapsulates most characteristics of the northern Rockies.

The state of Montana, like other Rocky Mountain states, has been heavily dependent on the resource extractive industry. At one time Montanans called their land "The Treasure State" to boast proudly of its minerals and timber (Toole, 1959). But with the long-term decline in metal mining, principally in the demise of the state's once all-powerful copper mining enterprise, the Anaconda Company, the current recessions in the oil, gas, and coal industries, and low timber prices, Montana policy makers and business leaders are just now beginning to see that perhaps tourism and outdoor recreation can be the cornerstone of a new era for the state's economy. Today, Montana advertises itself as "Big Sky Country" in its first tentative steps to sell its remaining undegraded environment (Lopach et al., 1983).

Public lands are the basis for the development of tourism and outdoor recreation. There are 27.7 million acres of federal land in Montana, almost 30 percent of the state's area. Of this amount 16.7 million acres are administered by the U.S. Forest Service (USFS), 8.1 million by the Bureau of Land Management (BLM), and 1.2 million by the National Park Service (NPS) (*The Battle for Natural Resources,* 1983). In addition to the wilderness lands encompassed by the Glacier and Yellowstone national parks, there are eight federal wilderness areas totaling 3.4 million acres under Forest Service administration. Of these the largest are the Bob Marshall (1,009,356 acres) and the 920,310 acre Absoraka-Beartooth wilderness areas (U.S. Department of Agriculture, 1985).

Within the public lands designated as wilderness there are in excess of 4,000 miles of hiking trails (Fraley, 1986). Among the attractions found is fishing for trout. In Montana's wilderness areas alone there are 500 productive alpine and subalpine lakes and thousands of miles of rivers and streams (Fraley, 1985).

According to recent surveys conducted on behalf of the Department of Fish, Wildlife, and Parks, Montanans make extensive use of their state's outdoor recreation resources (Frost & McCool, 1986; Wallwork, Lenihaw, & Polzin, 1980). For example, in 1985 the majority of residents reported participating in fishing, camping, and sightseeing activities. Large minorities also reported hunting, hiking, and backpacking. Almost two-thirds reported visiting a federal or state park during the past year (Frost & McCool, 1986). Nonresidents also have a high opinion of the state's outdoor recreation potential since 90 percent responding to a recent survey rated Montana's outdoor recreation as "good" to "excellent." Respondents cited the state's scenic beauty, its low population density, clean water, and clean air as the primary reasons for their positive evaluative judgments (Brock, et al., 1984). What then is the real and potential economic benefit of the travel and outdoor recreation industry for the state of Montana?

In a report for the Travel Promotion Division of the Montana Department of Commerce, Daily (1984) estimated that tourism pumped $225 million into the state's economy in 1983, a 9 percent increase over 1979. Nonresidents accounted for 56 percent of this amount. Approximately 20,000 jobs were generated by tourism, for an annual payroll of $106 million. Indeed, in 1985 tourism and travel surpassed mining and lumbering in income generated. Only agriculture and oil and gas wells contributed more (Lies, 1987).

Hunters and anglers are major sources of business income. For example, one estimate suggests that $150 million was spent by these individuals in 1980 (Graham, 1986). Nonresident anglers and hunters spent an estimated $53.1 million, while total spending for hunting and fishing may have reached $227.5 million in that year (Wilson, 1983).

Estimates concerning expenditures made by anglers have also been made. One study reports that an estimated $27 million was spent by anglers in 1982 for trout fishing alone (Kronberg & Tuholske, 1985). This estimate may not account, however, for the value contributed by nonresident anglers who come to enjoy the state's world famous blue ribbon trout fishery. A survey conducted by the statistics department of Montana State University on behalf of Trout Unlimited concluded that in 1982 the average nonresident angler spent $718 for food, travel, and other goods and services while in the state. Multiply that by the approximately 100,000 nonresident fishing licenses sold, the income generated by out-of-state anglers alone may have been as much as $24 million (Montana State University, 1982). Taylor and Reilly (1986) cite figures for guided hunting, fishing, and tourism. They report $34 million in direct expenditures and a total economic impact of $26 million for 1985.

Hunting and fishing are largely dependent on the preservation of publicly owned wilderness lands. Nonetheless, the state's long-term dependency on re-source extractive industries has created a distorted and one-sided perception that only these industries produce jobs and income. But additional data strongly suggest that wilderness (which means the prohibition of mining and logging) contributes a large measure of both to the state's economy.

For example, the Montana timber industry currently accounts for approxi-mately 8,000 jobs (about 4 percent of all jobs in the state) and is heavily subsidized (Emerson, 1986; Montana Department of Commerce, 1985). In most of the Montana national forests the Forest Service sells the public's timber below cost, which is defined as "sales in which the cost of sale development and administration exceed the timber sale receipts" (Jackson, 1986). The largest Forest Service expense in support of logging is road construction. In the Forest Service's Northern Region (comprising all of Montana and northern Idaho) road construction expenses exceed timber sale receipts. There are thirteen national forests in this region. All ten national forests in Montana sell timber below cost

(Emerson, 1986; Wilderness Society, 1987a). The net annual loss to the taxpayer is estimated to be $29 million (Schaeffer, 1986). It must be stressed that the problem is not peculiar to Montana. In 76 out of 123 national forests timber is sold below cost at an estimated loss of $2.1 billion between 1975 and 1984 (Emerson, 1986; Shaeffer, 1986). Currently evolving Forest Service plans, according to estimates made by the Wilderness Society, will result in similar future losses (Wilderness Society, 1987a).

Similar data have been compiled for the seven national forests that border Yellowstone National Park and which constitute the Greater Yellowstone Ecosystem (GYES). In all seven timber costs exceeded receipts by $7 million annually from 1979 to 1984 according to data gathered in 1987 (Cascade Holistic, 1987; Wilderness Society, 1987b). A congressional staff study points to the same conclusion. Between 1983 and 1985 money expended by the Forest Service for timber development in the GYES was $11.34 million while receipts from timber sales were $5.81 million (U.S. House Committee, 1986). Given that logging is accomplished at a net loss to the taxpayer with the below cost timber sales being in effect a public subsidization of the timber industry, any positive economic values that can be realized by not cutting the trees would seem to justify a careful reevaluation of the Forest Service mission. Yet no such reevaluation has yet taken place. The Forest Service continues to tilt its budgetary priorities strongly in favor of timber at the expense of alternative public uses for the public lands under its domain. For example, the 1987 budget for Forest Service Region 1 (the Northern Region comprising all of Montana and northern Idaho) allocated only 6.6 percent ($108,750) to outdoor recreation and a little more than 4 percent to fish, wildlife, soil and water conservation (Forest Service Budget Bureaucracy, 1987).

Though no comprehensive data exist for the entire state, available evidence clearly reveals significant and positive economic value is attached to natural areas. The data for the Greater Yellowstone Ecosystem are highly suggestive of the potential. Employment in the seven national forests bordering Yellowstone National Park is overwhelmingly derived from the area's outdoor recreational opportunities (Cascade Holistic, 1987; Wilderness Society, 1987b). According to the congressional staff study outdoor recreation accounts for 84 percent of all direct employment in the GYES. Logging, in contrast, accounts for only 10 percent of all direct employment. There are currently an estimated 5,548 direct and indirect jobs in outdoor recreation compared to 499 direct and 814 indirect or induced jobs associated with the timber industry (U.S. House Committee, 1986).

One of the public land areas bordering Yellowstone Park is Montana's Gallatin National Forest. Comprising 1.7 million acres, the Gallatin National Forest loses an average of $1.6 million in timber sales. This subsidy provides 54 to 189 jobs. In contrast, outdoor recreation provides for 1,171 to 1,517 direct and indirect jobs in the three counties whose jurisdictions encompass this national forest. The Forest Service's preferred alternative draft management plan for the area, however, seriously underestimated its outdoor recreation potential. The plan anticipates an increase in the harvesting of the marginal timber stands in the Gallatin National Forest, which will increase logging employment by approximately seventy-one jobs. These seventy-one new jobs will cost the taxpayers $646,000 in Forest Service expenditures annually or $23,000 per new job. Further, the Forest Service estimates that it will spend $2,355,000 per annum in timber development and realize gross receipts of $709,000. The result is a net loss of $1,646,000, a subsidized destruction of outdoor recreation opportunities (and employment) in order to underwrite a handful of jobs in the forest products industry (Cascade Holistic, 1985; Cascade Holistic, 1987; Wilderness Society, 1987b).

Finally, Power (1987) has provided an analysis of the economic value of wilderness in Montana's Rocky Mountain Front Area, which borders the Bob Marshall, Great Bear, and Scapegoat Wilderness Areas. According to Forest Service estimates, oil and gas development in the front may create three new jobs, while increased logging of timber considered marketable might also produce three new jobs. Clearly, outdoor recreation jobs, for example, outfitters, guides, sporting goods employment, and dude ranches, far outnumber potential resource extractive jobs that this area might reasonable spawn.

In summary, the data for Montana clearly point in one direction. The economic value of wilderness is clearly significant and grossly underestimated in comparison to estimates assumed for resource extractive industry. Data that are fully sensitive to the economic values associated with wilderness preservation need to be incorporated in public planning. Currently no such data exist, and existing data are often incomplete, contradictory, and/or based on questionable assumptions (U.S. House Committee, 1986). But even if such data did exist, no economical model can fully comprehend the value of wilderness. The jargon of economic science applied to public land policy formulation unnecessarily limits the value of wilderness to timber measured in thousands of board feet (mbt), grazing estimated by something called animal unit months (AUMs), and recreation calculated as recreation visitor days (RVDs). These measures, while useful, do not begin to capture the value of wild lands because some wilderness values are beyond monetary estimation, no matter how sophisticated the method.

CULTURAL AND PHILOSOPHICAL REASONS FOR PRESERVATION

There are many non-economic ways of thinking about natural resources and many classifications of uses of the natural environment have been offered. Brockman (1973) emphasized recreational uses. Carroll (1969) described their moral virtues and Cinchetti, Seneca, and Davidson (1969) described their alternative utilitarian purposes. More recently, Driver (1987) has completed a matrix distinguishing personal and social well-being, as well as a literature review of a wide variety of non-economic and economic values for natural resource recreation.

Perhaps the simplest reason for justifying the preservation of natural areas is that many people like them. In 1980, 175 million people used natural areas. The rates of use are far greater than population growth, particularly for mechanical uses like snowmobiling (Crandall, 1984). The problem with using such fundamental hedonism as a justification is that others may feel equally passionate about other activities that destroy natural areas. However much people like a natural trout or tree, or a scenic highway, or a redwood hot tub, the justification of how to allocate resources must transcend the simplistic consumer-driven economic model. Natural areas are too valuable to allow uninformed users operating in their own short-term self-interests to have the opportunity to destroy what is quite likely valuable beyond our comprehension.

Pantheistic societies believe each natural element has a spirit, a perspective that makes respecting and monitoring nature a way of life (Lenski & Lenski, 1987). Admittedly, the minimally destructive technologies of these cultures may have been the most important factors in protecting their environments. Nevertheless, their beliefs are conservationist. A similar perspective has been presented by philosophers and futurists to assure the preservation of species. For example, Van DeVeer and Pierce (1986) have discussed the intrinsic worth of nonhuman species. LeGuin (1985) has speculated that future societies faced with an economy that primarily relies on renewable resources will hold similar beliefs out of necessity. It may be that anything and everything that exists has value for the continuing processes of nature, whether or not the truth is comprehended, however tautological it may be.

An underlying and, until recently, rarely explored assumption governing the criteria that should be used to justify resource exploration is that humans are superior to other species (Regan, 1982). They are felt to have the right to determine the use of the environment because of this preferred status. This position has largely been ignored from St. Francis of Assisi to the present (Wallerstein, 1975). No intrinsic right of humans to dominate other species can be demonstrated other than our capacity to do so (Schmookler, 1984).

The best-known and most difficult attribute of wilderness to which to assign economic value are aesthetics, the perception of beauty (Goodpaster & Sayre, 1979). In the world of art and crafts objects gain value by how much people will pay to see, hear, smell, touch, or taste the things they want. The price of a painting or the popularity of a composition reflect their value as objects. Users are attracted to different aspects of nature. Many objects to which users might be attracted only exist in nature. For many, they can only be appreciated in their natural habitat. Animals or geothermal phenomena are more than created objects that can be preserved and appreciated in practically any context, as a great sculpture can. If at any moment, their value were to temporarily decline to a level permitting extinction, the process of which they are a part is simultaneously destroyed. An ecosystem without the direct interference of humans cannot be recreated.

NATURAL AND SOCIAL SCIENTIFIC REASONS FOR PRESERVATION

The loss of wilderness may mean the loss of precious and potentially irretrievable species that may be of direct adaptive benefit to humans. For example, some species of plants have pharmaceutical value. Many species are yet unrecorded (Scherer & Attig, 1983). Destruction of wilderness may eradicate such species before their potential is recognized and before they can be preserved for posterity. This problem is compounded if two or more potentially useful species are linked in a synergistic manner, a condition which would be extremely difficult to serendipitously discover outside of nature (Myers, 1979).

The additive effects of species toward a beneficial use points to another scientific value of wilderness that is scarcely acknowledged or understood. Wilderness has value as a natural ecosystem that cannot be duplicated. The system is a biological timepiece composed of inorganic and organic components. It is a natural laboratory in which natural history is stored. Without such a place there is no natural analogues to biological problems and solutions that emerge in systems where humans have unsuccessfully interfered (Singer, 1981).

The value of wilderness as a location for rest and recovery has been discussed since the late nineteenth century. Many of the figures cited in this chapter demonstrate how much time and money recreationists spend in various uses of the natural outdoors. The more troubling questions concern whether wilderness recreation has any intrinsic value and, if it does, how that might be measured. The questions behind these principles cannot be answered solely in a quantitative manner by economics (Dolan, 1969). In spite of the quasi-scientific notation of economics, on matters of general and long-term importance, the perspective is fundamentally grounded in philosophy.

The ultimate reason for maintaining vast areas of land that are relatively undisturbed by humans is that this land provides a sensitive marker for the well-being of the planet. In earlier times miners listened for the song of the canary to protect them from dangerous mine gases. When the bird stopped singing they left the mine—fast—if they could. A region of the planet is a far more varied and resilient environment than a mine shaft, but the principles of life are comparable. When flora and fauna of a natural system begin to die, it can signify that influences from external forces from a still broader system are imbalanced, as evidence concerning acid rain clearly demonstrates. Without wilderness, the most varied and sensitive long-term indicators of environmental deterioration may be missing.

The speculative quality of many of the considerations mentioned above regarding the value of nature are discomforting. They provide no precise and tangible answers of how to make decisions. They nonetheless may be the most crucial questions because they go beyond the limitations of cost-benefit analyses and other economic tools of analysis.

SUMMARY

In spite of the shortcomings of economic decision making, it provides one useful way of examining how a natural resource might be developed. The economic model has become the metaphor for rational decision making. It is considered primarily as a metaphor, a socially accepted way of thinking about how the world is supposed to operate. Pragmatically, it must be acknowledged and used because currently it has the most universal credibility.

It is evident that there is no single, clear, and concise way of conceiving or measuring what economic consequences of development mean, even for a relationship as simple as the relative contribution of resources of a limited geographic area when left in wilderness or when converted to salable timber.

Natural resources are valuable because they offer a variety of potential uses, which each compete with others. Competition in a natural ecosystem occurs simultaneously among all species that are biologically capable of occupying the same niche. In modern society human decision making determines the use of natural resources. Decision making in human-dominated systems replaces natural adaptation in a system void of humans. Rather than choosing the most adaptive allocation of land, air, and water, humans develop resources on the basis of social values incorporated into the social structure. Since values are cultural creations, development of resources based on values is also a result of human decisions. The competition between potential users of the environment is based on differing and opposing values rather than on the intrinsic worth of the resources.

In conclusion, the underlying values and assumptions of economics are simply inadequate to manage and preserve natural environments. Even though natural environments have proven their economic worth, the value of the natural environment can never be defended or understood in economic terms alone. Wilderness has irreplaceable cultural, scientific, and aesthetic worth. Any planning model must incorporate within it these incalculable contributions as well as economic ones.

REFERENCES

Athern, R. G. (1986). *The mythic western twentieth-century America.* Lawrence: University of Kansas Press.

Baden, J., & Stroup, R. L. (1981). *Bureaucracy vs. environment: The environmental costs of bureaucratic governance.* Ann Arbor: University of Michigan Press.

The battle for natural resources. (1983). Washington: Congressional Quarterly, Inc.

Boulding, K. (1969). Economics as a moral science. *American Economic Review, 59* (March), 1–12.

Brock, J. M., Larson, J. D., Huhs, W. F., Reilly, M. D., & Rogers, J. (1984). *Montana tourism marketing research project: Executive summary*. Helena: Montana Department of Commerce.

Brockman, C. F. (1973). *Recreational use of wild lands*. New York: McGraw-Hill.

Burch, W., Jr., & DeLuca, D. R. (1984). *Measuring the social impact of material resource policies*. Albuquerque: University of New Mexico Press.

Buttell, F. H., Geisler, C. C., & Wiswall, I. W. (1984). *Labor and the environment: An analysis of and annotated bibliography on work place environmental quality in the United States*. Westport, CT: Greenwood Press.

Carroll, P. N. (1969). *Puritanism and the wilderness*. New York: Columbia University Press.

Cascade Holistic Economic Consultants. (1985). *Review of the Gallatin Forest plan and draft environmental impact statement*. Eugene, OR: Author.

Cascade Holistic Economic Consultants. (1987). *Economic database for greater Yellowstone forests*. Eugene, OR: Author.

Catton, W. R. (1980). *Overshoot*. Urbana: University of Illinois Press.

Cinchetti, C. J., Seneca, J. J., & Davidson, P. (1969). *The demand and supply of outdoor recreation*. New Brunswick, NJ: Rutgers University Press.

Clawson, M. (1976). *The economics of national forest management*. New York: Resources of the Future.

Coffin, A. (1986). Economics of non-resident anglers. *Montana Troutline, 6* (May), 1, 11.

Crandall, D. (1984). America's national forest: An essential link in recreation supply. In A. E. Gamache (Ed.), *Selling the federal forest* (pp. 212–221). New York: Institute of Forest Resources.

Dailey, R. (1984). *The Montana travel industry, 1983*. Helena: Montana Department of Commerce.

Devall, W., & Sessions, G. (Eds.). (1985). *Deep ecology*. Salt Lake City: Peregrine Smith.

Dolan, E. G. (1969). *Tanstaafl: The economic strategy for environmental crisis*. New York: Holt, Rinehart, and Winston.

Driver, B. L. (1987). Benefits of river and trail recreation: The limited state of knowledge and why it is limited. In S. Seguire (Ed.), *Proceedings of the first international congress on trail and river recreation*. Vancouver: Outdoor Recreation Council of British Columbia.

Dubos, R. (1968). *So human and animal*. New York: Scribners.

Dumas, L. J. (1986). *The overburdened economy*. Berkeley: University of California Press.

Emerson, P. (1986). The below cost timber sale issue: Going against the grain? *Western Wildlands, 4* (Spring), 16–21.

Forest Service budget bureaucracy. (1987). *Wild Montana, 4* (Summer), 7.

Fraley, J. (1985). Should we manage it or leave it alone? *Montana Outdoors, 16* (July/August), 34–37.

Fraley, J. (1986). The joy of backpacking. *Montana Outdoors, 17* (July/August), 3–6, 24–25.

Friedman, M. (1980). *Free to choose*. New York: Harcourt, Brace, Jovanovich.

Friedman, M., & Friedman, R. D. (1962). *Capitalism and freedom*. Chicago: University of Chicago Press.

Frost, J., & McCool, S. (1986). *The Montana outdoor recreation needs survey*. Helena: Montana Department of Fish, Wildlife, and Parks.

Gamache, A. E. (Ed.). (1984). *Selling the federal forests*. New York: Institute of Forest Resources.

Goodpaster, K., & Sayre, K. M. (Eds.). (1979). *Ethics and problems of the 21st century*. Notre Dame: University of Notre Dame Press.

Graham, P. (1986). A reflection of choices. *Montana Outdoors, 17* (April/June), 20–22, 26.

Held, V. (Ed.). (1980). *Property, profits, and economic justice*. Belmont, CA: Wadsworth.

Humphrey, C. R., & Buttel, F. R. (1982). *Environment, energy, and society*. Belmont, CA: Wadsworth.

Irland, L. C. (1979). *Wilderness economics and policy*. Lexington, MA: Lexington Books.

Jackson, D. H. (1986). Below cost sales: Causes and solutions. *Western Wildlands, 12* (Spring), 11–15.

Junkin, D. (1986, June 9). A commission looks at outdoor recreation. *High Country News*, p. 4.

Kelman, S. (1981). *What price incentives?* Boston: Auburn House.

Kronberg, C., & Tuholske, J. (1985). *Forest plans and fisheries: Threat or promise*. Missoula: National Wildlife Federation.

Krutilla, J. V., & Fisher, A. C. (1975). *The economics of natural environments*. Baltimore: Johns Hopkins University Press.

LeGuin, U. (1985). *Always coming home*. New York: Harper and Row.

Lenski, G., & Lenski, J. (1987). *Human societies* (5th ed.). New York: McGraw-Hill.

Leopold, A. (1949). *A Sand County almanac*. New York: Oxford University Press.

Lies, C. H. (1987). U.S. Crop and Livestock Report Service. Personal communication.

Lopach, J., McKinsey, L., Playne, T., Waldren, E., Calvert, J., & Brown, M. (1983). *We the people of Montana*. Missoula: Mountain Press Publishing.

Mishan, E. J. (1976). *Cost benefit analysis*. New York: Praeger. Montana Department of Commerce. (1985). *Montana statistical abstract—1984*. Helena: Author.

Montana State University Statistical Research Center. (1982). *Survey of the economic impact of non-resident anglers in Montana—1982 season*. Bozeman: Trout Unlimited.

Morrison, D. E. (1978). Equity impacts of some major energy alternatives. In S. Warkov (Ed.), *Energy policy in the United States* (pp. 164–193). New York: Praeger.

Myers, N. (1979). *The sinking ark*. Oxford: Pergamon Press.

Peterson, G. L., & Randall, A. (Eds.) (1984). *Valuation of wildland resource benefits*. Boulder, CO: Westview.

Power, T. (1987). *The economic impact of wilderness classification for the Rocky Mountain front roadless areas in Montana*. Unpublished manuscript, University of Montana, Department of Economics.

President's Commission on Americans Outdoors [PCAO] (1987). *Americans outdoors: The legacy, the challenge*. Washington, DC: Island Press.

Regan, T. (1982). *All that dwell therein*. Berkeley: University of California Press.

Reid, R. T. (1987, February 12). From spuds to scenery: West shifts economic focus. *Washington Post*, pp. 20–21.

Reiger, J. F. (1975). *American sportsmen and the origins of conservatism*. New York: Winchester.

Schaeffer, R. (1986). Lumbering into oblivion. *In These Times*, November, pp. 19–25.

Schelling, T. (1968). The life you save may be your own. In S. B. Chase (Ed.), *Problems of public expenditure analysis* (pp. 127–162). Washington, DC: The Brookings Institute.

Scherer, D., & Attig, T. (1983). *Ethics and the environment*. Englewood Cliffs, NJ: Prentice-Hall.

Schmidt, J. C., & Boyer, J. (1983). An overview of coal leasing, mine development, and future production in the Powder River coal basin, Montana and Wyoming. *Coal Development VI*. Billings, MT: Bureau of Land Management.

Schmookler, A. B. (1984). *The parable of the tribes*. Berkeley: University of California Press.

Schnaiberg, A. (1980). *The environment: From surplus to scarcity*. New York: Oxford University Press.

Schwartz, W. (Ed.). (1969). *Voices for the wilderness*. New York: Ballantyne.

Scitovsky, T. (1978). *The joyless economy: An inquiry into human satisfaction and consumer dissatisfaction*. Oxford: Oxford University Press.

Singer, P. (1981). *The expanding circle*. New York: Farrar, Straus, and Giroux.

Stanley, G., & Lucas, R. (1986, May). *Shifting trends in backcountry and wilderness use*. Paper presented at the National Symposium in Social Science Resource Management, Corvallis, OR.

Taylor, S. V., & Reilly, M. D., (1986). *Economic impact of the outfitting industry on the state of Montana*. Bozeman: Montana State University School of Business.

Toole, K. R. (1959). *Montana: An uncommon land*. Norman: University of Oklahoma Press.

U.S. Department of Agriculture. (1985). *Land areas of the national forest system* (Forest Service Publication FS-3F3). Washington, DC: Author.

U.S. House Committee on Interior and Insular Affairs. (1986). *Greater Yellowstone ecosystem*. Washington, DC: U.S. Government Printing Office.

Van DeVeer, D., & Pierce, C. (1986). *People, penguins, and plastic trees*. Belmont, CA: Wadsworth.

Wallerstein, I. (1975). *The modern world system*. New York: Academic Press.

Wallwork, S., Lenihaw, M. L., & Polzin, P. E. (1980). *Montana outdoor recreation survey*. Helena: Montana Department of Fish, Wildlife, and Parks.

Walsh, R. G., Gillman, R. A., & Loomis, J. B. (1982). *Wilderness resource economics*. Denver: American Wilderness Alliance.

Wilderness Society. (1987a). *Forests of the future? An assessment of the national forest planning process*. Washington, DC: Author.

Wilderness Society. (1987b). *Management directions for the national forests of the greater Yellowstone ecosystem*. Bozeman: Author.

Wilson, J. (1983). *Direct expenditures for hunting and fishing in Montana—1983*. Unpublished manuscript.

Wyoming Game and Fish Department (1987). *Proceedings of the privatization of wildlife and public lands access symposium*. Cheyenne: Author.

Part III

Financing and Regulating Recreational Resources

6.

FINANCING OUTDOOR RECREATION IN THE UNITED STATES

William R. Mangun and John B. Loomis

In 1985, Marion Clawson wrote, "Outdoor recreation on publicly-owned areas is so firmly established in the modern American society that it can never be abolished or even heavily cut back." Apparently the Reagan administration was not aware of this when it eliminated the primary financial stimulus for outdoor recreation in the United States. In its 1982 budget proposal the Department of the Interior requested no funds be provided for the Land and Water Conservation Fund (LWCF). This proposal resulted in a political furor in Congress as states, local governments, and private conservation organizations lobbied vigorously to have these funds restored. Given the pressures of the federal deficit, however, Congress acquiesced to the administration's fiscal initiative and no outlays were made for the LWCF in fiscal year 1982.

Walsh and Loomis (1986) analyzed the contribution of recreation to national economic development as a background document for the President's Commission on Americans Outdoors (PCAO) and came to the conclusion that the American society benefits from expenditures by public agencies for parks and recreation. Their measure is a comparison between the value to the private sector of what it gives up to support a government recreation program (represented by taxes, user fees, and opportunity costs) and the value of the output that that government provides with the resources (represented by the willingness of citizens to pay for what the government produced, if they had to). Walsh and Loomis used this measure to determine whether total benefits substantially exceed government costs based on the limited aggregate U.S. data that are available.

Table 6.1
Benefits and Costs of Recreation and Park Programs by Level of Government,
United States, 1982

Level of government	Recreation visitor days	Net economic value[a]	Government expenditures
All government, total			
Million	3,100	$26,268	$8,876
Per household	36	305	103
Municipal and county			
Million	2,200	9,363	6,140
Per household	26	109	72
State			
Million	300	6,387	1,362
Per Household	3	74	16
Federal, total			
Million	600	10,518	1,375
Per household	7	122	16

[a]Municipal and county, $4.26, unit-day value from Water Resources Council (1983) represents the midpoint (50 points) in general recreation category, or $3.20 times 1.33 to correct for 12-hour recreation visitor days. State, $21.29, assumes that about two-thirds was wildlife related at $22 and one-third was park and recreation use valued at $20 (Andrews, 1984; Gibbs, 1983; Kalter & Gosse, 1969; Sorg & Loomis, 1985). Federal, $17.53, assumes that about one-half was wildlife related at $22 and one-half was park and recreation valued at $9.82 times 1.33 to correct for 12-hour recreation visitor days.

Source: U.S. Census of Government, 1982, and estimates from the authors.

For the year 1982, Walsh and Loomis estimated that government expenditures equaled about $2.50 per recreation visitor day (RVD). Approximately $8 billion in expenditures divided by 3.1 billion recreation visitor days yielded this value. The authors estimated that benefits in the same year averaged about $8.50 per RVD. By multiplying this figure by the number of visitor days, they determined that benefits amounted to approximately $26 billion. As such, this represents a roughly three to one ratio of benefits to costs, which represents a major overall benefit to society. Walsh and Loomis's data in Table 6.1 provide an overall picture of the benefits and costs of recreation and park programs for federal, state, and local government in the United States in 1982.

Of all the issues that the President's Commission on Americans Outdoors had to address, financing outdoor recreation may have been the most important. In public meetings across the United States, commission members were told about

Table 6.2
Direct Government Spending on Parks and Recreation

	1977-78	1980-81	1983-84	Change 1980-84 (%)
All governments	$6,732	$8,536	$9,882	+15.8
Federal	1,462	1,472	1,539	+ 4.6
State	1,013	1,329	1,388	+ 4.4
Local	4,257	5,735	6,956	+21.3

Note: Spending is measured in millions of dollars.

Source: President's Commission on Americans Outdoors, 1987 (as provided by the Conservation Foundation based on information from the U.S. Department of Commerce, Bureau of the Census).

the inadequate levels of funding for staff, facilities development, and maintenance that limit the use of public recreation facilities (PCAO, 1987). According to a study conducted by the Conservation Foundation, the problem is so severe at the state and local level that direct government spending for parks and recreation (adjusted for inflation) decreased 17 percent from 1980 to 1983. In contrast, similar spending for all programs fell only .04 percent (PCAO, 1987). From 1980 to 1984 federal and state governments appeared to have shifted a major share of the burden of funding recreation to local governments. Local government spending increased over 21 percent during this period, while federal and state spending only increased about 4 percent each (Table 6.2). Furthermore, the National Recreation and Park Association estimates that local park facilities rehabilitation unmet needs from 1981 to 1985 were $4.26 billion (PCAO, 1987). Similar funding problems exist at the federal level. Three of the major federal land management agencies that provide outdoor recreation services (Fish and Wildlife Service, Forest Service, and National Park Service) reported major shortfalls in funding for operations and maintenance (O&M) over the past decade. These agencies repeatedly made budget proposals for substantial amounts of money for O&M, but the Office of Management and Budget analysts continually lowered the requested amount. Consequently, recreation services are reduced and the facilities fall into a state of ill repair. For example, the U.S. Forest Service reports that from 1985 to 1987 the dollar amount of deferred maintenance more than doubled, to $297 million. The National Park Service reports that it needs $75 million a year for maintenance to stem deterioration. Together these two agencies report a $1 billion backlog in facilities rehabilitation (PCAO, 1987).

This means that existing recreational resources will continue to deteriorate and have to be replaced at a faster rate at higher costs in the future. Seven federal agencies with recreation responsibilities reported their recreation-related appropriations, ranging from $1.434 billion to $1.571 billion for fiscal years 1984, 1985, and 1986, to the President's Commission on Americans Outdoors (Table 6.3).

As a result of the above mentioned forces, there is a major shortfall in the financial support for outdoor recreation in the United States, which results from pressures in two directions. While demands for services increase, recreational opportunities continue to diminish due to the overcrowding of existing public recreation areas and recent cutbacks in fiscal resources. With the reorientation of federal budget priorities away from social programs, outdoor recreation programs have been reduced at all levels of government.

Although annual spending for recreation at all levels of government currently amounts to $9.8 billion, spending has not kept pace with inflation (PCAO, 1987). In 1962, the Outdoor Recreation Resources Review Commission (ORRRC) recognized the need for federal assistance to state and local governments for outdoor recreation through a specific recommendation for the establishment of a financial assistance program for the states for recreation land acquisition and facility development. In response, Congress enacted the Land and Water Conservation Fund Act (P.L. 88–578) in 1965 to provide for federal funding from offshore oil receipts to support state and local recreation planning, acquisition, and development programs on a matching basis, and to acquire lands and waters for federal recreation areas (Siehl, 1985). Through the LWCF the federal government has become the principal stimulus to spending for outdoor recreation in the United States. However, appropriations from the LWCF have fallen sharply since 1978 when the highest funding occurred ($905 million). For example, since 1982 most of the money has been spent on additions to federal lands and water systems. In 1986, localities and states received just one-sixth of the 1978 funding levels (PCAO, 1987).

Local, state, and federal recreation officials and resource managers told the President's Commission on Americans Outdoors that recreation funding is inadequate, especially for land acquisition and rehabilitation (PCAO, 1987). In 1986, the leaders of twenty-seven conservation organizations sent a joint letter to the PCAO recommending funding of $1.75 billion a year (Federal Parks and Recreation Newsletter, September 25, 1986). State and local officials appealed for an assured and stable source of federal funding to augment state and local investments in outdoor recreational facilities.

After considering the issue and listening to recreation advocates across the United States, the commission determined that more money is needed, the American public generally appears willing to pay for recreation, there are many present and potential sources of funds, many states and localities have developed innovative fund-raising programs, and there is wide support for some federal-level fund or funds to satisfy federal acquisition needs and complement and stimulate

Table 6.3
Agency Recreation-Related Appropriations, 1984–1986

	1984			1985			1986			Average
	Recreation operations and maintenance	Land acquisition	Capital improvements	Recreation operations and maintenance	Land acquisition	Capital improvements	Recreation operations and maintenance	Land acquisition	Capital improvements	of total funds
Fish & Wildlife Service	$ 148	$ 49	$ 27	$ 189	$ 85	$ 20	$ 205	$ 1	$ 1	3.1
Tennessee Valley Authority	11	0.1	0.3	3	0.1	0.3	4	0.1	0.2	3.2
Forest Service	110	40	14	111	50	19	113	28	18	11.0
Bureau of Land Management	23	1	---	24	3	0.1	26	2	---	3.8
Bureau of Reclamation	7	1	29	7	7	18	7	6	15	3.5
Corps of Engineers	140	---	8	163	---	10	176	---	4	11.0
National Park Service	616	129	81	627	96	139	614	98	113	85.0
Total	1,055	220	159	1,124	241	206	1,155	135	151	
Total appropriations per year	$1,434			$1,571			$1,441			

Note: Appropriations are measured in millions of dollars. Recreation operations and maintenance includes normal and ordinary maintenance, cultural resources, wilderness, trail maintenance, some natural resources management, and law enforcement. Land acquisition is primarily Land and Water Conservation Fund dollars returned for additional land acquisition. Capital Improvements is mainly construction of new capital facilities. Average percentage of total funds is the percentage of recreation in an agency's total budget.

Source: President's Commission on Americans Outdoors (1987).

state and local initiatives. Consequently, the President's Commission tentatively agreed that $1 billion per year is needed for funding of local, state, and federal recreation opportunities (Federal Parks and Recreation Newsletter, 1986).

In its final report, the PCAO recommended the establishment of a dedicated trust fund to provide $1 billion annually. The funds would come from a variety of sources such as a fixed percentage of offshore oil receipts (President's Commission, 1987) similar to the LWCF. One major difference between the LWCF and this proposal is that the new recommended approach is for an endowed fund that would earn its own revenue from interest on investment and not be subject to annual appropriations.

POLICY ISSUES

Financing outdoor recreation has become a major policy issue in the United States over the past two or three decades. It is difficult to pinpoint exactly when and how this occurred, but there are a number of contributing elements. High inflation rates in the 1960s and 1970s increased the costs of everything for which recreation administrators expended money. This, in turn, sharply increased operations and maintenance (O&M) costs. At the same time prices were increasing, another phenomenon was in effect pressuring resource managers to maintain admission prices and other user fees at a minimum. There was, and still is to a large extent, a widely held belief that public recreation resources should be provided at little or no cost to the public. As commercial recreational activities increase in cost due to inflation, public resources become even more desirable, and demand continues to grow.[1]

For a public policy issue to exist, conflict must exist between two or more societal groups in regard to a particular social condition (Dunn, 1981). Conservationists argue that all Americans are entitled to ready access to public lands. Economists and conservative politicians, on the other hand, argue that those individuals who receive services should pay their fair share. They are concerned about the free riders who benefit without paying for the services they receive. Hence, the policy problem for funding outdoor recreation fundamentally amounts to the issue of who should pay the costs—the average citizen or the user of the resource.

Policy proposals often include user payment strategies to assist federal, state, and local government agencies to recoup a substantial portion of their operating costs.[2] For example, federal budget proposals for fiscal year 1986 placed heavy reliance upon the increase of existing fees and the imposition of new fees upon recreational users as a means of generating additional income (U.S. Senate Committee, 1985). In fiscal year 1987, the Reagan administration raised admission fees to national parks, the first increase in prices in fifteen years.

For purposes of administrative efficiency, the price increases were targeted at the most heavily used facilities (e.g., Grand Canyon, Yellowstone Park, and Grand Teton Park). But the trend is toward greater use of fees. Seventy-one additional sites imposed fees for the first time (Armstrong, 1987). The funds are to be channeled back into the National Park Service system for resource management and not into the U.S. Treasury. Originally, however, the administration had intended to use 20 percent of the collected fees to reduce the federal government's deficit. Conservation organizations objected vigorously, however, and pressured the administration to rectify this inequity and this provision was removed. Although the emphasis of the Reagan administration on public-private interaction has led to greater employment of user fees, there are many other ways to finance outdoor recreation that are based on benefits received.

IDENTIFICATION OF POTENTIAL SOURCES OF REVENUE

The President's Commission on Americans Outdoors (1987) identified twenty-seven existing and potential sources for funding outdoor recreational activities on federal, state, and local public lands. These sources are:

1. general appropriations,
2. Outer Continental Shelf revenues,
3. dedication of existing revenues and revenues from new mineral development,
4. sale of surplus federal property,
5. excise taxes modeled on the Pittman-Robertson and Dingell-Johnson programs for wildlife and sport fish restoration,
6. recreation enhancement taxes,
7. summer gasoline tax,
8. Highway Trust Fund appropriations,
9. revenue bonds,
10. rechannelling or supporting existing sources like the Sikes Act for the management of wildlife on military lands of the Reclamation Act,
11. recreation fees,
12. public-private partnerships, cooperative agreements, challenge grants, expanded concession agreements,
13. volunteers,
14. donations,
15. development/impact fees,
16. land transfer taxes,
17. mandatory land dedication with new development,
18. billboard laws,
19. nonroad fuel taxes,
20. dedicated sales taxes,
21. special recreation taxing districts,
22. registration fees,

23. lotteries,

24. cigarette, liquor, accommodations taxes,

25. income tax checkoffs,

26. bottle bills,

27. surcharge on license fees.

In 1985 the National Recreation and Park Association (1986) surveyed all fifty states to identify innovative approaches that states were using to supplement traditional sources for land acquisition and recreation programs. This informative study, entitled *Special Revenue Sources for Parks and Recreation,* provides an invaluable source for further analysis of alternative financing arrangements for outdoor recreation.

Of the numerous potential sources of funds for recreation and examples of appropriate levels of government are land development fees (local government), equipment licenses and fees (state government), visitor fees (local, state, and federal), and excise taxes on recreational equipment (state and federal) (PCAO, 1987).

ANALYSIS OF SPECIFIC FUNDING ALTERNATIVES

Sources emphasized in this analysis include excise taxes on equipment (e.g., camping, backpacking, diving, and photographic equipment), entrance fees at federal facilities, and punitive taxes for the extraction of renewable and nonrenewable resources. Through the use of such alternative funding mechanisms, the financial shortfall for recreation could be lessened considerably. An approach like this would be acceptable to a majority of Americans according to the Market Opinion Research (1986) survey conducted for the President's Commission on Americans Outdoors. The consensus view shared by 78 percent of the respondents was that outdoor recreation should be paid for through a mix of taxes and user fees.

Criteria for Evaluating Funding Sources: Efficiency and Equity

There are two basic criteria of primary importance in determining the suitability of a potential funding source. These are efficiency and equity. Efficiency relates to the amount of revenue generated from a source and the tax or fee on producer and consumer decisions. The amount of revenue generated is an important criteria from the viewpoint of administrative nuisance and cost imposed by any fee or tax. The substantial costs to establish collection rates, collect the revenues, enforce collection, and so forth requires that significant revenues be realized. It costs only slightly more to administer a fund source to collect large amounts of money from a large tax base than to collect small amounts from a large tax base or to collect small amounts from a small tax base. Therefore, there are efficiency advantages to administering a few taxes/fees that generate substantial revenues rather than dozens of taxes/fees that individually generate little revenue. The tax/fee's performance against this criterion is evaluated in this chapter using revenue that could have been collected had the tax been in place in 1980 and the revenue that would be received in the year 2000. Both time periods are important. The 1980 date provides an indication of the immediate level of revenue that could be realized, while the year 2000 gives an indication of whether current revenues would rise or fall in the future. Because of the substantial up-front costs of establishing a program to administer tax/fee collection and the long-term funding needs of outdoor recreation, it would make little sense to target a product for taxation whose future outlook is bleak. A traditional concern among economists who study public finance relates to the potential for taxes/fees to distort consumer and producer choices. For example, if production and consumption of a particular good results in no spillover costs to society, then imposition of a tax is generally believed to result in a reduction in social well-being, the rationale being that artificially raising the price of the good above the social cost, will result in some consumers reducing their consumption. The loss in social well-being is often called the deadweight loss or excess burden of a tax. It represents the loss of well-being to the consumer (and producer) in excess of the tax revenue transferred to the government (Boadway, 1979; Musgrave & Musgrave, 1980).

To minimize the loss in social well-being associated with raising a given amount of revenue, economists recommend that tax rates/fees be set at high levels for price insensitive goods and lower levels for price sensitive goods (Baumol & Bradford, 1970; Boadway, 1979). To make this an operational criterion, a range of tax rates are recommended that reflect the price elasticity of demand for the various goods/services. The goal is to equate the excess burden per dollar of revenue raised.

In particular, a percentage of excess burden is calculated. This number represents the cents of excess burden per dollar of revenue raised. If economic efficiency were the only criterion, tax/fee rates would be set to equate the marginal excess burden of each source. However, economic efficiency is not the only criterion and the rates proposed here were modified to reflect equity as well. In addition, the production or consumption of some goods such as off-road motorcycles results in spillover costs in terms of habitat loss, soil erosion, and noise that are not reflected in the price consumers pay. Another example of negative spillover costs is congested recreation sites. If no fee is charged, people continue to enter, ignoring the negative effect of their presence on other visitors. In either of these cases, a tax/fee that raises the price of this good (visit) toward the true social cost results in a desirable reduction in consumption of the good toward the social optimum. This results in a gain in economic efficiency. Therefore tax rates for goods generating these negative spillover costs were often increased to reflect the gain to society from imposing the tax or fee.

The fairness of a tax can be evaluated using at least two standards. The benefits received criterion requires that those who receive the most benefit from a program pay more. The concept of benefits received strongly supports charging user fees such as entrance fees at recreation areas. In terms of excise taxes, benefits received requires that a high percentage of a product's buyers be recreation users and that most recreation users buy the good. For example, a large percentage of recreation users buy truck campers. Therefore, first priority for taxation would be goods that meet both of the benefits received factors. Since there are many different styles of recreation, benefits received may well be served by taxing a group of products that collectively are used by most recreationists, even though any one person may not use all of the products.

The benefits received criterion also requires that the entire burden of financing the provision of natural environments and open space not be borne solely by recreation users. In particular, studies (Walsh, Loomis, & Gillman, 1986) have shown that many nonvisitors derive substantial satisfaction from knowing that national parks, wilderness, and wildlife exist even if they never plan to visit them. The costs of managing a national park ecosystem independent of visitor use should not be recovered from recreation users but rather from society as a whole through the normal appropriations process.

Another criterion that is widely used by economists to measure the equity of a tax relates to the ability to pay. The difficulty comes in making this an operational concept. A standard approach is to classify taxes as to whether they are progressive, proportional, or regressive. A tax is considered progressive (regressive) if the tax rate increases as income goes up (down). A proportional tax means that the fee or tax payment is a constant percentage of income. To measure the degree of progressiveness or regressiveness of a tax, a Suits index (Suits, 1977) is used. The index takes on a value closer to $+1$ when the tax is progressive, a value close to zero if the tax is proportional, and a value closer to -1 if the tax is regressive. Such an index allows for comparison between taxes and facilitates evaluation of the overall progressivity of a group of taxes.

Data Sources

To evaluate how several excise taxes and fees rated against these four criteria, a number of data sources were used. These included the 1980 *National Survey of Fishing, Hunting, and Wildlife-Associated Recreation* (U.S. Department of the Interior, 1982), *Consumer Expenditures Survey* (U.S. Department of Labor, 1978; U.S. International Trade Commission 1981a; 1981b; 1983).

Analysis of Excise Taxes

Fundamental to the determination of the efficiency aspects of a tax or fee is estimation of demand equations for each particular product. Once estimated, the demand equation allows calculation of the tax revenue and percentage of excess burden that would occur at particular tax rates and likely future sales in the year

2000. The year 2000 forecasts are based on projections of U.S. population, income, and price of gasoline in that year. As such, the future tax revenues should only be interpreted as showing the direction of future change and likely order of magnitude and not exact predictions of future change, order of magnitude, or future revenues.

For products produced and consumed primarily by Americans, both demand and supply were estimated using two-stage least squares regression to account for the fact that the tax burden would be shared between producers and consumers in proportion to the relative elasticities of supply and demand, respectively. Where the U.S. supply was relatively small and imports provided a majority of U.S. consumption, the conventional assumption of past empirical studies of excise taxation were employed. In particular, Pechman and Okner (1974) and Musgrave and Musgrave (1980) were followed in assuming that the tax or fee is completely passed onto the consumer. With this assumption, ordinary least squares regression could be used to estimate the demand equations (Table 6.4). While the equations generally have acceptable correlation coefficients (R^2s), some of the variables are only marginally significant. This was often due to small sizes of most of the data sets (10-40 observations).

For products for which insufficient data existed to estimate a demand equation, the existing literature was used to obtain a price elasticity for the product or service. For several camping products price elasticity estimates from the sophisticated econometric work of Lareau and Darmstadter (1982) were used. Combining the price elasticity with current price and quantity allowed for estimation of tax revenues and percentages of excess burden for these products (Table 6.5).

As discussed earlier the ability-to-pay factor was quantified using the Suits index when data on consumption by income class could be obtained. For several of the goods, information about consumption by income class was not available. Therefore, information about the income elasticity was often used to determine whether the tax would be progressive or regressive. If a product had an income elasticity greater than one, the tax/fee would result in a progressive distribution of the tax burden. With an income elasticity greater than one, consumption increases by a greater percentage than the percentage increase in income. The same reasoning implies that goods with income elasticities approximately equal to one would result in a proportional distribution of the tax burden. Finally, if a product had an income elasticity of less than one (including negative elasticities), the distribution of the tax burden would be regressive.

To evaluate the benefits received linkage, a comparison of product sales to recreation users compared to total industry sales was made. If a substantial portion of total industry sales was to recreation users, the benefits received linkage was considered good. If, in addition, most recreation users purchased the good, the recreation benefits were considered quite strong. Data to perform these comparisons were drawn from a variety of sources, including Shaw and Mangun (1984).

Table 6.4
Results of Demand Equations

Product name	Dependent variable	Constant	Own Price	Psubs	Pcomp	Inc	Inc^2	Trend
Backpacks (OLS)	QCAP	.542	-.00098 (-2.50)	.00121 (2.52)		.00025	-.297E-7	
Four-wheel drives (TSLS)	Q	-5032431	-1149.7 (-2.66)	702.68 (1.67)	-58090 (-5.11)	6.98 (3.96)		
Off-road motorcycles (OLS)	(ln)Q	-22.77	-1.3088 (-1.012)			3.146 (4.90)		
Motorhomes (OLS)	Q	634.9	-.014 (-1.54)		-164.1 (-4.52)	.0008 (4.33)		-.141 (-2.278)
Photo equipment (Cameras) (OLS)	Q	-7.437	-.02469 (-7.85)			.187E-4 (3.31)		-.386 (2.461)
Film (OLS)	QCAP	-75.82	-1.188 (-1.08)			.0302 (8.75)		
Snowmobiles (OLS)	Q	20.51	-.003 (-1.95)			-.62E-5 (-6.93)		
Travel trailers (TSLS)	Q	-104.7	-.071 (-1.11)			-.963 (-5.587)	.000829 (2.32)	
Truck campers	Q	596	-.04659 (-2.467)			-3898 (-4.66)	-.198E-4 (01.11)	

Note: OLS = ordinary least square; TSLS = two-stage least square; QCAP = quantity per capita; Q = Quantity; (In) Q = natural log of Q; Psubs = price of substitutes; Pcomp = price of complements; Inc = income; and Inc^2 = income squared.

Table 6.5
Summary of Excise Tax Analysis

Product	Suggested tax rate (%)	1980 tax revenue	2000 tax revenue	Excess burden (%)	Ability to pay (Suits Index)
Backpacks	4	$ 0.8	$ 1.1	2.17	-0.15
Camp stoves	6	2.0	2.4	2.58	-0.15
Cross-country skis	5	3.1	3.7	nd	-0.29
Lanterns	6	2.6	3.1	2.58	-0.15
Sleeping bags	6	11.5	13.5	2.58	-0.15
Tents	6	10.4	12.2	2.58	-0.15
Folding camper trailers	1	0.4	0.1	1.90	-0.09
Truck campers	1	0.7	0.1	1.95	-0.09
Photo equipment	7	82.6	404.9	2.18	-0.13
Film	15	221.6	672.3	1.14	-0.13
Snowmobiles	2	3.6	0.1	2.33	nd
Off-road motorcycles	5	14.6	128.8	3.20	see text
Four-wheel drive vehicles	1	36.3	1,381.6	3.78	see text
Travel trailers	1	4.2	19.0	1.50	-0.09
Motorhomes	.5	1.5	33.7	2.69	nd

Note: Tax revenues are reported in millions of dollars.

Analysis of Entrance Fees

Evaluation of direct user charges such as entrance fees required information on visitation to recreation sites and an understanding of recreation demand. Visitation figures for the seven federal agencies with large recreation programs were assembled from a variety of sources including the *Federal Recreation Fee Report* (U.S. National Park Service, 1982), *Increasing Entrance Fees–The National Park Service* (General Accounting Office, 1982), and the *President's*

Private Sector Survey on Cost Control (1983). Projection of visitation to the year 2000 was made using rates of increase derived from the forecasts by Hof and Kaiser (1983). The revenue potential was calculated assuming that existing fees were raised by $1.00 per visitor at sites already charging an entrance fee and that a new $1.00 per visitor entrance fee were charged at sites currently having no fee. While there is substantial potential revenue from introducing fees at currently free areas, there would be increased collection costs in the form of buildings and employees that must be subtracted from the potential gross revenue.

RESULTS

Substantial revenue can be raised from excise taxes on some camping items, notably sleeping bags and tents (Table 6.5). These items have a good benefits received linkage since they are bought primarily by recreation users and most overnight recreation users require these items. Photographic equipment and film offer the potential for substantial revenue with little efficiency loss (as measured by the percentage of excess burden). The benefits received linkage is better than one might expect with 20 percent of photographic equipment expenditures being purchased primarily for photographing wildlife (U.S. Department of the Interior, 1982) and 67.4 percent being purchased to take pictures of nature (1982 Survey of Purchases, 1983). One reason photographic equipment expenditure has a good relationship to benefits received is that nature photographers spend an above average amount on cameras and lenses compared to the average buyer. Substantial revenues are possible from small excise taxes on four-wheel-drive vehicles and off-road motorcycles. While Table 6.2 indicates a 3.2 percent excess burden on off-road motorcycles, this may be largely offset since the tax also internalizes some of the external costs imposed on the environment and nonmotorized recreation users from the operation of off-road motorcycles.

All of the excise taxes for which data were available to calculate a Suits index would be regressive. A tax on cross-country skis would be about twice as regressive as the next most regressive source, camping equipment. A tax on folding camper trailers, truck campers, and travel trailers would be slightly regressive or nearly proportional.

The available data on expenditure patterns for off-road motorcycles and four-wheel-drive vehicles indicate that an excise tax would likely be very slightly regressive or nearly proportional (U.S. Fish and Wildlife Service, 1985, pp. 91–92).

As Table 6.6 indicates, entrance fees also have the potential to raise substantial revenue. Increasing fees at federal recreation areas already charging fees could raise $110 million annually, with the bulk of this coming from national parks. This is not too surprising since many national parks already have collection facilities and also receive millions of visitors annually. By contrast, the introduction of entrance fees on national forests and Army Corps of Engineers res-

Table 6.6
Revenue Sources from Entrance Fees

	Increase fees at existing fee areas		Charge fees at free areas	
	1980	2000	1980	2000
Federal Agency	$110.9	$133.1	$419.7	$503.6
Bureau of Land Management	2.73	3.28	3.0	3.6
Bureau of Reclamation	0.15	0.18	33.0	40.5
Corps of Engineers	8.75	10.50	151.8	182.1
Fish & Wildlife Service	0.05	0.06	1.4	1.7
Forest Service	27.55	33.06	207.4	248.8
National Park Service	71.11	85.33	15.7	18.8

Note: Fees are reported in millions of dollars.

ervoirs has the greatest potential to raise revenue. This is generally due to the legal constraint that these agencies cannot currently charge for simply providing access but only when they provide facilities such as for camping. Charging a one dollar per visitor fee at national forest wilderness areas alone could result in several million dollars of revenue each year with little additional costs since many wilderness areas already have an elaborate permit process that regulates use.

The excess burden from an across the board imposition of entrance fees at all federal recreation sites would be quite small since the demand for this type of outdoor recreation is quite price inelastic. When the increase in fee is viewed in the context of an increase in total trip costs (e.g., transportation, food, etc.), the range in price of outdoor recreation would be small. Coupled with a price inelastic demand, there would be little reduction in visitation if this fee (or fee increase) were established at all federal sites.

In an absolute sense, the ability-to-pay effects of entrance fees to federal sites would be minimal since most of these sites are sufficiently remote from urban areas as to require automobile ownership. However, entrance fees would likely be slightly regressive since visitation is relatively income inelastic.

FUNDING RECOMMENDATIONS

Since outdoor recreation is provided at several levels of government, in a range of settings from urban parks to remote wilderness areas, and involves a wide range of recreational activities with radically different equipment requirements, a mixture of funding sources are needed to optimize attainment of efficiency and equity. Entrance fees would clearly be an element in federal recreation areas, but logistics and equity would strongly argue against entrance fees for provision of urban parks and open space. Excise taxes on many items of camping equipment would allow for indirect charges for outdoor recreation in settings where collection of user fees would be infeasible (e.g., dispersed recreation). Excise taxes on items such as four-wheel-drive vehicles and off-road motorcycles would not only raise revenue but would internalize some of the costs imposed on the environment and other nonmotorized recreationists.

Raising revenue is only part of the solution to funding outdoor recreation. Distribution of the funds in line with the demands for different types of recreation provided at different levels of government requires careful analysis. Future research is needed on formulas for appropriate distribution of money raised from excise taxes to each level of government and how those governmental units should target funding to provide land areas and facilities for the recreation users who paid the taxes.

In the final analysis, there is a legitimate need for continued and expanded general appropriations for outdoor recreation. Many areas that provide outdoor recreation are also dedicated to preserving wildlife and nationally significant natural environments (e.g., Yosemite, Yellowstone, etc.). Management of these areas bestows a public good type of existence value on a majority of citizens, whether they will be visitors or not (Krutilla, 1967; Walsh, Loomis, & Gillman, 1986). Other more common types of recreation areas, such as local parks and golf courses, provide aesthetic open space enjoyed by many persons who may rarely visit the particular park. At either of these extremes (e.g., Yellowstone or a city park) it is economically inefficient to rely solely on funds derived from visitors to purchase, protect, and manage natural environments that happen to also provide recreation. Optimal funding of outdoor recreation requires a package balanced among the different types of recreation users and the many indirect users of the recreation environments.

Excise taxes, entrance fees, and general appropriations are capable of raising the $1 to $1.7 billion needed for adequate funding of outdoor recreation. Analysis by Walsh and Loomis (1986) indicates that such sums would be socially wise investments that would return benefits to the recreation user several times greater than the costs. The benefits to society as a whole, in terms of reduced medical bills from a physically and mentally healthier population, imply that the provision of adequate land and facilities for outdoor recreation may be a wise investment for many Americans.

Table 6.7

Approximate Annual Increases in Recreation Attendance at the National Park System, National Forests, and State Parks, by Periods of Generally Similar Rates of Change, 1924–1981

National Park System			National Forests			State Parks		
Average annual increase			Average annual increase			Average Annual increase		
Period	Visits	%	Period	Visits	%	Period	Visits	%
1924- 1941	1.1	19	1924- 1942	0.3	10	---	---	---
1948- 1956	4.0	9	1947- 1964	6.6	13	1946- 1958	18.1	8
1958- 1970	8.9	10	---	---	---	1958- 1970	20.5	6
1971- 1981	13.0	6	1967- 1980	6.5	4	1970- 1980	5.2	4

Source: Clawson (1985). All visits are reported in millions.

NOTES

1. Demand for outdoor recreation has risen significantly throughout the century as evidenced by visitations to national parks, national forests, and state parks. Clawson (1985) reports that the average annual increase in visits to national parks grew from 1.1 million in the 1924–1941 period to 13 million annually in the 1971–1981 period. Similarly, visits to national forests rose from .3 million annually to 6.5 million annually in 1962– 1980. Although the rate of increase in visits to state parks declined considerably from the 1946–1958 period (18.1 million annually) to the 1970–1980 period (5.2 million annually) the total number of visitors still continued to climb consistently (Table 6.7).

Clawson (1985) indicates that the area and number of publicly owned recreation areas has increased during the past thirty-five years. But he reports that using acreage as an indicator of the available supply of outdoor recreation may be flawed. Increased amounts of acreage fails to be a true indicator for the actual upward trend in the intensity of use per average acre. Acreage is a poor measure for at least two reasons: (1) it does not necessarily correlate well with capacity to accommodate recreationists; and (2) many areas are open to outdoor recreation but are not primarily managed for it (e.g., wilderness areas, national forests, or Alaska National Interest Land Conservation Act lands). Therefore, data on the supply of outdoor recreation tend to be insufficient to provide an accurate picture. Nevertheless, the PCAO Report (1987) indicates that in 1986 there were 778.4 million acres of public recreation land in the United States (federal, 707.7 million [90.9%]; state, 62 million [8%]; county/regional, 5.7 million [0.7%]; municipal, 3 million [0.4%]). Similarly, the total number of recreation areas identified on public lands in 1985 was

109,718 (federal, 67,685 [61.7%]; state, 19,884 [18.1%]; county/regional, 20,375 [18.6%]; municipal, 1,774 [1.6%]).

2. User fee programs, however, seldom generate more than one-half of the operating costs.

REFERENCES

Andrews, K. (1984). *Recreation benefits and costs of the proposed Deer Creek Reservoir.* Cheyenne: Wyoming Recreation Commission.

Armstrong, S. (1987, June 11). Folks aplenty forecast in parks despite fee hike. *Christian Science Monitor,* p. 21.

Baumol, W., & Bradford, D. (1970). Optimal departures from marginal costs pricing. *American Economic Review, 60,* 265–283.

Boadway, R. (1979) *Public sector economics.* Boston: Little, Brown.

Clawson, M. (1985, February). Trends in the use of public recreation areas. In *Proceedings of the 1985 National Outdoor Recreation Trends Symposium II* (pp. 1–12). Clemson, SC: Clemson University, Department of Parks, Recreation, and Tourism.

Dunn, W. (1981). *Public policy analysis: An introduction.* Englewood Cliffs, NJ: Prentice-Hall.

Federal Parks and Recreation Newsletter. (1986). *4* (18), p. 4.

General Accounting Office. (1982). *Increasing entrance fees—National Park Service* (GAO/CED–82–84). Washington, DC: U.S. Government Printing Office.

Gibbs, D. (1983). *A comparison of travel cost models which estimate recreation demand for water resource development: Summary report.* Washington, DC: U.S. Bureau of Reclamation.

Hof, J. G., & Kaiser, H. F. (1983). *Projections for future forest recreation use* [Bulletin WO–2]. Washington, DC: U.S. Forest Service.

Kalter, R., & Gosse, L. (1969). *Outdoor recreation in New York State* [Special Cornell Series No. 5]. Ithaca, NY: Cornell University.

Krutilla, J. V. (1967). Conservation reconsidered. *American Economic Review, 57,* 777–786.

Lareau, T., & Darmstadter, J. (1982). Energy and consumer expenditure patterns: Modeling approaches and projections. *Annual Review of Energy, 7,* 262–292.

Market Opinion Research. (1986). *Participation in outdoor recreation among American adults and the motivations which drive participation.* Washington, DC: President's Commission on Americans Outdoors.

Musgrave, R., & Musgrave, P. (1980). *Public finance in theory and practice.* New York: McGraw-Hill.

National Recreation and Park Association. (1986). *Special revenue sources for parks and recreation: A survey of the states.* Alexandria, VA: Author.

1982 survey of purchases of 35mm SLR cameras and accessories. (1983, March 13). *Newsweek,* p. 54.

Outdoor Recreation Resources Review Commission. (1962). *Outdoor recreation for America.* Washington, DC: U.S. Government Printing Office.

Pechman, J., & Okner, B. (1974). *Who bears the tax burden?* Washington, DC: The Brookings Institute.

President's Commission on Americans Outdoors [PCAO]. (1987). *Americans outdoors: The legacy, the challenge*. Washington, DC: Island Press.

President's Private Sector Survey on Cost Control. (1983). *Report of the task force on user charges, May 26, 1983*. Washington, DC: U.S. Government Printing Office.

Shaw, W., & Mangun, W. (1984). *Nonconsumptive use of wildlife in the United States* [Service Resource Publication No. 154]. Washington, DC: U.S. Fish and Wildlife Service.

Siehl, G. (1985). *Outdoor recreation: A new commission is created*. Washington, DC: Congressional Research Service.

Sorg, C. F., & Loomis, J. B. (1985). *Empirical estimates of amenity forest values: A comparative review* (General Technology Report RM–107). Fort Collins, CO: U.S. Forest Service, Rocky Mountain Forest and Range Experiment Station.

Suits, D. (1977). Measurement of tax progressivity. *American Economic Review, 67*, 747–752.

U.S. Department of Labor. (1978). *Consumer expenditures survey, 1972–1973*. Washington, DC: U.S. Government Printing Office.

U.S. Department of the Interior. (1982). *National survey of fishing, hunting, and wildlife-associated recreation: National summary*. Washington, DC: U.S. Government Printing Office.

U.S. Fish and Wildlife Service. (1985). *Potential funding resources to implement the Fish and Wildlife Conservation Act of 1980*. Washington, DC: U.S. Department of the Interior.

U.S. International Trade Commission. (1981a). *Photographic cameras: Summary of trade and tariff information*. Washington, DC: Author.

U.S. International Trade Commission. (1981b). *Sporting goods: Summary of trade and tariff information*. Washington, DC: Author.

U.S. International Trade Commission. (1983). *The U.S. auto industry: U.S. factory sales, retail sales, imports, exports, apparent consumption and suggested retail prices, 1964–1984*. Washington, DC: Author.

U.S. National Park Service. (1982). *Federal recreation fee report—1982*. Washington, DC: U.S. Department of the Interior.

U.S. Senate Committee on Energy and Natural Resources. (1985, June 27). *Hearings before the subcommittee on public lands, reserved water, and resource conservation: Recreation user fees*. Washington, DC: U.S. Government Printing Office.

U.S. Water Resources Council. (1983). *Economic and environmental principles and guidelines for water and related land resource implementation studies*. Washington, DC: U.S. Government Printing Office.

Walsh, R. G., & Loomis, J. B., (1987). "The contribution of recreation to national economic development." In *Literature Review*. Washington, DC: President's Commission on Americans Outdoors.

Walsh, R. G., Loomis, J. B., & Gillman, R. A. (1986). Value option, existence and bequest demands for wilderness. *Land Economics, 60*, 14–29.

7.

RATIONING THE CONGESTED RECREATIONAL FACILITY: MARKET VERSUS POLITICAL INSTRUMENTS

Robert H. Patrick and Stephen B. Lovejoy

The growth in demand for recreation over the past two decades has been tremendous, while supply may actually be declining.[1] As a result of this situation recreational facilities in the United States are becoming increasingly congested. This overcrowding of facilities has led many administrators and managers to hire more personnel, restrict access to certain features, or attempt to enforce some type of visitor limitation by rationing (reservations, queueing, etc.). Relatively higher levels of visitation, even below the physical capacity of the area, may lead to external costs for recreational users in the form of reduced enjoyment due to crowding and deterioration of the natural setting. Most recreational professionals recognize that congestion can reduce the value that visitors place on their experience. However, there has been little empirical estimation of these congestion costs[2] and less attention toward devising market mechanisms that account for the cyclical nature of the congestion problem.[3] Further consideration of both aspects is necessary to design recreation management policies that will efficiently reduce the negative effects of congestion.

The market, rather than political entities, should ration scarce recreational resources. Fisher and Krutilla (1972) establish the basic tenet that optimal management of a recreation resource requires a charge per user that is the sum of the marginal congestion cost and the marginal cost to the environment. Economically efficient resource allocation dictates that those willing and able to pay the marginal cost of their consumption activity be allowed to consume the good. By this criteria users who are willing to pay the congestion cost that their consumption imposes on other users are allowed to use the recreational facility.

Conversely, simply restricting the number of visitors may allow admittance of users who would not visit the facility if such a fee were in place. Societal welfare can be improved by allowing access to those who value the amenity more highly. In addition, appropriately chosen congestion fees eliminate excess demand problems and provide additional revenues for recreational site maintenance, improvement, and so forth.

One market mechanism that holds some promise is the use of congestion fees or peak time charging for recreational users. Many other sectors of the economy (e.g., long distance telephone, time-sharing on computers, electricity, etc.) utilize such fees in attempts to even the load on fixed capacity. Determining an efficient congestion fee, however, is complicated by the fact that congestion of recreational facilities varies not only over time of day but also over time of year and spatially, making a standard fee across recreational areas and times of use relatively inefficient. While some observers might suggest continuously varying the level of the congestion fee as the number of visitors varies, the transactions costs of such a mechanism would probably prohibit its use. Fee systems in which relatively higher congestion fees would be used during weekends and holidays would aid in internalizing such congestion externalities. However, such a scheme should be viewed as just the first step in more efficiently allocating recreational resources.

In this chapter a method for implementing congestion fees based upon temporal characteristics is described that could provide significant improvements over present attempts to control congestion. The methodology advances the use of an optimization model for determining efficient user fees for congested recreational sites. This model suggests the magnitude of user fees and the actual timing of such fees as are necessary to reduce the congestion in overcrowded recreational sites to an allocatively efficient level. Considerations in actual application and data necessary for empirical estimation are also discussed.

CONGESTION EXTERNALITIES

Externalities are uncompensated direct effects of the actions of one economic entity on the welfare or productivity of another or others. Externalities are especially important in the context of public policy because the individual or economic agent does not pay the entire marginal cost (or receive all the marginal benefit) associated with any action affecting consumption or production by others. Efficient resource allocation and management decisions require that these external effects be measured and explained. [4]

The efficiency justification for congestion fees is the internalization of the cost imposed by an individual user on other users through the effects of the additional demand on the enjoyment of the latter. For example, congestion on highways causes delays in travel that would generally represent some costs in terms of additional travel time. The case of outdoor recreation leads to a different type of external cost as a result of congestion, namely a reduced value attributable to the individual recreational visit. Congestion may be considered as a consumption externality that affects individuals' satisfaction derived from the recreational experience or, conversely, as a production externality in the household production framework.[5] Either approach implies that the optimal level of use of a congested recreation facility is generally less than the open access level due to external costs. When an individual chooses to stay at a site a longer length of time, congestion increases for this additional period of time, and other users' value of the experience declines. This extra cost is ignored by individuals (they equate their marginal benefit to the average cost of congestion, analogous to the typical common property problem). Restricting the number of entrants to the facility or park, however, does not insure that the resource is efficiently allocated (in a Pareto sense). Some visitors may not be willing to pay the marginal cost of congestion that they inflict on others, while others who would be willing to pay an additional fee for congestion may be excluded.[6] Welfare improvement could be accomplished by charging entrance fees, the optimal price being equal to the external congestion cost of the marginal visit.[7]

Congestion costs generally occur above a certain threshold of visitor numbers, which would naturally be affected by the type and capacity of the recreational facility. Clearly when demand is below this threshold, no congestion fee should be charged since no costs are imposed on others by an additional user. The technological capacity of recreational facilities has not been considered binding in optimal pricing because it is never reached in a strictly spatial sense due to the demand reducing effect of congestion. This is of little consequence to the congestion problem. The congestion threshold would likely be reached well before the technical capacity. However, the issue does point to the uniqueness of congestion charges in relation to recreational facilities. The fee would be expected to vary substantially across recreational facilities of different sizes and attributes. Additionally, there are effects of visiting a different recreational area when fees are imposed that change the relative costs of the outing. These substitution effects should also be considered in the design of efficient fees.

Defining the capacity of a recreational facility is of course an aggregate problem.[8] To accomplish this objective, however, one must begin at a disaggregate level to determine the implications of user interactions for the benefits each individual derives from his own activities. Before congestion costs can be adequately reflected in management policies or investment plans for a given facility, it is necessary to identify the individual effects of user interactions.

The questions addressed in this chapter can best be summarized with the following example—a park. If a manager's goal is to maximize the benefits associated with the use of the park, then he or she must somehow optimally balance two opposing forces of demand. Additional users will add to the aggregate benefit derived from the services provided by the park through the increased number of visitors. (It is assumed that the number of visitors would increase until there are no additional net benefits to an additional visitor.) The presence of these additional users, however, may interfere with the enjoyment derived by other users, imposing congestion costs. Thus, a full accounting of the benefits derived from the use of the park will recognize these congestion effects as real losses in the benefits derived from the facility. A trade-off is involved between the additions to total benefits from more users versus the costs they impose in terms of the reduced benefits of other users. Managerial actions based on efficient resource allocation must ultimately incorporate consideration of this fundamental trade-off. The problem is exacerbated by the fact that the demand for recreational sites generally varies over periods of time too short to continually adjust the supply of recreational facilities. Therefore, there will be excess capacity (relative to threshold congestion levels) in some time periods resulting in varying costs of congestion. Important questions arise concerning the magnitude of congestion fees to be charged, as well as the exact time periods that they should be in effect. If fees cannot be adjusted continually to reflect current congestion costs, there is the additional consideration of the level of demand upon which the fee should be based (e.g., minimum, median, maximum).[9]

OPTIMAL CONGESTION FEES WITH VARYING DEMAND

Setting a single congestion fee for any particular level of congestion would be efficient only for that period of time in which the level of congestion does not change. During other time periods in the demand cycle the price or level of congestion fee would be too high, implying inefficient resource allocation. This system would produce inefficient results because users willing to pay the optimal congestion costs they impose on others would not be allowed to visit the site, while at other levels of congestion too many users are allowed. For example, in Figure 7.1 the choice of demand D_1 is chosen as the base and the approximate efficiency losses are represented by the shaded areas. (Too many consumers use the facilities for D_3 and too few for D_2; of course the congestion effect itself mitigates this tendency to some degree.) MCC represents the increasing marginal cost of congestion. Equality of the MCC curve and the demand curves gives the efficient fee levels, f^*_1, f^*_2, and f^*_3. When visitation is above threshold congestion levels, the choice of any base to set a single congestion fee when demand varies over the demand cycle leads to inefficiencies in time periods during which levels of demand differ from the base.

If demand actually varied discretely over periods of time with constant demand within a period, as represented in Figure 7.1, the choice of congestion charges and the time periods in which these should be charged would be relatively easily determined. However, demand would generally vary substantially over the demand cycle (Schechter & Lucas, 1978) as shown in Figure 7.2. With continuously varying demand, the optimal congestion charge would also vary continuously with nonconstant marginal congestion costs. In other words, since marginal costs of congestion increase with the level of use above the threshold level (Baumol & Oates, 1975), the optimal congestion fee would increase for each additional

Figure 7.1
Optimal Congestion Fees with Varying Demand

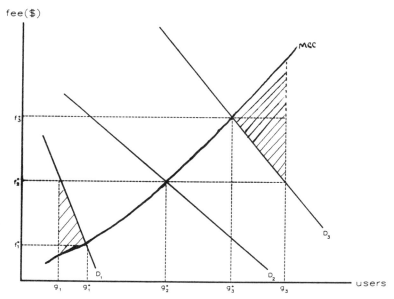

Note: Efficiency losses are approximated by the shaded areas when demand varies over time and only a single congestion fee is charged. q_i^* repesents the efficient outcomes. When the fee is based on the optimal congestion level at q_2^* then there are $(q_3 - q_3^*)$ too many visitors for period 3 and $(q_1 - q_1^*)$ too few visitors in period 1.

visitor. Unfortunately, transaction costs would increase considerably with such a pricing scheme. In addition, it may not be politically or institutionally feasible to charge consumers by order of entry (which is implied by the continuous pricing). The natural implication for facilities, such as for camping, would be to base the fee on the marginal use for each day. Again, varying fees from day to day may not be possible, but days of similar characteristics should be grouped in choosing a standard fee for these days. Alternatively, for an urban park with variation throughout the day, the day could be broken into a number of fee periods. Of course care must be taken in this latter instance since the incentives would be for people to arrive, if possible, before the peak fee is in effect even though they may stay throughout the peak period. Given the appropriate data, the proper fees are relatively easily determined numerically.

Generally, a limited number of discrete pricing periods must be chosen. In this case the choice of congestion fees must be determined simultaneously with the periods of time these fees are to be in effect. The simultaneous choice of the number of fee periods, the magnitude of fees in each period, and the times at which the fees switch would take place would be determined numerically. A criterion generally used to determine an economically efficient allocation of resources is the maximization of the sum of consumer and producer surplus with

Figure 7.2
The Demand Cycle

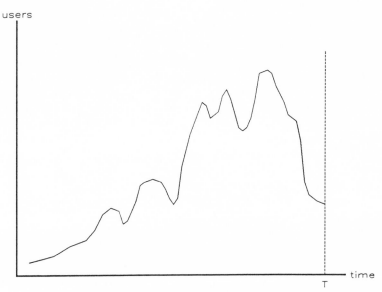

Note: Demand generally varies substantially over the demand cycle (which may be a
season or year depending upon the use and type of facility).

externalities internalized. Alternatively, the maximization of revenue to the recreational facility could be the objective, which would lead to a lower visitation
level than would the efficient fees. The minimum necessary information to
optimize such a scheme is an estimate of demand as a function of the fee, a
congestion measure, and time (within the demand cycle).[10] An estimate of costs
for additional fee periods (within that institutionally allowed) is necessary to
determine the optimal number of periods (without costs to implementation, or
restrictions on the number of fee periods, the optimal would be continuously
varying the fee for each user above the congestion threshold level). Additionally,
prices of substitute activities and the fees in other periods for the considered
recreational facility or facilities would lead to the more precise choice of an
optimal management policy. Through these variables the substitution of visitation
at one park for that at another, as well as the substitution of visitation across
time periods at the same area could be examined.

In regard to how the congestion variable affects demand, congestion would
most likely be defined differently for different recreational demands. Measurement of congestion may be different for different uses of the recreational facility.
For example, in hiking congestion may be defined by the number of others
encountered on the trail. With skiing congestion may be defined by the length
of lift lines as well as the number of skiers on the slopes.[11]

The authors of existing literature on congestion externalities mention the concept of a demand cycle (e.g., Dorfman, 1984), but the formal analyses have been in terms of a particular point in time or have assumed that congestion was constant through time.[12] However, such is not generally the case. It appears that the existing peak load pricing literature could easily be applied (other than formally extending the congestion externality model to include cyclical demand). The congestion problem, however, has qualitative differences that must be taken into account.

The demand for the congested facility may, or may not, be of a discrete length of time. That is, for some services the demand may be for a particular length of time (i.e., guided tours through parks or overnight camping), while for others (outdoor recreation in general) the length of the visit (demand) may be discretionary. An asymmetry within the peak load model exists in that demand may be substituted from peak time to other points in time within a pricing period due to varying demand. This is not a problem in the traditional literature, for example, public utilities, since there are no incentives to substitute consumption from one point in time to another point within the same pricing period if there is no price difference. Additionally, in this regard, the individual's demand for the facility may actually increase if the congestion effect on demand is greater than the price (fee) effect. Given the varying demand (and hence varying levels of congestion through time) and increasing costs of congestion (Baumol & Oates, 1975), the optimal solution, if there are no transaction costs, is continuously varying congestion charges. In most actual situations, however, government-imposed surcharges cannot vary from transaction to transaction. Therefore, it should be advantageous to group consumers who are relatively homogeneous with regard to the time of consumption (and possibly congestion evaluations) into periods of time over which the congestion fee would not vary.

Patrick (1989) developed optimization models for choosing allocatively efficient congestion fees and fee switching times. In his models, if a fee were charged that is equivalent to the marginal congestion cost imposed by an additional visitor, the optimal fee would vary with each increment in visitor numbers, increasing (decreasing) with each visitor when congestion is increasing (decreasing). Of course times in which aggregate visitation is below the congestion threshold would have a zero fee. However, if continuously varying fees are not possible, socially optimal entrance fees are chosen simultaneously with fee switching times, as the choice of one would affect the optimal choice of the other. The switching times are chosen so that, at the time of fee change, welfare at the initial fee and congestion level is equal to welfare at the new fee and congestion level at that fee. Thus, it is simply insured that at the fee switching times welfare cannot be improved by leaving the existing fee in effect for an additional increment in visitation as indivisibilities may prohibit equality at some levels of congestion.

There are several additional considerations in determining the optimality of cyclical congestion fees. Given the possibility and technological feasibility, of implementing time-of-use (TOU) fees, the costs of implementing such fees must be considered. Substitution (analogous to arbitrage in the temporal sense) possibilities must be limited or the policy will simply shift the peak times of congestion, possibly creating times of higher congestion than originally existed at other points of time in the demand cycle. In addition, when demand is discretionary, a barrier to users arriving before the higher congestion fees are in effect must exist. Otherwise the user may just show up in a low or zero fee period and stay through higher fee periods.

If TOU congestion fees are not a feasible policy, then the question as to the optimal congestion charge, if any, over the varying recreational demand cycle still must be addressed. In this case the fee to be charged over the demand cycle is set to equal the average of the demand weighted marginal cost of congestion (at each increment in visitation) over the demand cycle. This is not simply a fee based on the average congestion level since the costs at higher levels of visitation receive a relatively higher weighting. Such a fee would minimize the efficiency losses depicted in Figure 7.1.

CONCLUSION

This chapter illustrated nonmathematically (see Patrick, 1989, for a technical treatment), an improved mechanism for estimating optimal congestion fees for recreational facilities. As congestion of facilities, particularly public facilities, increases, managers and policy makers are searching for methods to reduce usage in acceptable manners while maximizing societal benefit of the facilities. This chapter assists the reader in following the issues underlying the problems of fixing and assessing congestion fees. While the methodology suggested here is not a panacea, it does provide a mechanism for achieving greater societal benefits from the inventory of public recreational facilities. In addition, this chapter offers managers an operational technique for constructing a congestion fee structure and informs them of many of the potential pitfalls in the development of such a structure. This work marks the beginning of analysis of market-type mechanisms used for rationing and preservation that are more efficient alternatives to traditional governmental rules and regulations.

NOTES

1. Harrington (1987) presents figures on demand growth and supply decline.
2. McConnell (1977) and Cicchetti and Smith (1973; 1976) are notable exceptions. The measurement of congestion and evaluation of the willingness to pay for congestion reductions are not detailed here as these studies provide the basis. The cyclical nature of congestion and optimal resource management are of more concern in this chapter.
3. Smith (1981) and McConnell (1977) are exceptions. Additionally, Dorfman (1984) briefly touches upon the cyclical nature of demand.
4. Of course transaction and/or information costs may outweigh benefits. Naturally this is an empirical question.
5. See Deyak and Smith (1978) for an example of the household production function

approach and McConnell (1977) for an example of congestion as a consumption externality.

6. This is correct only if consumers do not have homogeneous recreational preferences. The empirically relevant case is that of heterogeneous preferences. Freeman and Haveman (1977) discuss the optimal congestion fee when consumers have heterogeneous tastes.

7. Additional obvious advantages of charging fees over simply restricting access is the elimination of excess demand for the facility and additional revenue with which to operate. McConnell and Duff (1976) discuss issues with regard to excess demand.

8. Fisher and Krutilla (1972) examine optimal capacity determination for outdoor recreation facilities. The discussion in this chapter is based on a given capacity.

9. There is also the question of optimal capacity of recreational facilities which is beyond the scope of the present chapter. The main concern here is with the management of an existing stock of facilities.

10. Oliveira and Rausser (1977) discuss the estimation of recreation demand through time. However, there is no consideration of congestion in their study.

11. See, for example, Cicchetti and Smith (1976).

12. Smith (1981) considers a two period peak load congestion model in which demand is constant within each period. However, this model fails to capture some of the complexities of varying consumer demand with congestion externalities and thereby ignores potentially important policy considerations. He does, however, present an excellent discussion of the timing of recreational demands that are important elements in optimal policy as well as necessary data.

REFERENCES

Anderson, L. G. (1980). Estimating the benefits of recreation under conditions of congestion: Comments and extension. *Journal of Environmental Economics and Management, 7* (December), 401–406.

Baumol, W. J., & Oates, W. E. (1975). *The theory of environmental policy.* Englewood Cliffs, NJ: Prentice-Hall.

Cicchetti, C. J., & Smith, V. K. (1973). Congestion, quality deterioration, and optimal use: Wilderness recreation in the Spanish Peaks Primitive Area. *Social Science Research, 2* (March), 15–30.

Cicchetti, C. J., & Smith, V. K. (1976). *The costs of congestion: An econometric analysis of wilderness recreation.* Cambridge, MA: Ballinger Publishing.

Deyak, T., & Smith, V. K. (1978). Congestion and participation in outdoor recreation: A household production function approach. *Journal of Environmental Economics and Management, 5,* 63–80.

Dorfman, R. (1984). On optimal congestion. *Journal of Environmental Economics, 11* (June), 91–106.

Fisher, A., & Krutilla, J. V. (1972). Determination of optimal capacity of resource-based recreation facilities. *Natural Resources Journal, 12,* 417–444.

Freeman, A. M. III, & Haveman, R. H. (1977). Congestion, quality deterioration, and heterogeneous tastes. *Journal of Public Economics, 8,* 225–232.

Harrington, W. (1987). *Measuring recreation supply.* Baltimore: Johns Hopkins University Press.

Haveman, R. H. (1973). Common property, congestion, and environmental pollution. *Quarterly Journal of Economics, 87,* 278–287.

Layard, R. (1977). The distributional effects of congestion taxes. *Economica, 44,* 297–304.

McConnell, K. E. (1977). Congestion and willingness to pay: A study of beach use. *Land Economics, 53,* 185–195.

McConnell, K. E. (1980). Valuing congested recreation sites. *Journal of Environmental Economics and Management, 7,* 389–394.

McConnell, K. E., & Duff, V. A. (1976). Estimating net benefits of recreation under conditions of excess demand. *Journal of Environmental Economics and Management, 2,* 224–230.

Oliveira, R. A., & Rausser, G. C. (1977). Daily fluctuations in campground use: An econometric analysis. *American Journal of Agricultural Economics, 59* (May), 283–293.

Patrick, R. H. (1989). Optimal cyclical congestion (Working Paper 89–7). Golden: Colorado School of Mines.

Schechter, M., & Lucas, R. C. (1978). *Simulation of recreation use for park and wilderness management.* Baltimore: Johns Hopkins University Press.

Smith, V. K. (1981). Congestion, travel cost recreational demand models and benefit evaluation. *Journal of Environmental Economics and Management, 8,* 92–96.

Stevens, T. H., & Allen, P. G. (1980). Estimating the benefits of recreation under conditions of congestion. *Journal of Environmental Economics and Management, 7,* 395–400.

8.

PRIVATE MANAGEMENT OF PUBLIC RECREATION: IS IT COST-EFFECTIVE?

Steven E. Daniels

The actions of public land management agencies are increasingly constrained by finances, and activities that incur budget deficits are being closely scrutinized. Curtailing or eliminating programs that do not yield positive net revenue is one obvious response but may not be entirely consistent with long-term social needs. The ability of a particular agency function to return a profit may not be related to the provision of positive net social value. For example, the social value of a program to educate underprivileged inner-city children about natural environments might exceed their ability to pay the program's full cost. A farcical example of a potentially profitable program with negative social value is the use of public land and personnel to produce marijuana. Clearly there is no necessary correlation between profitability and social value in some programs.

A two-step decision process can be an alternative to merely reducing the size or number of unprofitable programs. The first step is to separate the activities that are unprofitable both financially and socially from those that are unprofitable to the agency but beneficial to society. The former activities can justifiably be eliminated, but dealing with the latter group is more difficult. These activities should be retained because of their social value, but given the current fiscal environment alternative means of financial support must be considered.

Based on the contention that providing many types of outdoor recreation, specifically developed camping, is socially valuable but unprofitable at the agency level, this chapter examines private management of public campgrounds as a way to reduce costs. The analysis is based on a case study of United States Department of Agriculture Forest Service campgrounds in the Seeley-Swan valley of western Montana. The case study consists of two concessionaire campgrounds and four traditionally managed campgrounds. Apart from this managerial difference, the campgrounds have similar locations, physical attributes, services provided, and serve similar users. Thus, the traditionally managed campgrounds function as an experimental control against which the concessionaire campgrounds are compared.

Both the general topic of developed camping and the specific case study were chosen because they are symptomatic and illustrative of greater resource allocation problems facing many practicing recreational resource managers. The potential of this research extends beyond these six campgrounds to the extent that lessons learned in the analysis of campground recreation are applicable to other campgrounds and are also relevant, by inference, to many other forms of public recreation. That is, this approach applies to the range from dispersed to concentrated outdoor recreation, for example, everything from wilderness hiking to hotel living at Old Faithful. Moreover, recent Forest Service experiments with concessionaire management are being closely monitored by managers who may adopt the technique. This analysis gives timely insight on how, or if, they should proceed.

ANALYTICAL APPROACH

The efficiency of concessionaire-managed campgrounds depends on the cost structure of the campgrounds and the provisions of the concessionaire contract. Contracts for concessionaire campgrounds generally contain the following three features: (1) the concessionaire is responsible for the daily operation of the campground and for maintenance at a contractually specified level; (2) the concessionaire is allowed to keep all user fee revenue as payment for services rendered; and (3) the contract is offered annually on a sealed bid basis.

The concessionaire's profit is implicitly equal to the fee revenue minus the cost of operation and the bid. Economic theory provides some insight into the relationship between a concessionaire's bid, his operating costs, and Forest Service operating costs. Given the assumption of perfectly competitive concessionaires operating with full information, the bid (adjusted for a normal profit) equals the producer's surplus from Forest Service management if the concessionaire and the Forest Service have similar production functions and face similar prices. If concessionaires are more efficient than the Forest Service, the bid is above the producer's surplus from Forest Service management because the concessionaire's costs are lower. This relationship between the efficiency of concessionaire management and the size of the bid is the core of this analysis. The costs efficiency of concessionaire management is addressed by comparing the concessionaire's bid to the Forest Service–generated producer's surplus.

Equation 1 shows the economic situation facing the concessionaires.

$$P^*Q_c - \int_0^{Q_c} C(Q)dQ \geq B \tag{1}$$

where P = user fee; Q_C = use; $C(Q)$ = concessionare's cost function; and B = bid, adjusted for normal profit.

In other words, revenues minus costs should be greater than or equal to the bid. The bid equals the difference between revenues and cost when competition increases the bid until only a normal profit remains. Furthermore, the more efficient firms have lower cost functions and can bid higher while remaining profitable.

The Forest Service, on the other hand, faces Equation 2.

$$P^*Q_c - \int_0^{Q_c} C_{FS}(Q)dQ = PS \tag{2}$$

where $C_{FS}(Q)$ = Forest Service cost function and PS = producer's surplus generated by Forest Service management.

The following comparison tests the cost effectiveness of concessionaire management:

$$B \geq P^*Q_c - \int_0^{Q_c} C_{FS}(Q)dQ \tag{3}$$

or

$$B \geq P^*Q_c - [AFC_{FS} + \int_0^{Q_c} VC_{FS}(Q)dQ] \tag{3'}$$

where AFC_{FS} = annual fixed cost of Forest Service management and $VC_{FS}(Q)$ = variable cost function of Forest Service management.

Several factors affect the relationship in Equation 3'. The concessionaire must have lower annual fixed or variable costs than does the Forest Service for Equation 3' to hold, if perfect competition and full information are still assumed. Dropping these assumptions complicates the situation considerably. Competition presumably has a positive effect on the bid size, and in the absence of competitive pressure, profit maximizing concessionaires bid the minimum dictated by law or by game theory. Relaxing the perfect information assumption has an ambiguous effect on the bid; if the bidders underestimate (overestimate) the potential profit, the bids are lower (higher) than an *ex post* calculation of Equation 3′ indicates.

The economic implications of Equation 3′ can be summarized as follows. If $B >$ revenues − costs then concessionaires are either more efficient than the Forest Service, or concessionaires are less efficient, but overestimate profitability. If $B <$ revenues − costs then concessionaires are either less efficient than the Forest Service, or concessionaires are more efficient, but underestimate profitability, or there is insufficient competition.

Relaxing the full information assumption insures that the results will be ambiguous. This ambiguity is acceptable because it reflects the environment in which both the concessionaire and the Forest Service are operating. Concessionaire management is a new policy and both the Forest Service and concessionaires have imperfect information, which may combine to increase the cost of concessionaire management. These start-up costs are presumably temporary but are nevertheless part of the total cost of shifting from traditional Forest Service to concessionaire management. Assuming perfect information ignores these start-up costs; the ambiguity of imperfect information must be endured in order to present realistic costs.

EMPIRICAL ANALYSIS

The case study examines six Forest Service campgrounds in the Seeley-Swan valley of western Montana. The Seeley-Swan is a long narrow valley bordered by the Swan and Mission mountains to the east and west, respectively. The valley is a popular recreation spot, easily accessed by 42 percent of Montana's population. It is relatively unknown, however, to the out-of-state campers who tend to travel just north and south of it on their way to Glacier and Yellowstone national parks, respectively. In sum, the Seeley-Swan valley provides an important, although not unique, recreation opportunity for a regional market.

The six campgrounds in the Seeley-Swan valley are all quite similar with the most notable exception that the northern two are concessionaire managed and the southern four are traditionally managed. All are on small lakes in the valley floor, are of similar size and construction, equally remote, face the same local markets for purchasing labor and materials, and receive roughly equal use. In short, the factors that would affect the operating costs of these campgrounds are constant across the group, providing a control group of traditionally managed campgrounds and an experimental group of concessionaire campgrounds.

Solving Equation 3′ requires data for three of its four variables. The bid (B) and the fee revenues ($P*Q$) are both available from Forest Service records. The variable costs of Forest Service management ($VC_{FS}(Q)$) are derived by applying variable cost functions developed by Daniels (1986) for the four traditionally managed campgrounds. This latter step assumes that if the Forest Service managed the campgrounds currently under concessionaire management, the variable costs would be equal to the variable cost on the four campgrounds

Table 8.1
Physical and Economic Data from the Concessionaire Campgrounds, 1984

	Campground	
	Holland Lake	Swan Lake
Physical Data		
Number of sites	55	43
Number of RVDs	8584	12648
Economic Data (in dollars)		
Bid revenue	500	1510
Fee Revenue	9452	9576
Variable costs		
Compliance checking	973.00	141.02
Garbage Collection	616.76	609.02
Maintenance/cleanup	224.70	227.55
Fee management	490.87	632.42
Total	2296.33	2610.01
Critical value for annual		
fixed cost[a]	6655.67	5455.99

[a]Critical value is the annual fixed cost above which the bid exceeds the producer's surplus generated
    by Forest Service management.

the Forest Service currently manages. This appears reasonable, given the similarities between the campgrounds.

The cost structure of the concessionaire campgrounds is displayed in Table 8.1. The critical values for annual fixed cost are derived by reorganizing Equation 3' and expressing it as an equality.

$$\text{AFC} = P^*Q_c - (VC_{FS}(Q_c) + B) \tag{4}$$

The bid exceeds the Forest Service producer's surplus if, and only if, the annual fixed cost of Forest Service management exceeds this critical value.

DISCUSSION

The critical annual fixed costs for the concessionaire campgrounds and the observed annual fixed costs for the four traditionally managed campgrounds are

Table 8.2

Comparison of Annual Fixed Costs: Critical Values for Concessionaire Versus Observed Values for Forest Service Management

Campground	Annual Fixed Cost
River Point	$4495.40
Swan Lake	5455.99
Lake Alva	5837.39
Big Larch	6131.21
Holland Lake	6655.69
Seeley Lake	7802.10

Note: Swan Lake and Holland Lake are under concessionaire management; the others are traditionally managed.

presented in Table 8.2. The annual fixed costs are not different between the groups, which supports the conclusion that concessionaires and Forest Service managers are equally efficient. In other words, concessionaire management was neither more nor less cost-effective than traditional management on the six campgrounds analyzed.

By extending this analysis to consider two issues not captured in the cost functions, concessionaire management can be shown to have some small advantages over traditional management. First, concessionaires are an effective way for local recreation managers to avoid the taxing effects of the Twenty-Five Percent Fund Act of 1908. This law requires that 25 percent of forest receipts, including recreation revenues, be remitted to the county in which the revenues were generated, to fund roads and schools (USDA, 1983). The rational revenue maximizing manager recognizes this as an *ad valorem* tax that shifts the demand curve and responds by maximizing after tax revenues. Concessionaire management allows a large portion of the tax to be avoided because under traditional management total fee revenue (equivalent to gross income) is subject to the 25 percent tax; under concessionaire management only the concessionaire's bid (equivalent to net income) is taxed. The combined tax on the Seeley-Swan valley concessionaire campgrounds for 1984 was $502.50, but under traditional management it would have been $4,757.

Second, there are nonpecuniary advantages to concessionaire management, namely that the Forest Service can reallocate manpower to other projects. This implies that concessionaire management appears to be Pareto improving, since the concessionaire makes a profit and the Forest Service can reallocate its recreation staff to other useful tasks. Given the endemic personnel shortages in recreation programs, this may be the most significant consideration for recreation managers.

Concessionaire management is not without disadvantages, however. One major uncertainty regards the experiential quality of concessionaire campgrounds. Forest Service facilities consistently provide high quality recreation opportunities. It remains to be seen if concessionaires also provide such exemplary service. The Forest Service has long pursued a good host philosophy—it is even mentioned in the recreation management objectives section of the Forest Service Manual (USDA, 1985, Section 2302.2). Concessionaires are constrained by profit maximization and may merely be adequate hosts. Moreover, to the extent that fee revenues are only a small fraction of total recreation benefits, concessionaire behavior that marginally reduces revenues could produce a large reduction in the total benefits, thereby decreasing net social benefits of the campgrounds. If recreators do not like concessionaire management, continued use of concessionaire managed facilities amounts to focusing on immediate revenue issues while ignoring the larger issues of recreation provision. In addition, the cost of any problems with a concessionaire that required litigation would outweigh the benefits for several years.[1]

These results roughly parallel those of Scott and Gartner (1987), which is the only other refereed analysis of concessionaire-managed Forest Service campgrounds of which the author is aware. Their approach was to compare gross receipts with estimated campground operation and maintenance costs derived from existing cost function estimates (Gibbs & Van Hees, 1981) to identify potential concessionaire campgrounds in the Siuslaw National Forest. While they found only one of seventeen campgrounds met this criterion, they acknowledged potential benefits through Forest Service reallocation of resources to other recreation activities.

SUMMARY

Concessionaire management of public campgrounds has some reasonable, but not overwhelming, advantages. The bids offered by concessionaires are comparable with the producer's surplus the Forest Service managers would generate and have the advantages of reducing the remittance required by the Twenty-Five Percent Fund Act of 1908 and freeing Forest Service employees to perform other tasks. The bids are not large enough, however, to support the hypothesis that concessionaires are more efficient than Forest Service managers. Moreover, the Pareto improvements resulting from concessionaire management are small, and problems with concessionaires can potentially outweigh the benefits.

NOTE

1. These reservations about the quality of concessionaire management are based on

two observations from 1984 experiences at the Holland Lake and Swan Lake campgrounds. First, a concessionaire employee hit a female recreator—certainly not evidence of good hospitality. Second, fee envelopes submitted at the four traditionally managed campgrounds included recreator complaints about recent experiences at the concessionaire facilities and admonitions to continue traditional management.

REFERENCES

Daniels, S. E. (1986). *Efficient provision of recreational opportunities: The case of U.S. Forest Service campgrounds*. Doctoral dissertation, Duke University, Durham, NC.

Gibbs, K. C., & Van Hees, W. S. (1981). Cost of operating public campgrounds. *Journal of Leisure Research, 13* (3), 243–253.

Scott, R., & Gartner, W. C. (1987). An economic feasibility analysis for concessionaire management of campgrounds in the Siuslaw National Forest. *Western Journal of Applied Forestry, 2* (3), 91–94.

U.S. Department of Agriculture (1983). *Principle laws relating to Forest Service activities* (Agriculture Handbook #453). Washington, DC: U.S. Government Printing Office.

U.S. Department of Agriculture. (1985). *Forest Service manual*. Washington, DC: U.S. Government Printing Office.

9.

FOUNDING PRINCIPLES AND CONTEMPORARY PUBLIC POLICY: THE CASE OF THE OFFICE OF MANAGEMENT AND BUDGET AND THE SPORT FISH RESTORATION PROGRAM

Lloyd G. Nigro and William D. Richardson

It has become almost an article of faith among conservative economists and policy makers that user fees and excise taxes are often efficient alternatives to collective goods approaches to public services (Mushkin & Vehorn, 1980; Savas, 1982). In addition to their economic rationale, these charges are also put forward as politically efficacious because only the self-interested beneficiaries pay and nonusers are not visibly affected. Accordingly, each consumer decides whether or not to participate. Presumably, the choice is made on rational grounds having to do with individual preferences and calculations balancing the costs and benefits associated with a particular good or service. Likewise, governmental provision of these goods and services depends on the extent to which there are consumers willing to pay a price that at least equals the cost. While they are not put forward as a complete substitute for the market, user charges and taxes are a step in that direction. They assume self-interested behavior by individuals, and they facilitate the rational calculation of benefits and costs so valued by economists (Frieden, 1979; Friedman, 1962; Gilder, 1981; Goldwin & Scambra, 1980; 1982; Smith, 1904; Sowell, 1981). Savas, a leading exponent of user charges to limit the size of the administrative state, argues:

Gaining political acceptability of any new charge is always a problem, of course, but the more clearly the service is a private or toll good, with individual, identifiable beneficiaries, and the more that service is permitted to deteriorate due to underfinancing, the more acceptable a user charge becomes, like an increase in mass-transit fares. (1982, p. 133)

The virtues of this approach need not be limited to economics and political acceptability, however. The character of the participating citizens is also a relevant concern, as the forms of political action and administration with which user charges are associated tend to promote some of those traits upon which the American regime is based.

The founders of the American republic relied heavily upon individualism and acquisitiveness in their constitutional design. The American character was seen to be self-centered to the point that the private world is usually more important than the general welfare as a guide to behavior. The individual, therefore, was expected to make the improvement of his own conditions the basis for making political and economic choices. The founders successfully argued for a republic on the grounds that individualism was a predictable, if not uplifting, trait whose negative features might better be controlled through a managed clash of interests than by reliance on the regime's capacity to reform the individual (Tocqueville, 1969; Diamond, 1979; Goldwin, 1979; Horwitz, 1979). Acquisitiveness is intrinsic to the American character set forth in founding thought. In the tradition of John Locke and Adam Smith, James Madison believed that acquisitiveness served as a kind of moral code for the commercial society because, to be successful, one must be willing to take risks, to exercise self-discipline, to maintain a reputation for honesty, to be industrious, and to delay gratification (Cropsey, 1980a; 1980b; Diamond, 1979; Hamilton, Madison & Jay, 1961; Moulds, 1964; Parsons, 1969; Smith, 1904).[1]

As Madison recognized, these character traits, while necessary to sustain a regime that is both democratic and commercial, are a comparatively low moral foundation upon which to build a republic. This criticism is often made by those who believe that the regime and its citizens would benefit (in ethical if not material terms) from seeking more noble ends (Hofstadter, 1979). However, in contrast to the classical concept of the polis, which saw the regime as a comprehensive system for the formation of character, the Madisonian point of view accepts the modern image of human nature as essentially self-interested. According to Martin Diamond:

the new science of politics could dispense with those laws [concerned with character formation] and, for the achievement of its lowered ends, could rely largely instead upon shrewd institutional arrangements of the powerful human passions and interests. Not to instruct and to transcend these passions and interests, but rather to channel them became the hallmark of modern politics. Politics could now concentrate upon the "realistic" task of directing man's passions and interests toward the achievement of those solid goods this earth has to offer: self-preservation and the protection of those individual liberties which are an integral part of that preservation and which make it decent and agreeable. (1979, p. 47)

SPORT FISHING INTERESTS AND THE OFFICE OF MANAGEMENT AND BUDGET

User charges and excise taxes are among the many shrewd arrangements to which Diamond refers. In political as well as economic terms, they tap and channel self-interest. The public agencies responsible for the administration of programs funded by user fees and excise taxes must avoid obscuring or breaking down the connections between user interests, program contents, and the ways resources are allocated. Support for these programs depends on the perception that funds collected through these means are not being made available to non-contributors (free riders) or other programs. If either of these diversions occurs, a crucial linkage to self-interest and participation is broken. The channeling process works both ways, for these funds must be spent on specific programs, thereby greatly limiting administrative discretion.

Administrative attempts to divert or redefine the uses to which such funds may be put predictably arouse opposition from vigilant proponents and contributors, especially if they have been active participants in the development of the program. A confrontation between David Stockman of the Office of Management and Budget (OMB) and sport fishermen over the uses of funds collected under the Federal Aid in Sport Fish Restoration Program serves as an object lesson of how to undermine a program with very strong participant support for its user charges and excise taxes. More broadly, this episode illustrates how public administrators may attempt to exercise discretion in the pursuit of worthy objectives that are nonetheless in conflict with founding assumptions about the American character and its place in the regime. It might also be interpreted as an example of what Stockman (1986) meant when he acknowledged that his approach to federal budgeting failed to fully recognize the role of self-interest in the American political process.

The Federal Aid in Sport Fish Restoration Act (1950) was passed in response to a perceived need to augment state efforts to manage and restore sport fishing with federally collected excise taxes on equipment. These funds were collected by the Department of the Treasury and apportioned to the states according to a formula based on a state's geographic area and its ratio of licensed sport fishermen to total population. Revenues collected under this act provided about $30 million annually to the states (Williamson, 1985). In 1979, combined state and federal expenditures for fisheries management were about $139 million. These funds were inadequate for the purpose of simply maintaining current resources, however, and pressure on these resources was increasing. In response to this situation, concerned groups of conservationists, state agencies, equipment manufacturers, and sport fishermen waged a protracted campaign to increase federal support through additional taxes. This effort culminated in the Wallop-Breaux expansion of the original legislation, which was then signed into law by President Reagan in July 1984.

The Wallop-Breaux legislation significantly increased program funds in four ways by (1) expanding the types of fishing-related equipment subject to federal excise taxes, (2) diverting $45 million of marine fuel taxes from highway construction to boating safety programs, (3) redirecting another $45 million in marine fuel taxes to the sport fish restoration program, and (4) taking another $20 million in duties previously paid on imported fishing gear from the treasury and allocating it to the restoration program. In total, the funds available to the fisheries program were increased by approximately $75 million annually. The legislation, therefore, was the product of the efforts of a coalition of self-interested individuals who had voluntarily joined in the effort to increase the resources available to all of them. Very clearly, the expectation was that these funds would be used for improving fisheries management and boating safety.

However, much to the ire of the fishermen and boaters, in December 1984 (after the election) David Stockman revealed that most of the new money (about $70 million) might not be available for the intended purposes. Reducing the federal deficit, it seemed, was a higher priority at the OMB, and Stockman proposed to keep the fuel tax and customs receipts as a contribution to that effort. In a June 28, 1985 letter to Senator Wallopp, Stockman argued that diverting these funds was justified for two reasons: (1) revenues from pleasure boat and fishing tackle customs duties are not excise or user fees, and therefore should go directly into the general fund, and (2) that diverting motorboat fuel tax revenues to fisheries programs instead of spending them on boating-related matters (e.g., supplementing Coast Guard operations) is inequitable. Needless to say, the fishing and boating coalition viewed matters differently. In a 1985 memorandum to its membership, the American Recreation Coalition characterized OMB's stance as a breach of faith, for ''We accept that there is no real free lunch, but when we pay for lunch we don't expect to starve.'' The coalition aggressively lobbied against Stockman's proposal, and Wallop and Breaux were eventually able to block it by mobilizing public opinion and the Congress.

PRIVATE AND PUBLIC INTERESTS IN THE AMERICAN REGIME

The argument in favor of capturing tax revenues in this manner, of course, is that they are better used to help solve the problems of the general public as opposed to those of the special interests by asserting that the public interest was being promoted over that of a narrow faction by reducing, however modestly, the national debt. The fishing and boating interests, however, angrily contended that Stockman had arbitrarily taken their money and given it to other interests, especially the military.

This dispute was rooted in a fundamental disagreement over the roles self-interested factions and public administrators were intended to have in the American regime (though we are not contending here that Stockman or the sport fishing interests thought about the dispute in these terms). In this case, Stockman's position apparently violated one of the basic principles upon which the founders relied: the structure and process of American government was supposed to moderate and channel the self-interested acquisitiveness of the citizens. As the founders would have anticipated, this particular program is widely supported by sport fishermen and boaters because it appeals directly to their interests—so much so that they even lobbied for increased taxes on the equipment and fuel they used. It also may be argued that the resulting improvements in fisheries management and boating safety benefit not just these special interests, but the general public as well. However, the OMB approach sought to substitute its concept of the public interest for a policy that explicitly sought to bridge or accommodate private and public interests.

One of the earliest and most insightful commentators on self-interested behavior in the American regime was the nineteenth-century French philosopher Alexis de Tocqueville (1969). His observations regarding the state's impact on the character of the American people are especially relevant to the issues discussed here. For example, Tocqueville argued that voluntary associations (such as that of our fishermen) are crucial to the proper functioning of American democracy. Not only do these associations lessen the need for government, but they also teach their members the skills and citizen virtues that serve to moderate certain undesirable features of individualism and acquisitiveness. In his words:

[M]any of my contemporaries . . . claim that as the citizens become weaker and more helpless, the government must become proportionately more skillful and active, so that society should do what is no longer possible for individuals. They think that answers the whole problem, but I think they are mistaken.

A government could take the place of some of the largest associations in America, and some particular states of the Union have already attempted that. But what political power could ever carry on the vast multitude of lesser undertakings which associations daily enable American citizens to control? . . . The more government takes the place of associations, the more will individuals lose the idea of forming associations and need the government to come to their help. . . . The morals and intelligence of a democratic people would be in as much danger as its commerce and industry if ever a government wholly usurped the place of private associations. (p. 515)

Tocqueville refers to at least two perils he believed threatened the citizen virtues and habits necessary to an effective democracy: (1) as government expands, individuals increasingly will become dependent and passive; and (2) greater dependency will encourage the government's complete assumption of responsibilities that previously were performed by voluntary or private association (p. 510). President Reagan and David Stockman often expressed similar concerns.

According to Tocqueville, political and economic liberty are fostered by voluntary associations of citizens acting to define and express their interests within a framework of decentralized democratic government. However, liberty is threatened by democracy's tendency to encourage a centralization of power. Tocqueville believed that this centralizing process could make it easier for public administrators to impose policies better designed to serve the majority. These are certainly concerns with which the Reagan administration had considerable sympathy, and one suspects that Stockman would have heartily agreed with the following:

Every central power which follows its natural instincts loves equality and favors it. For equality singularly facilitates, extends, and secures its influence. One can also assert that every central government worships uniformity; uniformity saves it the trouble of inquiring into infinite details, which would be necessary if the rules were made to suit men instead of subjecting all men indiscriminately to the same rule. Hence the government loves what the citizens love, and it naturally hates what they hate. (Tocqueville, 1969, p. 673)

Ironically, led by Stockman, the OMB behaved in a manner designed to confirm Tocqueville's suspicions regarding central governments, for it tried to treat these revenues as part of the general fund. In so doing, it displayed the centralizing tendencies Tocqueville feared and, in the process, punished the fishermen and boaters for exercising their interests in a manner that also promoted a larger public interest. As individuals, the concerned beneficiaries believed that by working for the good of this larger community they would thereby also advance their own interests. In other words, the user tax system is a device that allows individual self-interest to be expressed and channeled into socially beneficial activities.

The Stockman stratagem, if successful, would likely have produced an effect almost diametrically opposed to that described by Tocqueville (and desired by the founders) because it is an approach likely to undermine a process by which citizens may learn to understand the connections between their private interests and those of a larger community. Tocqueville commented on the American tendency to individualism, which he described as "a calm and considered feeling which disposes each citizen to isolate himself from the mass of his fellows and withdraw into the circle of family and friends; with this little society formed to his taste, he gladly leaves the greater society to look after itself" (1969, p. 506). However, he did not consider individualism to be a basic character flaw requiring coercive state remedies, for it "is due more to inadequate understanding than to perversity of heart" (p. 506). The American citizen could learn to understand the connections between his self-interest and the general interest through participation in the management of public affairs.

This would be in accord with the founders' perception of individualism and acquisitiveness as reliable democratic character traits that could be moderated through a variety of means. To the extent that the Reagan administration was in fact pursuing a return to decentralized government, individual self-reliance, and voluntarism, the Stockman approach in this instance was all the more anomalous.

CONCLUSION

The conflict between the OMB and the sport fishermen is instructive because it illustrates how public administrators may or may not act in ways that are congruent with the understanding of American character that guided the founders and so impressed Tocqueville. In its initial formulation, the Federal Aid in Sport Fish Restoration Program seems well fitted to the founders' expectations regarding the proper role of the state and its administrative agencies. Stockman's attempt to divert these excise tax revenues, however, was an example of how administrators may, for whatever reason, frustrate public policies having the potential to tap effectively individualism and acquisitiveness. It also appeared to be a strategy designed to discourage the formation of those voluntary groups that may function to translate narrow self-interest into actions that promote the common good.

The OMB's position that the needs of the nation as a whole should be met before those of relatively small special interest groups was surely one that should not be dismissed lightly. Such a majoritarian argument must, of course, carry considerable weight in a democracy. However, it should be remembered that the founders were intent on protecting the liberties of minorities precisely because of the dangers they faced from majorities and their representatives. The sport fishermen in this particular instance may be considered to be such a threatened minority.

In the American regime, public administrators must often make decisions that require them to balance general against special interests. Usually they are instructed to seek policies that best serve the interests of the general public. However, if the role of public administration in America also includes a responsibility to promote the purposes of the founders, administrators should attempt to develop and implement policies which do so. An important element of this responsibility is a willingness to consider the consequences of public policies in these terms.

NOTE

1. In addition to individualism and acquisitiveness, the founders also considered the importance of such traits as reputation, civility, moderation, and courage. For a general discussion of these see Almond and Verba (1963) and McWilliams (1979). The concept of moderation falls within the general idea of justice, especially that part of it known as distributive justice. For an introduction to the topic, see Aristotle (1975, Book V, Chapter III) and Plato (1968, Book IV). On courage or risk taking see the works of Adam Smith.

REFERENCES

Almond, G. A., & Verba, S. (1963). *The civic culture*. Princeton, NJ: Princeton University Press.

Aristotle. (1975). *Nicomachean ethics*. Cambridge, MA: Harvard University Press.

Cropsey, J. (1980a). Capitalist liberalism. In J. Cropsey (Ed.), *Political philosophy and the issues of politics* (pp. 53–75). Chicago: University of Chicago Press.

Cropsey, J. (1980b). The invisible hand: Moral and political considerations. In J. Cropsey (Ed.), *Political philosophy and the issues of politics* (pp. 76–89). Chicago: University of Chicago Press.

Diamond, M. (1979). Ethics and politics: The American way. In R. H. Horwitz (Ed.), *The moral foundations of the American republic* (2nd ed.) (pp. 39–72). Charlottesville: University of Virginia Press.

The Federal Aid in Sport Fish Restoration Act. (1950). *U.S. Statutes at Large*, 81st Congress (2nd session), *64*, 430–434.

Frieden, B. J. (1979). The new regulation comes to suburbia. *The Public Interest, 55* (Spring), 15–27.

Friedman, M. (1962). *Capitalism and freedom*. Chicago: University of Chicago Press.

Gilder, G. (1981). *Wealth and poverty*. New York: Basic Books.

Goldwin, R. A. (1979). Of men and angels: A search for morality in the Constitution. In R. H. Horwitz (Ed.), *The moral foundations of the American republic* (2nd ed.) (pp. 1–18). Charlottesville: University of Virginia Press.

Goldwin, R. A., & Scambra, W. A. (Eds.) (1980). *How democratic is the Constitution?* Washington, DC: American Enterprise Institute.

Goldwin, R. A., & Scambra, W. A. (Eds.) (1982). *How capitalistic is the Constitution?* Washington, DC: American Enterprise Institute.

Hamilton, A., Madison, J., & Jay, J. (1961). *The federalist papers* (No. 10). New York: American Library.

Hofstadter, R. (1979). The founding fathers: An age of realism. In R. H. Horwitz (Ed.), *The moral foundations of the American republic* (2nd ed.) (pp. 73–85). Charlottesville: University of Virginia Press.

Horwitz, R. H. (1979). John Locke and the preservation of liberty: A problem of civic education. In R. H. Horwitz (Ed.), *The moral foundations of the American republic* (2nd ed.) (pp. 129–156). Charlottesville: University of Virginia Press.

McWilliams, W. C. (1979). On equality as the moral foundation for community. In R. H. Horwitz (Ed.), *The moral foundations of the American republic* (2nd ed.) (pp. 183–213). Charlottesville: University of Virginia Press.

Moulds, H. (1964). Private property in John Locke's state of nature. *The American Journal of Economics and Sociology, 23,* 179–188.

Mushkin, S. J., & Vehorn, C. L. (1980). User fees and charges. In C. H. Levine (Ed.), *Managing fiscal stress* (pp. 222–234). Chatham, NJ: Chatham House.

Parsons, J. E., Jr. (1969). Locke's doctrine of property. *Social Research, 36* (3), 289–411.

Plato. (1968). *The republic*. New York: Basic Books.

Savas, E. S. (1982). *Privatizing the public sector*. Chatham, NJ: Chatham House.

Smith, A. (1904). *The wealth of nations*. New York: G. P. Putnam's Sons.

Sowell, T. (1981). *Markets and minorities*. London: Basil Blackwell.

Stockman, D. (1986). *The triumph of politics*. New York: Harper and Row.

Tocqueville, A. de (1969). *Democracy in America*. Garden City, NY: Doubleday.

Williamson, L. (1985, May). Doing the budget two-step. *Outdoor Life*, p. 56.

Part IV

Public Demand and Preferences for Outdoor Recreation

10.

RECREATION POLICY AND PLANNING OPTIONS WITH NATIONWIDE RECREATION SURVEY DATA

Joseph T. O'Leary, Francis A. McGuire, and F. D. Dottavio

A major responsibility mandated to the Secretary of the Interior by the Outdoor Recreation Coordination Act of 1963 (Public Law 88–29) is the preparation and periodic updating of the Nationwide Outdoor Recreation Plan. The plan sets forth the needs and demands of the public for outdoor recreation and the current and foreseeable availability of outdoor recreation resources to meet those needs. The plan is required to identify critical problem areas and to recommend solutions. The act further requires the Secretary of the Interior to "prepare and maintain a continuing inventory and evaluation of outdoor recreation needs and resources of the United States." Other federal agencies also require information on people's recreation behavior and concerns for planning, policy development, and program evaluation. Some of these requirements are mandated by law, as in the case of the Forest Service's "RPA Assessments" under the Forest and Rangeland Renewable Resources Planning Act (16 U.S.C. 1600–1614).

The Nationwide Recreation Survey (NRS) is central to the acquisition of information on recreation pursuits, constraints, and concerns of the American people. The NRS provides a macroscopic, top-down look, rather than a site-specific management orientation.

Opinions vary concerning the development of information for policy and planning and the complaint that the right kinds of nationwide recreation data are not available for proper management. Contrary to the prevailing opinion, good data have been collected in the NRS, but for a number of reasons they have not been available or adequately used.

Four key issues that need to be explored are as follows: (1) there is nothing inherently wrong with the questions being asked on the surveys; (2) the timing and availability of the data are a problem; (3) the nationwide survey should be viewed as an innovation; and (4) there are significant planning and policy applications.

THE SURVEY QUESTIONS

Throughout the 1970s there was concern about the status of recreation data gathering at the national level. Many national report writers discussed improving the collection and utilization of these data. Two key reports provided major anchor points for understanding at that point in time.

As a byproduct of preparing for the 1977 nationwide survey, Kirschner Associates (1975) did a comparative examination of several nationwide recreation surveys conducted from 1960 through 1972. Similarly, at the first nationwide trends symposium, Bevins and Wilcox (1980) presented an in-depth analysis of national recreation surveys. The purpose was "to review the findings and methodologies of the various nationwide recreation surveys and to further evaluate the feasibility of using such studies as the basis for identifying trends" (Bevins & Wilcox, 1980, p. 1). Bevins and Wilcox's basic conclusion was that surveys provided a basis for evaluating short-run changes during the 1960s and 1970s, but enough changes had occurred during the latter 1970s and early 1980s to warrant additional information about how adjustments had taken place. In their conclusion they noted that one of the most difficult problems encountered in the review was the inconsistency (contact persons, length of time measured for participation, time of the season, activity definition, etc.) encountered between the different surveys. Many of the survey efforts were apparently tailored to reflect the individual interests of the persons responsible for conducting the survey or to address an issue in vogue at the time. The goal of comparability was often sacrificed along the way. A good example of this is the Kirschner Associates (1975) comments of the review of the 1972 Nationwide Outdoor Recreation Survey. "Nothing revealed that the survey was incorrectly designed. Its limitations are those placed upon it by the type of information sought and the specific requirements of an economic analysis (p. 13). . . . We have been able to find nothing intrinsically wrong with the 1972 survey. Although the survey is not comparable, it does contain useful information that would be helpful to planners and researchers" (p. 15).

The efforts to deal with these issues were often confounded by changes in agency agendas and personnel, items not unique to the nationwide recreation survey, but also evident at the state and local level. A good example of a nonresponse to Kirschner Associates' comments is that the 1977 nationwide survey was again different from those surveys that had been conducted previously so that it also lacked the comparability noted in the 1972 survey.

The survey for 1982 and 1983 represented an attempt to replicate parts of the

1960 survey. In addition, it included many of the questions recommended as necessary for inclusion by the Kirschner Associates report. The activity participation section, motivations, constraints, and the important activity questions served as a core and were all reasonably comparable to those of 1960. Most of the remaining survey questions requested other kinds of information that was specific to the interests of particular agencies. In general, there was nothing wrong with the questions on the survey. For the information people sought from the survey when it was initiated, it is a good effort. The exception that appears to have emerged after the fact was the inability to obtain regional disaggregations of these data, a position apparently taken by the Bureau of the Census to maintain confidentiality. Although not the fault of anyone initially connected with the survey, this decision by the Bureau of the Census has probably created future barriers to interagency cooperation.

TIMING AND AVAILABILITY OF THE DATA

The major problem associated with the growth of the national recreation survey information base is that much of the data are never carefully studied and applied to policy and planning. Many individuals are unaware that the information is available. The data are not readily accessible due to geographic distance, the lack of technical personnel to assist in the complex task of working with a large data set, missing data and documentation, or other unfavorable conditions of availability and access. Further, the computer tapes and the most simple analysis have taken inordinate amounts of time to emerge from the groups responsible for the data, often leaving the information perceived as dated.

It would appear that leisure data in general, and the NRS in particular, are being underutilized both in terms of their contribution to specific decision making and policy formulation, and their role in theory building. Part of this problem stems from the emphasis placed on initial data collection (especially in terms of funding) as opposed to the analysis and evaluation stages. As Burch (1971) and Knott and Wildavsky (1980) point out, data and information are not knowledge without analysis and in some cases action. The need to address this data question more effectively was recognized in the 1980 National Working Conference of the National Program for Forests and Associated Rangelands, at which several of the most important national problems identified focused on the availability of information transfer for basic and applied recreation data to citizens, managers, and policy makers. A number of symposia, conferences, and meetings conducted by such agencies as the Bureau of Outdoor Recreation, the National Park Service, and the National Academy of Sciences point out the lack of a national clearinghouse or data center on recreation and leisure research. These agencies and others see the surveys, planning studies, and other research conducted under the sponsorship of public and private bodies as containing gaps and overlaps that preclude their use for replication or as complements to one another.

Various researchers and administrators throughout the United States suggest that only 5 to 10 percent of the collected recreation data have been adequately studied. Many data are neglected in the rush to examine new data, as new studies begin, or as programs are ended. In September 1974, the Bureau of Outdoor Recreation convened a conference on outdoor recreation research needs. The major recommendation of this meeting was the establishment and maintenance of practical storage, retrieval, and dissemination systems for quantitative recreation data, scientific literature, research methods, and on-going research projects. In addition, conference members called for the establishment of leisure data banks on an international, national, and/or regional basis to gather and utilize data on recreation resources, facilities, and behavior. Such data banks are already operational throughout Europe and Canada. At least one repository with leisure data now exists in the United States at the Institute for Survey Research at the University of Michigan. In 1974, the publication *The Recreation Imperative* (U.S. Senate, 1974) contained a very explicit recommendation:

It is recommended that an Interdisciplinary Research Center for Environmental Quality and Outdoor Recreation Research be established at one or more existing institutions and provided with long-term financing through core grants from the Federal Government and interested foundations. (p. 375)

The *National Urban Recreation Study* (U.S. Department of Interior, 1978) suggests that increased attention be given to research and its applications. The study further states that although the Heritage Conservation and Recreation Service has a mandate (P.L. 8–29) to sponsor, engage, and assist in recreation research and to assemble and disseminate research information, this mandate has never been effectively implemented.

The early draft report of the current President's Commission on Americans Outdoors (PCAO) again underlies the need to inventory and organize the broad range of past and current data collection efforts.

Knott and Wildavsky (1980) describe these centers as "knowledge brokerage houses" where material is analyzed, interpreted, and from which relevant information is disseminated to interested clients. The key to the function of a leisure data center is the evaluation, analysis, and dissemination of the material in the center. Data gathering is important; however, the even more important next step is to identify what is available and how it was compiled, and to develop a policy-relevant theory for organizing the data that do exist (Knott & Wildavsky, 1980). The repository idea is only one step. The key is proactive and aggressive analysis. Without a great deal more knowledge and information development, the current state of affairs will create more problems for the future study of leisure. A data center might provide a focus, but the analysis activity must be the thrust.

INNOVATION AND DIFFUSION OF THE SURVEY DATA

When all the nationwide recreation surveys conducted during the last twenty-five years are examined, it appears that the goal for which each of the national surveys had been undertaken was achieved—generating the kind of information necessary for preparing an outdoor recreation plan (although the most recent effort is not completed). It is not clear that there was any other implicit or explicit purpose in collecting these data. Certainly, policy analysis and planning application never appear to have a goal. Similarly, there does not seem to be any serious attempts to actively follow up on calls for extending the application of the data (one notes the rather narrow application of the information in the national plan).

Part of the problem in extending application is the narrow range of people with a vested interest in using the data. Until 1982 and 1983, the Department of the Interior was the only entity with an expressed need for these data. The interagency approach to the survey conducted in 1982 and 1983 has met with mixed success. There remains limited utilization of these data three years after the fact. In particular, this is strange because the 1986 Market Opinion Research (MOR) survey for the National Geographic Society (NGS) and the PCAO reported outdoor recreation data patterns that are virtually the same as those found in the survey of 1982 and 1983. Personal communication with the MOR group has indicated that at least some of the staff members consider the older survey to be better because it has many more cases. Certainly, it is the prerogative of the NGS to spend its money on this survey, but what may be more important is that the 1986 Market Opinion Research survey reinforced the larger and continuing utility of the data from 1982 and 1983.

In the existing environment of agency mandates, goals, and objections, any attempt to elicit greater support for conducting these kinds of surveys would require an orientation that treats both the survey and the data/information as potential innovations. Innovation-diffusion research provides some structure within which this could be done. Based on the personal experience of making these data available to various people and groups, it should be done. However, the key in effective diffusion is that the orientation to working with a nonparticipating client must be on the clients' terms and compatible with the client's needs (Rogers, 1983).

To accommodate organizational innovation there is a need to consider it as a process that identifies organizational problems and links the problems to the innovation (i.e., what National Park Service problems does the NRS help to solve?); refines and clarifies the innovation so that it coincides with the mission of one organization (i.e., does the NRS help the National Park Service accomplish the purpose set forth in the 1916 Organic Act?); and makes routine the innovation as part of the regular operation of the organization (i.e., is the provided data considered invaluable to the on-going operation of the National Park Service?).

One of the key problems in attempting to deal with this process and the national recreation survey data is that many officials responsible for policy and planning maintain (even facetiously) that they do not use NRS type (or any other) data to make decisions. In fact, this is not the case. They use NRS type of data, but they do not always need the detail that is associated with the traditional reports.

In general, they appear to want to know facts like YES/NO, or HIGH/MEDIUM/ LOW. They would be happier with a simple graph rather than detailed tables. Certainly based on the way in which NRS information has been delivered in the past, presenting the material in a simple, graphic form could be viewed as an innovation.

The Bureau of Outdoor Recreation (BOR) and the Heritage Conservation and Recreation Service (HCRS) had no line management responsibility in which these data could be readily transferred as innovations. Therefore, in the 1960s and 1970s the application of the survey was focused on the national recreation plan. In terms of the organizational innovation process, the problem was the need to complete a plan. For HCRS, the Nationwide Outdoor Recreation Survey was a means to address mandates of the Secretary of the Interior, and thus it was considered an appropriate activity for the agency.

The survey of 1982 and 1983 represented the first time the mandate to provide information to the Secretary of the Interior was carried out within the National Park Service (NPS), the entity which has absorbed HCRS. With planning and management as key responsibilities of the NPS, the opportunity to use the NRS for something other than the preparation of a national plan was now present. By the time the merger of HCRS with the NPS occurred, however, the format for the NRS for 1982 and 1983 was well established. Whether future surveys should attempt to align NRS objectives more closely with the mission of the National Park Service is debatable. For the NRS to be accepted as a legitimate function of the NPS, this match is critical. The disadvantage of this alignment is that the other traditional functions served by the NRS would likely be diluted.

It is possible that this survey represented a benchmark in moving toward the use of the national data for management and planning. The participation of the U.S. Forest Service and the Bureau of Land Management was tied to legislative requirements to develop planning and management information for the resource planning function. This is in fact being done. The Administration on Aging sought information that could be used to assist in future program development for volunteer efforts with older Americans.

The National Park Service has not embraced using the nationwide survey as part of its planning process. However, the document "Planning for Units of the National Park System" appears to provide an entrée into the planning process for application of these types of data through the General Management Plan. The Statement for Management (SFM) describes the need for analysis of influences on management and use and major issues and problems. In addition, there is a need for visitor use information. The existing NRS data contains information on national park use, as well as some information on visitation at specific parks and when this visitation took place. These data could be used as a basis for describing visitor use and how it has changed over time. The activity information about which the Forest Service inquired would also help planners in the National Park Service to anticipate trends and the need for changes.

IS THERE POLICY APPLICATION?

Trying to improve the application and dissemination of the NRS represents a linchpin for future recreation policy analysis. Again, this particular objective does not appear to be one that was originally specified for the survey effort (using the overview from the scope of work specified for the 1982–1983 survey as a basis for the statement).

Knott and Wildavsky (1980) suggest four approaches that might be used to improve the dissemination of policy resources. The first approach includes passive exchanges and more sophisticated computer retrieval systems for those already in a position to use the data and information. A second option is to reach out to the needy policy maker by subsidizing analysis or conference and meeting participation to facilitate interaction. A third alternative would be to focus on emerging policy issues like energy or tourism, using artificial dissemination of particularly interesting information as a way of enhancing natural dissemination. Finally, when the lack of policy knowledge is the real problem, shift resources away from dissemination to the development of knowledge. This is certainly one of the arguments so persistent in the government reports and would provide a focus and major role for the knowledge brokerage houses.

A VIEW TO THE FUTURE

The 1987 report from the President's Commission on Americans Outdoors (PCAO) underscores the concern for management and analysis of data and raising professional consciousness about its use. In the solicited reports that were submitted by the states and in the commission's evaluation of recreation infrastructure needs, the recommendation for more data and better analysis and coordination emerged. In general, there are concerns that many jurisdictions have no idea what land or facilities are owned and who or how many people use open space facilities. The PCAO recommendations point toward a need for better information systems that incorporate recreation accounts or indicators, research, long-term maintenance, and partnerships within and between the public and private sectors in information networks. Twenty-three different information needs were identified by the commission. The results for these recommendations if carried out are probably more data requiring better organization at the national, state, and local levels than has been seen in the past. Whether or not this can be achieved depends to a large extent on the ability of those involved to think about these data using the approach used for the use of the NRS.

An appropriate role for the national participation survey is to monitor trends for planning and policy application as part of the recreation accounts or indicator system. In many respects this approach is much like that described for social indicator studies except it is focused specifically on the area of outdoor recreation and incorporates both physical and social measures. The notion is that the data are gathered and analyzed to guide, monitor, and evaluate actions and policies that have been put in place or which could be initiated to affect opportunities, facilities, participation, and so on in the recreation area.

Social indicators are described in the *Social Indicators Newsletter*:

What are social indicators? We take them to be statistical time series that measure changes in significant aspects of society . . . thus, a social indicator . . . may be a time series which at present contains very few points. The aspect of society it measures may not be deemed "significant" by all observers. But the social indicator expresses something about the composition, structure, or functioning of that society, and expresses it in quantitative terms that can be compared with similar measures in the past or the future. (Social Science Research Council, 1973, p. 1)

Burch and DeLuca (1984, p. 184) describe how social indicators can have utility for testing theoretical models. They are components in a sociological (including sociopsychological, demographic, and ecological) model of a social system or some particular segment or process thereof. They can be collected at a sequence of points in time and accumulated into a time series, and they can be aggregated or disaggregated to levels appropriate to the specifications of the model.

On the one hand, NRS surveys provide precisely the type of information that allows for an examination of change in outdoor recreation factors over time. A good example of this was cited earlier in Bevins and Wilcox (1980) when they compared results from the various nationwide surveys to determine the nature of change. Similarly O'Leary, Peine, and Blahna (1980) used data from the 1960, 1965, and 1977 national surveys to ascertain changes in activity participation by age group for the first National Trends Symposium. The results demonstrated that there appeared to be some age group participation changes, although some of this was tempered by methodological differences between the surveys. Just as we periodically attempt to examine population changes from census data, the recreation data provide the same opportunity.

While it will not be easy to organize a recreation accounts system, the issue here is not whether the data are available to act as social indicators; the question continues to be how to present the material in a form that various audiences will find interesting and useful. This again is an innovation/application issue that has not been easy to resolve in the past and will continue to pose problems in the future.

CONCLUSION

One question that arises is whether the national surveys should be abandoned. The recommendation from the PCAO about continuing to monitor national recreation participation and involvement suggests that the decision to stop should be thought through carefully. The problem, often identified as being with the survey, does not appear to be with the survey at all. Rather, it is with determining what information is sought and how the information about patterns and trends in the country is delivered. There is no reason to believe that simply choosing a new, more topical area, or adding new data collection needs as noted by the PCAO, would change the need to improve the way in which any of this information is being disseminated. In effect, unless alternative delivery mechanisms are developed and existing techniques improved, the choice of a new area of interest will not be an improvement or guarantee the long-term viability of any program.

A significant problem with most government agencies engaged in the business of collecting recreation data is little or no time to study the data in detail. There were never agendas outlined for more condensed or detailed reports, subtopic exploration, specific policy issues or questions, or more sophisticated analysis to test hypotheses and answer questions in a more comprehensive and succinct manner (Hakim, 1982). An emphasis on secondary analysis possibly incorporating university personnel must be explored if policy and planning problems are to be addressed in the short run. Without this type of initiative, a long-term solution to the problems involved in utilizing recreation data, particularly in terms of indicators, is unlikely. However, with adequate planning, understanding recreation futures could become more meaningful and significant than ever before.

REFERENCES

Bevins, M. I., & Wilcox, D. P. (1980). *Outdoor recreation participation: Analysis of national surveys, 1959–1978* (Bulletin 686). Burlington: Vermont Agricultural Experiment Station.

Burch, W. R., Jr. (1971). *Daydreams and nightmares: A sociological essay on the American environment.* New York: Harper and Row.

Burch, W. R., Jr., & DeLuca, D. R. (1984). *Measuring the social impact of natural resource policies.* Albuquerque: University of New Mexico Press.

Hakim, C. (1982). *Secondary analysis in social research.* London: George Allen and Unwin.

Kirschner Associates, Inc. (1975). *Interim report: Evaluation of five previous nationwide citizen surveys.* Washington, DC: Author.

Knott, J., & Wildavsky, A. (1980). If dissemination is the solution, what is the problem? *Knowledge: Creation, Diffusion, Utilization, 1* (4), 537–578.

National Academy of Sciences. (1969). *A program for outdoor recreation research.* Washington, DC: Author.

O'Leary, J. T. (1985, February). Social trends in outdoor recreation. *Proceedings of the National Outdoor Recreation Trends Symposium II* (pp. 24–36), Myrtle Beach, SC.

O'Leary, J. T., Peine, J., & Blahna, D. (1980, February). Trends in selected day use activities. *Proceedings of the National Outdoor Recreation Trends Symposium I* (pp. 205–214), Durham, NH.

President's Commission on Americans Outdoors [PCAO]. (1987). *Americans outdoors: The legacy, the challenge*. Washington, DC: Island Press.

Rogers, E. M. (1983). *Diffusion of innovations*. New York: The Free Press.

Social Science Research Council. (1973, March-July). *Social Indicators Newsletter*. Washington, DC.

U.S. Department of the Interior, Bureau of Outdoor Recreation. (1974). *Proceedings of the outdoor recreation research needs workshop*. Washington, DC: U.S. Government Printing Office.

U.S. Department of the Interior, Bureau of Outdoor Recreation and School of Natural Resources, University of Michigan. (1963). *Proceedings: National conference on outdoor recreation research*. Ann Arbor, MI: Ann Arbor Publishers.

U.S. Department of the Interior, Heritage Conservation and Recreation Service. (1978). *National urban recreation study: Executive report*. Washington, DC: U.S. Government Printing Office.

U.S. Senate, Committee on Interior and Insular Affairs. (1974). *The recreation imperative*. Washington, DC: U.S. Government Printing Office.

11.

Deriving National Outdoor Recreation Policy from a Limiting Demand Participation Model

Francis P. Noe, Robert E. Snow, and Gary Hampe

Public support for the out-of-doors has achieved widespread consensus through sustained reinforcement from the conservation movement in the United States. In particular, outdoor recreation has certainly received considerable public backing at the state and federal level. Governments have set aside large tracts of land for such public use, much of it preserved as wild land, forests, parks, and reserves. "Outdoor recreation may not have quite the deep emotional commitment that public education has, or even that those newcomers Social Security and Medicare have, but it is strongly defended by most people" (Clawson, 1985, pp. 10–11). Despite the staunch support received from the public through trade, professional, and conservation associations, outdoor recreation has received "little attention by policy analysts" (Light & Groves, 1978, p. 405). It obviously lacks the harsh sting of the pressing social problems associated with crime in the streets, health care, aging, and other issues that are more disruptive to institutions and individuals. Perhaps these problems cause a greater sense of urgency since they cause pain and frequently threaten life. They almost universally take precedence over issues that bring joy and pleasure. Add to that the strong competition outdoor activities receive from the commercial entertainment and leisure industry, and it is no wonder that social concern for the out-of-doors may be far less than most of us would wish. That kind of judgment admits de facto a value system in America that is partially responsible for allocating priorities and directing decisions about the outdoors.

But how is the value of recreation to be measured in American society? The question was answered in early recreational studies by measuring rates of participation over time. Today the standard demand measure is devised by taking frequency counts at entrances/exits, by measuring use in terms of days, hours, or by acquiring more qualitative evidence by counting responses to categories specifying choices such as "often," "some," or "never." La Page (1976) philosophically bemoaned the absence of reliable indicators for recreation as reported by the Office of Management and Budget. Participation was then, as now, the only variable listed.

Rates of participation were grounded in the early history of outdoor recreation research. A numbers game was played that became important in pushing the issue of recreation to the forefront. A review article by Lincoln Ellison (1942), summarizing recreation in the outdoors from the late 1800s to the 1940s, reported growth in the "increase of use" and "changes in quality of use." Admittedly, "long-time figures" on recreation use were scarce. Despite this obstacle, Ellison was still able to piece together a series of figures over time indicating trend lines, which showed that the "curves for both national forests and national parks agreed in showing great increases" (p. 631). On the other hand, Gallup's (1986) public opinion polls on recreation activities since 1959 have shown at best more modest increases or merely a sustained level of growth in most outdoor activities. Not all research or opinion polls were necessarily skewed upscale, although many key influential national surveys still tended in that direction.

Projection errors in large-scale government-sponsored research have leaned toward the optimistic end of the growth spectrum. Cordell and colleagues (1985) confirmed such divergence in previous projections and studies reporting actual use for those years in which future estimates were made by the Outdoor Recreation Resources Review Commission (ORRRC) and then the Bureau of Outdoor Recreation. Overestimates of recreation projections were supposedly more a result of a lack of precision and unspecifiable information than intent. Claims of improved accuracy by recent demand models, however, have not stood the test of time. The most recent demand models project a slackening growth in recreation into the year 2000, which is strengthened by positive correlations with projections of population growth, changes in the gross national product, and shifts in disposable income. Because of the rather pervasive emphasis on demand models in the past, much of the quantitative data gathering efforts have been directed at determining answers to the question of present and future demand for outdoor recreation. Unfortunately, preoccupation with demand has suppressed other avenues of potentially productive inquiry for policy makers.

DEMAND DOMINATES RECREATION RESEARCH

There is nothing intrinsically erroneous with attempting to determine what Americans demand in their free time. A problem arises when that issue dominates the attention of recreation policy makers. Light and Groves (1978) stated that,

such calculations ignore the full range of potential recreation opportunities which could be offered. As a result, this method tends to perpetuate existing programs and facilities and encourages further development of the same. Secondly, such calculations neglect the benefits, satisfactions and achievements obtained by a person during and after the activity. (p. 407)

The problem of dealing with outdoor recreation behavior is greatly simplified by dealing exclusively with participation rates. Recreation policy is reduced to favoring only those recreationists who are the majority of users. Supplying their needs to the exclusion of others all but assures recurring success of being recognized again in future surveys. It almost guarantees that researchers and policy makers will be spared surprises except for the occasional fad which is easily forgiven. A report from the last nationwide recreation survey stated that "the resulting pattern is similar to the findings of the 1960 and 1965 surveys" regarding recreation (U.S. Department of the Interior, 1984, p. 1). Upon closer examination of the activities that received a majority of responses, swimming, walking for pleasure, picnicking, driving for pleasure, sightseeing, visiting zoos, fairs, amusement parks, and attending sporting events were chosen repeatedly by close to 50 percent of those surveyed. Neither is it surprising that the 1986 President's Commission on Americans Outdoors reported identical findings from a national telephone survey sponsored by the National Geographic Society.

Given the general nature of those recreational activities and their accessibility, it is difficult to imagine how anyone could not participate in any one of these activities on an annual basis. Perhaps this is another example of what La Page (1971) called "cultural fogweed" that results in a subculture when the government and researchers have implicitly reached an agreement. "Since public recreation agencies measure success by counting heads . . . the conclusion seems to be saying something about scientific freedom" (p. 91), which results in suppressing more meaningful lines of inquiry. Equally pessimistic was Neil Cheek (1979) who commented that "the accident of history which has transformed [sic] the debacle of visitation statistics upon us, which cannot easily be transformed into original observations, is perhaps our albatross." Despite this reality, there are researchers both in and out of government who recognize that they are not truly representing recreation benefits by identifying the value of a recreation policy with the popularity of an activity.

SOCIAL BENEFITS LINKED TO DEMAND

Stereotyping recreation research as being totally insensitive to noneconomic values would be callous because many of those conducting the research have sounded a loud call for reforms in recreation policy. Ellison (1942), who performed an early quantitative policy review, was concerned with whether the "great increase" in numbers still enabled the people to absorb the benefits of the wilderness environment, to offset "the apparent dilution of quality" (p. 634). He felt quality recreational experiences relied on how well the needs of a public were satisfied, needs thought of more in noneconomic terms. Admittedly, the psychological language of self-esteem, social prestige, self-reliance, escapism, companionship, and aesthetic enjoyment on Wagar's (1966) list of needs was a departure in considering the outcomes of recreation policy. It was certainly not an approach to estimating use since few needs could be measured with proven empirical scales or reliably tested given the field's sensitivity to such techniques and theory. The policy issue of identifying and measuring human values and benefits remained particularly problematic in recreation and progressed very little during this time. Lucas (1978) again raised the issue a little more than a decade later, pointing out that again "human benefits are represented primarily by visitor days. There is a need for some measure of more ultimate benefits produced by these visitor days." Some possibilities for policy evaluation such as individual development and health were identified, but many were merely referenced in general terms. Because of the lack of precision, Lucas concluded that there are "many assertions of various individual benefits, but little documentation" (1978, p. 3). Kelly (1981) drew together a compendium of short position papers titled the *Social Benefits of Outdoor Recreation*. For the most part, these papers focused on evaluating personal and social benefits, which marked a significant advance in recreation policy evaluation in that it sounded a call to researchers to explore this untested area. The very first page of the compendium captures one's attention when Angus Campbell, the late director of the Institute of Social Research, was quoted as saying that "people are talking about values that cannot be counted in dollars" (Kelly, 1981, p. 1). This was a reminder that societal values and norms, which organize and motivate behavior in society, may also directly influence recreational policy choices.

SOCIETAL VALUES AND DEMOGRAPHICS LINKED TO RECREATION DEMAND

If recreation demand can be gauged more adequately and its direct links to societal values and norms understood, then policy makers can escape the tautological recreation policy determination process discussed earlier. In that circular reasoning process, activities that enjoy high usage rates are assumed to be those most highly prized by the public. This assumption undergirds the continuation of the policies supporting the activity.

What follows is an alternative method for defining recreation demand, using a model that links the demographic characteristics, values, and attitudes of those participating in an activity to these demands. The following general model from social psychology, which related preferences for a particular behavior (recreation demand) to societal values and demographic characteristics of participants, is evaluated (see Figure 11.1).

After determining the demand for particular types of outdoor recreation, this model is evaluated by a series of stepwise discriminate analyses. These determine the relative salience of demographic characteristics and values/attitudes as differentiators of demand for particular recreation activities.

Figure 11.1
General Model of Recreation Preferences, Values, and Demographic Characteristics of Participants

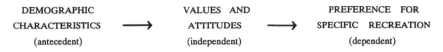

Given empirical support, this model forms a new basis for evaluating the impact of current recreation policies based on the popularity-of-an-activity approach discussed earlier. The model can be used to determine who benefits (demographic characteristics) from a current or proposed policy supporting a specific activity. In addition, it helps delineate what values are being reinforced by a current or proposed policy. The model is a first attempt to overtly include values in the evaluation of outdoor recreation policy.

After empirically demonstrating the application of the model, the conclusion section discusses how this approach can be used to enhance the recreation policy formation process. The next section details the data used to evaluate the model and how the demographic and value orientation constructs were operationally defined.

METHODOLOGY FOR THIS NATIONAL SURVEY

Sample

A United States national random telephone survey was conducted to obtain information about leisure preferences. The U.S. Bureau of the Census estimates that approximately 93 percent of all American households contain telephones. General statistical characteristics of this telephone sample were distinguished by a fairly total enumeration of all households. The sample was stratified to all counties by their size and systematically drawn from an array of working telephone blocks that contained three or more residential numbers. Sixty percent of all possible blocks were without a single listed residential number. A system developed and employed by Survey Sampling, Inc. eliminated nonresidential numbers from the pool of 330 million possibilities. Since unlisted telephones are randomly assigned to all blocks, they were also included along with listed numbers. The chances of encountering a listed telephone is about 0.6 in each block, but since unlisted numbers are an urban phenomenon, varying even among city areas, further stratification was done to equalize the probabilities.

Interviewers were assigned numbers and up to twelve call-backs were required before reaching final dispositions. The few cases not resolved after twelve call-backs were declared ineligible. From 2,148 attempts, 1,607 interviews were completed, resulting in a 66.5 percent completion rate. An additional 104 interviews were partially completed, accounting for an additional 4.3 percent contacted, while 29.2 percent of the eligibles contacted refused to be interviewed. The survey achieved a higher than average completion rate when compared to average completion rates for general public telephone surveys.

Since describing U.S. working adults was of primary interest, the interviewers screened out individuals over the age of sixty-five and under the age of twenty-one. As a result, teenagers and retirees were systematically eliminated from the survey. To gauge the representativeness of the sample, its demographics were used as a benchmark against the 1980 census. The sample closely paralleled the census except for females being slightly overrepresented, and income-education being somewhat skewed upward. This slight bias is more likely a result of the age groups deliberately excluded from this study than sampling error.

Variables

The Leisure Survey instrument contained sets of variables that provided possibilities for evaluating the leisure preference model discussed earlier (Figure 11.1). Antecedent variables define a set of key influences that shape the outcome of the relationships among independent and dependent variables. Antecedent variables in the model are key social demographic characteristics that identify major differences among leisure preference groups. Sex, age, race, and social economic status (SES) factors (including education, occupation, and income) have repeatedly been shown to influence leisure choices and preferences. Leisure studies have documented relationships, variations, and clarifications of direct and indirect associations among these variables. To measure these variables, the leisure survey used self-reports of age, sex, and completed years of education. Job titles and description of occupations were coded following Treiman's (1977) international prestige scores. Total household income before taxes was requested at intervals of $10,000 by a checklist and ethnic background was obtained by self-definition.

Independent variables are norms and values, or the attendant beliefs that establish a basis for behavior. Part of what individuals really like to do in their free time is leisure activity and how these leisure activities are organized may well be based on socially acceptable norms and values. To use the language of the functionalist, norms answer the question of how to act in an appropriate manner. They furnish an ideological map on how to adjust to the demands of society and also provide essential moral justification for one's actions. Values answer the question of what is worthy of pursuit. They provide a set of goals to motivate individuals. The telephone survey instrument contained items indexing norms and values that may guide choices in leisure participation.

The normative questions were constructed from an examination of leisure studies and the social psychological literature. Twenty-one items were screened and pretested to form a general normative scale. A modified Likert routine was used to solicit responses. Items included in the normative scale sought opinions on how leisure activities are perceived to be organized in society. Cronbach's alpha and factor analytic techniques were applied to the items resulting in three clusters of normative judgments based on competition, sociability, and relaxation. The factor scores were used to define scales along the dimensions of competition, sociability, and relaxation, which proved to be reliable measures.

Value-oriented questions included items characterizing free-time activities using dichotomized pairs of bipolar concepts representing a belief about leisure. The items were offered with a neutral position separating them. Respondents were also given the option of "don't know" and "not applicable" responses. The value items evaluated how those interviewed characterized their free-time activities. Choices such as intellectual-nonintellectual, skilled-unskilled, and competitive-noncompetitive are pairs identifying beliefs about leisure. Eighteen items comprised the value scale that was pretested and refined from a larger pool of items. Three value-oriented scales emerged from the data representing beliefs on skilled-unskilled, active-passive, and safe-risk meanings accorded to leisure activities.

The dependent variables were measured with an open-ended strategy when questioning the public about leisure preferences. These responses were categorized into clusters or treated individually following the work of Yu (1985), Kaplan (1960), and Noe (1974), which provided a more parsimonious pattern to the data set. Two questions were asked that identified a favorite activity first and then determined what activity would never be pursued. Rather than using checklists that name many activities, this less structured approach was thought to characterize more accurately the most salient interests by relying on self-recall. Furthermore, asking what would be eliminated as a leisure option was added as a question in order to demarcate the outer limits of cultural choice. The contrast between what is most favorite and what is never done may establish a pattern of leisure salience. Such a strategy has never been tested. More traditionally, participation studies have offered respondents a checklist and measured commitment by how frequently an activity was engaged in over time. Kelly (1983) pointed out that a rather different picture of participation patterns in leisure occurs when the "accessible and informal attributes" are considered separately (p. 331). Core or habitual patterns of activity such as walking for pleasure or sightseeing are recognized for inherently possessing mass appeal because of easy access and lack of formality. In order to determine those recreation characteristics that distinguish nonhabitual from simple core choices, open-ended questions asking about favorite and least preferred preferences were sought to define the leisure lifestyles that better differentiate Americans.

MEASURING DEMAND FOR RECREATIONAL ACTIVITIES

Table 11.1 details the favored and unfavored recreation activities of working adults (twenty-one to sixty-four years old) in the survey. These data contrast with previous studies that gauged demand for recreation activities by asking how frequently a respondent engaged in a particular activity. Table 11.1 approaches

Table 11.1
Adult Recreation Preferences and Dislikes

	Recreation preferences	Recreation dislikes
Activity type[a]	favorite response (n = 1607)	never response (n = 1601)
Immobility (resting, etc.)	14.4	1.3
Golf	5.0	11.1
Exercise/health	7.0	11.4
Group association	2.3	0.1
Beach/swimming	4.2	2.3
Risk/skill	3.4	21.5
Mobility (traveling, etc.)	3.7	0.7
Popular arts (crafts, etc.)	8.7	1.0
Fine arts (theatre, etc.)	6.8	1.4
Camping/hiking	8.6	0.4
Fishing/hunting	8.8	3.2
Games/gambling skill	4.9	5.5
Sports	10.4	13.1
Boating	2.9	2.6
Others	2.5	1.3
Don't know	0.7	23.1
Total	100.0	100.0

[a]See Kaplan (1960), Noe (1974), and Yu (1985) for a detailed description of activities included in the leisure designations.

demand in terms of a respondent's self-evaluation and defines the salience of an activity by how often the respondents choose that one activity from all other possible activities.

For example, recent articles in the *Journal of Leisure Research*, such as Stamps and Stamps (1985), report that golf is ranked in the top five recreation activities when leisure activities are ranked by the percentage of the respondents indicating that they participated in that behavior as a leisure experience. If the data in Table 11.1 are treated in similar fashion, golf would rank toward the bottom of the list. This divergence in results strongly indicates that how one gauges demand will determine the outcome of analyses attempting to define the relative salience of recreational activities.

In addition to documenting recreation demand in terms of selection of a favorite activity, Table 11.1 contains data on respondents' dislike of recreation activities. These data also illustrate that the overall demand for an activity is not only determined by who passionately likes the activity, but it is also influenced by those who passionately dislike an activity. For example, golf appears to be a high demand recreation activity since one in twenty adults (5%) report golf as their favorite activity. However, twice as many (11.1%) adults intensely dislike golf as prefer it. These data obviously suggest that previous studies defining demand for recreation activities in terms of relative frequency of participation may have erroneously measured demand by ignoring the negative dimension of the choice. Thus, defining public policy using the relative frequency definition of demand may be risky business because the policy may alienate more people than it serves.

Given the fourteen types of generic recreation preferences in Table 11.1 and the model predicting demand in Figure 11.1, the general analytic problem remains of describing whether or not sets of demographic or value/attitude indicators can differentiate those who prefer or conversely those who intensely dislike specific recreation activities. As a partial answer to this question, Table 11.2 presents a limited summary of results from the discriminate analyses. First, we analyzed whether preference (demand) for a particular activity could be differentiated on the basis of demographic variables. A second set of value/normative variables was also analyzed separately. Finally, the demographic and value/normative variables were analyzed together. Based on chance alone, one would expect these variables to correctly predict preferences for an activity roughly 50 percent of the time. The increase in correct differentiation of preference over 50 percent when using a set of variables indicates the degree to which the variables differentiate those who prefer an activity from those who do not. If demand for a particular recreation activity is related to values/norms and demographic characteristics, then use of these variables should increase our ability to differentiate group membership over the 50 percent levels.

As shown in Table 11.2, the degree to which independent and antecedent variables or their combination can differentiate preference for recreation activities varies by the type of recreation activity. In general, values and norms are better differentiators of preference for an activity than are demographic characteristics. The rate of differentiation is highest when values, attitudes, and demographic variables are used in combination to separate preference and nonpreference groups. This suggests both considerable covariation among both types of predictors as well as possible slight interactive effects among the types of variables. For example, the model combining demographics and attitudes can differentiate those who prefer risk-taking forms of recreation (i.e., sky diving, automobile racing, scuba diving, etc.) from those who do not 81 percent of the time. This would seem to suggest that the model can allow us to differentiate what types of people prefer risk-taking types of recreation accurately. Yet, for other types of recreation activities, such as exercise (68%) and gaming/gambling (66%), the

Table 11.2
Summary of Discriminant Analyses Differentiating Recreation Preferences on the Basis of Values/Attitudes, Demographic Characteristics, and Their Combination

	% cases correctly classified					
	Preferences			Dislikes		
Activity[a]	Demo- graphics	Attitudes values	Combined variables	Demo- graphics	Attitudes values	Combined variables
Immobility	54.72	<66.54	68.11	56.21	<70.06	64.52
Golf	67.88	=67.32	69.83	56.96	<57.36	58.82
Exercise/ health	64.78	>62.22	70.36	48.49	<55.02	48.89
Association	62.28	<66.83	68.18	93.60	>78.72	98.10
Beach/ swimming	59.27	<61.09	66.13	63.58	<65.70	69.01
Risky	63.96	<76.72	76.77	55.71	>52.83	55.23
Mobility	58.47	<65.08	66.74	67.28	>65.05	72.01
Popular arts	60.15	<66.96	65.96	72.07	>68.20	78.25
Fine arts	57.63	<64.51	65.89	69.55	>61.41	71.05
Camping/ hiking	56.48	<72.7	59.81	63.46	>54.05	68.67
Hunting/ fishing	71.56	>62.32	73.39	65.02	>62.32	73.39
Games/ gambling	63.98	>57.81	61.65	50.22	<58.17	60.23
Sports	58.99	<60.63	63.90	55.21	<56.80	55.00
Boating	71.26	>63.6	74.90	60.33	>56.39	65.17

[a]See Kaplan (1960), Noe (1974), and Yu (1985) for a detailed description of activities included in the leisure designations.

rate of differentiation is much lower. In addition, the right half of Table 11.2 generally indicates that it is more difficult to differentiate people on the basis of what they do not like rather than on the basis of what they prefer.

COMPARISON OF DEMOGRAPHIC AND VALUE/ NORMATIVE MODEL

In the previous data analyses, both demographic and value/normative variables influencing demands were separately treated at a very general level of comparison. In order to evaluate the hypothesis that a value/normative model is a more sensitive predictor of recreational choices, sufficient evidence that specific value/ normative beliefs are more accurate predictors of demand and more cogent as a theoretical explanation is presented. Table 11.3 summarizes the results of a discriminate analysis that evaluates the relative merit of either a demographic or value/normative model as being a more dominant force in predicting the outcome of a decision choosing a favorite/unfavorite recreational activity. In only one case did demographic factors predict better than the normative/value model. However, there were only three out of the total set of recreational activities in which demographic characteristics did not contribute to some degree. Demographic factors largely related to status or class conditions and age functioned in an important support capacity in the recreational demand process.

A brief summary of the results in Table 11.3 will best describe the direction of these findings. Immobile activities such as reading or writing prose, poetry, listening to music, watching television, relaxing, resting, or loafing were preferred by those individuals who did not share values or norms that supported a physically active, exciting, challenging, difficult, and risky recreational lifestyle. The strength of this relationship was sufficient and acceptable but not overwhelming.

Golf was primarily predicted by those individuals who supported norms and values that were challenging or difficult, physically active, exciting and competitive, and from a demographic viewpoint were in the upper income bracket. The strength of this relationship was also acceptable but modest.

Exercise activities such as running, jogging, aerobics, racquet or handball, tennis, and power lifting were treated as a class of activities whose followers support an active, competitive, exciting leisure lifestyle, possess a higher occupational status, are achievement oriented, more educated, and less intellectually motivated in their leisure lifestyle and definitely more youthful. The strength of the relationship was good.

As noted in Table 11.3, voluntary association membership, while mentioned by those surveyed in the national sample, contained too few negative replies to construct a proper discriminate analysis. Perhaps the public identifies service and social community organizations more with obligatory requirements than discretionary opportunities.

Swimming at a beach, tanning, sailing, canoeing, visiting seashores or lakes

Table 11.3
Discriminants of Values, Norms, and Demographic Influences on Recreation Demand Choices

Recreation Activity	Standardized Discriminant Coefficients[a]		Eigen-value	Canonical Correlation	Centroids (Group)		Classification Accuracy[b] (-)	(+)
Immobility	Active	.567	.17	.38	(-)	1.30	(-) 71.4	28.6
	Challenge	.431			(+)	-.13	(+) 28.3	71.7
	Risky	.418					classified = 72%	
Golf	Challenge	.698	.17	.38	(-)	-.27	(-) 70.7	29.3
	Active	.397			(+)	.64	(+) 34.8	65.2
	Income	.392					classified = 68%	
Exercise/	Challenge	.455	.28	.46	(-)	-.40	(-) 72.6	27.4
health	Occupation	.411			(+)	.68	(+) 32.6	67.4
	Skill	-.357					classified = 70%	
	Achievement	.352						
	Education	.323						
	Age	-.303						
Beach/	Skill	.604	.03	.18	(-)	.53	(-) 75.8	24.8
swimming	Age	.567			(+)	.06	(+) 40.2	59.8
	Socialize	.526					classified = 62%	
Risky	Risky	.768	.23	.43	(-)	-.19	(-) 77.8	22.2
	Challenge	.405			(+)	1.18	(+) 38.8	61.2
	Education	.366					classified = 75%	
	Skill	-.357						
Mobility	Socialize	-.647	.22	.43	(-)	-.88	(-) 83.3	16.7
	Risky	.632			(+)	.24	(+) 40.2	55.6

144

Table 11.3 (continued)

Recreation Activity	Standardized Discriminant Coefficients[a]		Eigen-value	Canonical Correlation	Centroids (Group)		Classification Accuracy[b] (-) (+)	
	Residence	.551					classified = 61%	
	Income	-.442						
Popular	Active	-.721	.46	.56	(-)	-1.86	(-) 90.9	9.1
arts	Age	.542			(+)	.24	(+) 9.7	90.3
	Skill	.523					classified = 72%	
	Socialize	.408						
	Education	-.401						
Fine arts	Active	-.615	.21	.42	(-)	-1.11	(-) 78.6	21.3
	Education	.586			(+)	.19	(+) 28.3	71.7
	Skill	.536					classified = 72%	
	Occupation	-.500						
	Age	.442						
	Socialize	.400						
Camping/	Income	.747	.04	.21	(-)	.90	(-) 50.0	50.0
hiking	Age	.697			(+)	.05	(+) 36.4	63.6
							classified = 63%	
Hunting/	Active	-.509	.41	.54	(-)	1.08	(-) 78.0	22.0
Fishing	Competition	-.463			(+)	-.37	(+) 23.0	77.0
	Income	.414					classified = 77%	
	Skill	.381						
	Challenge	.368						
	Residence	.324						
Games/	Relax	.817	.15	.36	(-)	-.36	(-) 64.0	36.0

Table 11.3 (continued)

Recreation Activity	Standardized Discriminant Coefficients[a]		Eigen-value	Canonical Correlation	Centroids (Group)		Classification Accuracy[b]	
							(-)	(+)
Gambling	Risky	.446			(+)	.40	(+) 23.0	64.1
	Occupation	-.405					classified = 64%	
	Residence	.324						
Sports	Active	1.080	.36	.51	(-)	- .58	(-) 66.7	33.3
	Risky	-.312			(+)	.62	(+) 55.6	44.4
							classified = 69%	
Boating	Active	.592	.86	.68	(-)	-1.00	(-) 76.5	23.5
	Risky	.559			(+)	.88	(+) 22.0	78.0
	Age	-.370					classified = 77%	

[a]All Association discriminants included normative and value variables indicating relaxing, competition, activeness, socializing, risking, challenging, and skill orientations. Also included are demographic variables indicating age, residence, income, occupation, sex, education, and race. Only those variables pooled within group correlations above .30 are reported in this table. A complete data set is available from the authors.

[b]As with the group centroids, the (−) sign indicates that a respondent would never engage in that leisure activity while the (+) sign indicates that the leisure activity is the respondent's most favored choice.

were favored by individuals who did not support intellectual or creative values, and demographically tended to be younger. These same individuals were also socialized within their own class or stratum, feeling uncomfortable about associating outside their own peer level. The strength of the relationship, however, was very low with an eigenvalue of just .03.

Risk-associated activities like motorcycling, racing, skiing, and scuba diving were predicted by individuals who possess risky, novel, and challenging values associated with their leisure lifestyles. They were more highly educated but were also less accepting of skilled or intellectual orientations in their leisure choices. The strength of the discriminate relationship was good.

Mobile activities including traveling, sightseeing, and flying were supported by individuals who believe in socializing outside their own class and have higher incomes. Those individuals favoring mobile activities tend to be from more urban residences and are willing to take greater risks and search for novelty in their leisure lifestyle. Again the strength of the relationships was good.

Popular arts including gardening, farming, woodworking, remodeling, automobile repair, cooking/dining, crafts like sewing and knitting are favored by the less physically active, more passive educated public. Supporting these kinds of activities are those who are also older individuals who regard skills, intellectual/ creative activities, along with associating within a closed-class circle as being important. The strength of the relationship was one of the highest.

Fine arts including dance, music, theatre, photography, painting were favored by those in the survey who valued a physically inactive, noncompetitive, delicate leisure lifestyle and shunned higher occupational status. Furthermore, more highly educated older individuals who supported the fine arts also valued intellectual and open socialization within class groups. The strength of the relationships were modest.

Outdoor recreational activities such as camping, hiking, walking, backpacking were favored by the younger and less wealthy individuals surveyed. No values or norms motivating leisure choices were powerful enough to enter the discriminant equation. The strength of the two demographic variables was low in comparison to other eigenvalues.

Hunting and fishing activities were favored by those individuals seeking an exciting experience who were more competitive individuals valuing professional skills or needing to be in control in their leisure lifestyle. Lower income, more rural individuals also valuing a simple, relaxing unintellectual experience favored hunting and fishing. The strength of the relationship was very good.

Games of skill and chance were basically favored by those who appreciated the element of luck and valued risk-taking behavior, were lower in occupational status and lived in an urban residence. The strength of the relationship, however, tended to be among the lower eigenvalues found.

Sports, such as baseball, bowling, basketball, and softball, were among those favored by the active participants who valued excitement and competitiveness but were also nonrisk individuals. The strength of this relationship was quite good.

Finally, boating was strongly favored by those surveyed who regarded an active, exciting, risky lifestyle as being more important in their lives. They also tended to be younger individuals.

For the most part, the value/normative variables were superior to the demographic variables in predicting recreational preferences. However, the demographic variables contributed to the explanation and should not be overlooked in the application of the model.

CONCLUSION

The data in Table 11.1 indicate that demand for recreation activities is influenced by the method used to measure recreation preferences. In contrast to previous research using closed-ended checklists, the current research paints a different picture of demand in this country using an open-ended approach, asking respondents to specify their favorite recreation activity. Table 11.2 indicates that once demand is properly identified, what groups of people prefer which types of activities can be distinguished. From a policy perspective, the general model differentiating recreation preferences (Figure 11.1) can be used to evaluate who benefits from current recreation policy favoring certain types of activities and to evaluate the impact of proposed alternative recreation policies. For example, one could evaluate who would benefit from a public policy favoring government sponsorship and development of golf recreation facilities, who would be displeased with the policy, and which values/attitudes are reinforced by this policy. In the case of golf, such a policy would tend to make those who are white males, older, wealthy, higher educated, and having highly competitive values very happy. On the other hand, the same policy would alienate a group roughly twice as large who tended to be female, younger, poorer, less highly educated, more often nonwhite, and preferring more social interaction than those favoring golf. In referring back to Table 11.3, the crucial factors in determining preference or demand were the values supporting a challenging and active leisure lifestyle, and wealth or income in that order. Public policy must be formulated on the basis of weighing options either for or against a course of action. The approach taken herein sought to accomplish that objective both in the formulation and analysis of the national survey data. This strategy was sorely absent and lacking in previous research efforts seeking to identify the limits of demand in recreation. In addition, the social benefit is emphasized in terms of values and norms held by the public as a force in society for motivating action. Finally, the inability of other studies to predict demand correctly on the basis of demographic variables leads to more salient social factors, such as values and norms that generally proved more significant.

To the extent that policy evaluation should involve the specification of demand and the concomitant of demand for support of specific recreation activities, this more complex model offers one useful way of dealing with this issue. In calling for an integrated approach to explaining recreation preferences, Solan (1982) observed that "the task for the study of outdoor recreation seems to be one of describing the patterns of meanings/values, searching for their complements in social structure (sharing and commonality) and relating these variations to choice of recreation activity" (p. 3). This effort to integrate should encourage others to break further with past research in public policy that has narrowly defined recreational demand.

REFERENCES

Cheek, N. (1979). Visitor monitoring panel review. *National Park Service Report, Southeast Region, Atlanta, GA*. Atlanta: National Park Service.

Clawson, M. (1985, February). Trends in the use of public recreation areas. In *National Outdoor Recreation Trends Symposium II* (pp. 1–12). Myrtle Beach, SC.

Cordell, K., Fesenmaier, D., Leiber, S., & Hartman, L. (1985, February). Advancements in methodology for projecting future recreation participation. In *National Outdoor Recreation Trends Symposium II* (pp. 89–109). Myrtle Beach, SC.

Ellison, L. (1942). Trends of forest recreation in the United States. *Journal of Forestry, 40* (8), 630–638.

Gallup Organization. (1986, April 2). Consumer taste. *The Wall Street Journal*, Section 4, p. 13D.

Kaplan, M. (1960). *Leisure in America: A social inquiry*. New York: John Wiley.

Kelly, J. (1981) *Social benefits of outdoor recreation*. Washington, DC: U.S. Forest Service.

Kelly, J. (1983). Leisure styles: A hidden core. *Leisure Sciences, 5* (4), 321–338.

La Page, W. (1971). Cultural fogweed and outdoor recreation research. *Proceedings of the recreation symposium, Northeast Forest Experiment Station* (186–193). Upper Darby, PA.

La Page, W. (1976, October). A plea for mediocrity in recreation research goals. *Proceedings of the research roundtable meeting of the Bureau of Outdoor Recreation*. Washington, DC.

Light, S., & Groves, D. (1978). Policy issues in recreation and leisure: An overview. *Policy Studies Journal, 6* (8), 404–412.

Lucas, R. C., (1978, August). *Wilderness policy and management problems: Possible applications of psychology*. Paper presented at the meeting of the American Psychological Association, Toronto.

Noe, F. P. (1974). Leisure life styles and social class: A trend analysis, 1900–1960. *Sociology and Social Research, 3* (58), 286–294.

Solan, D. (1982, October). A macro value-determined model of outdoor recreation behavior. *Proceedings of the NRPA/SPRE Leisure Research Symposium*. Louisville, KY.

Stamps, S., & Stamps, M. (1985). Race, class, and leisure activities of urban residents. *Journal of Leisure Research, 17* (1), 40–56.

Treiman, D. (1977). *Occupational prestige in comparative perspective*. New York: Academic Press.

U.S. Department of the Interior. (1984). *Preliminary findings of the 1982–80 nationwide recreation survey*. Washington, DC: National Park Service.

Wagar, A. (1966). Quality of outdoor recreation. *Trends, 3* (3), 9–12.

Yu, J. (1985). The congruence of recreation activity dimensions among urban, suburban, and rural residents. *Journal of Leisure Research, 17* (2), 107–120.

12.

DEVELOPMENTAL PRESSURES ON RECREATION AREAS: PUBLIC DECISION MAKING AS A "GALVANIZING" EFFECT AMONG LOCAL CITIZENRY

Dennis L. Soden

The volatile political environment within which development of small-scale hydroelectric facilities occurs has been characterized as one of astronomical polarization. With few exceptions, the development of small-scale hydroelectric facilities has met with considerable opposition as a result of the mix of attitudes, preferences, and beliefs that come together in the public decision-making process. In settings in which traditional outdoor recreation activities are challenged by developmental interest, opposition has been especially vocal and strong in its challenge to development.

In this environment, a collective decision through public decision-making processes is often exceedingly difficult to achieve. In the course of the activities that take place with respect to small-scale hydroelectric development, each of the major actors—individual citizens, interest groups, government officials, and developers—has pursued strategies believed to maximize the interests particularly important to it. With particular attention paid to group dynamics, the two case studies that follow are used to illustrate how individual and group conceptions of the public interest are tied to outdoor recreation and how this interest emerges as a result of public decision making.

The two case studies—Elk River Falls in the Elk Creek Falls Recreation Area of the Clearwater National Forest in northern Idaho and the Horsepasture River in western North Carolina, which was granted National Scenic River status in 1986—provide excellent examples of the settings in which traditional outdoor recreation activities are challenged by developmental interests. In both instances, the issue of small-scale hydroelectric development became highly politicized. Local interests including those previously not politically active, became galvanized in their efforts to protect their favored outdoor recreation sites.

The case studies summarized here are based on two larger studies (Soden, 1985; 1987b), which employed concepts distilled from the literature of public choice theory—an increasingly well-accepted approach to the study of public policy and political issues (Lovrich & Neiman, 1984; Mueller, 1979). It is an approach that has proven to be well suited to the study of natural resource-related issues (Soden, 1987a; Sproule-Jones, 1982). The public choice literature suggests a number of attributes or characteristics that capture the essence of the public decision-making/collective-action process. The postulated traits were used to consider the political behavior that small-scale hydroelectric development at Elk Creek Falls and on the Horsepasture River engendered to see if galvanized public interest was, in fact, achieved.

A central tenet of public choice theory is that individuals, and by implication collectives, act in their own self-interest when making decisions. Proponents of public choice theory attempt to use this core assumption to study collective choices that are made in political and organizational settings. While falling far short of explaining all individual or aggregate behavior, public choice research suggests that the hypothesis of self-interested motivation provides the best single basis for predicting how people will act in a given social and/or political setting (Buchanan & Tollison, 1984; Mitchell, 1979). What constitutes self-interest, however, is often difficult to determine, particularly in cases in which rewards or the ends of action (i.e., beauty, peace of mind) cannot be measured in monetary terms. In the case of small-scale hydroelectric development, the way benefits or costs accrue to alternative choices, such as preservation of traditional recreation areas, is perceived as direct behavior. Of course, that perception of benefits may be very different across a set of individuals or elected officials—or even among expert policy analysts.

The study of citizens', group representatives', and developers' behavior relative to the implementation of small-scale hydroelectric projects in the Pacific Northwest (Idaho) and the Southeast (North Carolina) illustrates that there is considerable difference in the perceptions of self-interest entertained by the various actors involved. Yet, despite these differences, previously unrelated groups can join together in opposition to the development of traditional recreation areas. It is necessary to understand that the perceptions and behavior of relevant actors in the case studies direct the political reality of small-scale hydroelectric development and the applicability of the public choice approach to the study of natural resource issues. With this as background, the utility of the framework for analysis provided by the theory of public choice (Soden, 1985; 1987a) is assessed for its ability to explain the political and social dynamics relevant to small-scale hydroelectric development, especially as those dynamics materialize in the form of a galvanized citizenry in the concrete setting of case studies.

A PROFILE OF THE ELK CREEK FALLS PROJECT

The Elk Creek Falls area is approximately fifty miles northeast of Lewiston, Idaho, near the town of Elk River, a boomtown of the premiere days of the northwest timber industry that since the late 1970s has fallen on hard times. The town of Elk River is not dying, but like many other towns in the northwest whose economy rested on a single industry, Elk River did not recover from the economic recession of the late 1970s and early 1980s. The town is nestled in a picturesque mountain valley, but visual assessment of the boarded up homes and empty lumber mill quickly illustrate that Elk River has enjoyed far better days.

The Elk Creek Falls site covers a 3,600 foot reach of river characterized by a series of waterfalls, pools, and riffle segments common in mountain streams. Within the reach, a series of drops of sixty to ninety feet occur. The proposed Elk Creek Falls project site has been a long-term regular scenic destination of day hikers and is the central focus of the Elk Creek Falls Recreation Area, managed by the Palouse Ranger District of the U.S. Forest Service (USFS). The opposition that developed about the Elk Creek Falls project is closely tied to the characteristics of the town of Elk River located four miles away.

The Elk Creek Falls proposal entailed development on public lands that are administered by USFS. The Forest Service played a key role as mediator between environmental actors and the developer and acted as the lead government agency during the application for license phase. In this position, the Forest Service called for an in-depth environmental analysis in response to concerns that the public domain, and thus the public interest, were threatened by private development. The result was a final Forest Service position in opposition to the project on environmental grounds. The attention given to the Elk Creek Falls proposal was very emotional, resulting in nearly 100 letters to editors and local newspaper editorials during 1984 and 1985 focusing primarily on the recreation and esthetic value of rivers (Soden, 1985; 1987b).

A PROFILE OF THE HORSEPASTURE RIVER PROJECT

The Horsepasture River has a long history as a popular warm weather recreation spot. It lies in the southwest corner of North Carolina amid the Southern Highlands and Blue Ridge areas of the Appalachian Mountains. Near the town of Asheville, North Carolina, the Rainbow Falls portion of the river occurs in a four-mile stretch where the Horsepasture River drops 1,700 feet over the Blue Ridge escarpment. At this point the river plunges through a steep-sided gorge before flowing into Lake Jacassee in Transylvania County, just north of the South Carolina state line. With a 1,700 foot drop, the Rainbow Falls has held obvious attraction for hydroelectric developers, especially after the passage of the Public Utilities Regulatory Policies Act of 1978 (PURPA).

As a whole, the mountainous area of North Carolina is characterized as a "region faced with an environment peculiarly sensitive to land speculation and development which is goaded by private and corporate pecuniary 'self-interests' operating largely in locally permissive political arenas'' (Gade, Stillwell,& Rex, 1986, p. 200). As a result, evidence of environmental neglect, if not actual destruction, is rapidly accumulating. While region-wide action is required, history has recorded only highly localized opposition and solutions. Reaction to the proposed development of a small-scale hydroelectric facility on the Horsepasture River initially led to a generally localized response, but much like the scenario that has occurred regarding hydroelectric development elsewhere, publicity over the proposed project thrust the Horsepasture River into the region-wide and national arena.

The case studies are not sufficiently revealing of motives, resources, and vulnerabilities to determine what optimal strategy either proponents or opponents of development should attempt to develop as a means for achieving their desired ends. However, the case studies do provide some useful information about the behavior of participants that indicates if self-interest, the foundation of public choice theory, is the key predictor of behavior in this area. The case studies allow for the determination of whether, contrary to the axioms of public choice theory, some factor other than self-interest emerges to explain the behavior of individuals, interest groups, and developers concerned with the issue at hand.

SUMMARY OF FINDINGS

The studies were based on eight research questions distilled from the logic of public choice theory, independent from the analysis of recreation interests in opposition to small-scale hydroelectric facilities (Soden, 1985; 1987a). Briefly, these questions ask:

1. Is the property nature of the resources threatened by development seen as a "commons" by participants involved?

2. How does individual citizen activity and response pertain?

3. To what extent can a multiple agenda be identified among policy actors?

4. To what extent do general political beliefs, attitudes, and preferences affect policy positions?

5. To what extent does group behavior affect policy making?

6. How do informal interactions affect decision-making processes?

7. How does the possession or lack of policy-relevant knowledge affect decision making, and, if knowledge levels are low among participants in the policy process, whom do they trust as sources of information about small-scale hydroelectric development?

8. How likely is it that an effective/workable decision will be achieved?

In the simplest terms, public choice theory relies on the proposition that actors in the policy process are self-interested and behave rationally in accordance with their perceptions of their self-interest after assessing the relative costs and benefits associated with a particular subject of choice.

The evidence collected in the course of the case studies came from two general types of sources. First, content analyses were conducted of the media (newspaper articles and letters to editors) and documents (Federal Energy Regulatory Commission [FERC] permit applications and government agency files) linked to the projects involved. Second, key participants in the public decision-making process, for example, USFS district rangers, city and county officials, interest group representatives, and developers, were interviewed using an instrument designed to obtain responses relative to the identified tenets of public choice theory and the set of research questions. This occurred throughout 1984 and 1985 in the case of Elk Creek Falls and continues to be monitored through regular contacts with the participants. The Horsepasture River was under similar study from the fall of 1985 through late 1986, at which time the run of the river was granted National Scenic River status by the 99th Congress. By using a mixture of research techniques—multiple case studies, personal interviews, document study, and content analysis—the case studies were well analyzed and a clear understanding of the public decision-making process was obtained.

The particulars of the case studies are, however, far from being identical. In the case of the Elk Creek Falls project, the project site is located within an existing recreation area of the Clearwater National Forest and from inception involved many government agencies. The Horsepasture River proposal, in contrast, brought together actors in an effort to protect the threatened run of the river by placing it under government control. Yet, in both cases, the result has been the same—developmental pressures and the characteristics of public decision making acted as a galvanizing factor among local citizens in opposition to development of traditional recreation areas.

Galvanization involved a process by which actors previously politically unrelated or even at odds with each other joined forces in opposition to development. Three key characteristics in the case studies emerged relative to galvanization. First was the fact that those of lower education and lower socioeconomic levels become fervent in their opposition and at times led local opposition to the projects. They became united and involved with groups that were more often politically involved in environmental issues and were made up of individuals with higher levels of education and from higher socioeconomic levels. These individuals joined activists in expanding public involvement beyond the more standard set of environmental issue participants (Cigler & Loomis, 1983, pp. 4–5). Second, in light of the technical complexity of the issue, they showed considerable ability to quickly learn the intricacies of the obscure issues involved, such as impoundment effects on in-stream flows, fisheries impacts, and shoreline management. Third, the galvanization process witnessed obtained a boost at critical points when general public interest appeared to be waning because of the aid of a government agency. For example, in the case of Elk Creek Falls, the Forest Service opposed the proposed project in 1986, a point that will most likely halt the development. Similarly, in the case of the Horsepasture River, in 1984 then Secretary of Energy Donald Hodel noted federal opposition to the project, which led to the demise of the proposed project and opened the door for National Scenic River status.

From the perspective of public choice theory, the two case studies suggest that self-interested motives appear to guide the behavior of actors both for and against small-scale hydroelectric development. Developers attempt to maximize the benefits afforded to them through PURPA, while collectives representing the concerns of outdoor recreationists and individual citizens form a unified front in opposition. Finally, the actions of government officials, representing the interests of the agencies to which they belong, through their participation in the decision-making process support the notion of the utility of the self-interest construct. The goals of the Forest Service to insure recreation as a multiple-use strategy, the efforts of state legislators, U.S. Congressmen, and U.S. Senators, as well as the efforts of then Secretary of Energy Hodel, are all examples of the self-interest of government agencies and their representatives.

Relative to the research questions that directed the case studies, the following conclusions are suggested. First, the political economy concept of "commons" when development is seen as working against the long-term goals of the joint users of the resources involved is prevalent among those with preservationist leanings (namely, the interest group representatives and some government personnel), but does not appear to be a concern of developers. Further, the ability to protect rivers for recreation and preservation may hallmark strategies that will aid those who fear a "tragedy of the commons" when protective management plans do not exist.

"Consumer sovereignty," a key concept upon which public choice theory rests, involves the fulfillment of individual citizens' wants and desires, and it is apparent in the behavior of interest group members, in individual responses to development, in letters to newspapers and government agencies, in individual citizens' participation in public meetings, and in individuals' seeking and taking advantage of access to government officials in rural western North Carolina and northern Idaho. It is reasonable to conclude that particular individuals carry more weight in the decision-making process. Because of the reliance on old boy networks, some opponents to development, who reside in the rural areas of the case studies, command greater respect and fellowship than others. In contrast, the individual developers in both cases are viewed as nothing short of carpet-baggers, seen in one instance as trying to "Californicate" the area, in reference to the developer's origins. Individual roles are an important factor that cannot be minimized.

A strong multiple agenda exists. Nearly everyone involved agrees that the renewable nature of water resources makes them important in our energy calculus. In general, broad support was found to exist for small-scale hydroelectric development. However, little support exists among local citizens for either project because of the considerable significance attached to traditional recreation uses of the areas. Despite general support for small-scale hydroelectric development, local opposition formulated a not-in-my-neighborhood attitude about hydroelectric development. An ordering of priorities that placed the recreation uses of water systems above those of energy use also emerged. Thus, the concept of a multiple agenda may serve as an excellent clue to behavior about what underlies the galvanization that occurs.

General political beliefs, values, and policy preferences tend to be organized along a preservationist/developmentalist continuum. In both case studies, strong beliefs about how to manage water resources are exhibited in a developmentalist mode by small-scale hydroelectric developers and proponents. In contrast, a strong preservationist position is exhibited by opponents, including the numerous interest groups involved and many representatives of government agencies. More than any other factor, environmental beliefs are the best predictor of the policy position taken either in support for or opposition to development.

Group behavior plays an important role in both case studies. As public attention to the issue began to wane, group pressure continued against development, very notably in the ability of groups to mobilize resources in a highly professional manner on short notice. Collective action by outdoor recreation advocates in opposition to hydroelectric development was the major impediment to development in both cases. Groups have played a major role in establishing the agenda about the proper use of scarce natural resources. Group behavior is firmly rooted in the beliefs and attitudes that individual members hold. The strength of their belief is a barrier of which developers are typically unaware when they undertake projects.

Informal activities and interactions are much in evidence in both cases. Informal actions may help to speed up the decision-making process, but the analysis suggests that the projects may be unique because of the rural settings in which informality is more of a norm than it might be in urban environments. Under different conditions, such as a proposal in a more urbanized area, informal action may be less of a standard procedure, and the easy access would not exist.

The holding of public policy-relevant knowledge affected both individual and group acts in the public decision-making process. Knowledgeable actors actively use public policy-relevant knowledge to state their positions. Position statements backed with knowledge about hydroelectric development impacts are more concrete and thus less likely to be discounted as an emotional response. Developers hold information as a private good, holding it as long as possible, thereby cutting the response time available and limiting wide dissemination as a means of preventing possible adverse reaction to their plans. The level of technical information needed to fully comprehend the entirety of small-scale hydroelectric issues is enormous. The results of the case studies tend to indicate that most individuals rely on traditional sources of information, with which they share beliefs and attitudes, to understand the issue at hand (e.g., developers seek information from energy companies while preservationists seek information from environmental groups). Low levels of information holding were quickly overcome, however, by opponents making them formidable actors within a complex policy area.

An effective and workable decision favoring outdoor recreation proponents emerged as a result of collective action among various actors working within their perspective of the public interest—reflective of their self-interest. Despite the intricacies and complexities of the issue, the process of public decision making led to a not so uncommon scenario. Outdoor recreationists and their supporters relied on collective action in both cases and created a series of events, concerns, and responses with which developers were unprepared to deal.

CONCLUSION

The strategies of participants in the public decision-making process described here vary according to the unique dynamics that arise in each case of proposed small-scale hydroelectric development. While these strategies may vary, in general consistencies across each case do exist. Public choice theory provides a useful theoretic approach for examining such consistencies. The approach is useful not only for explaining and predicting policy positions and political behavior, but, it is also well organized, parsimonious, and heuristic. Public choice theory provides a set of testable statements about relationships obtained between key concepts. A set of statements about potentially important phenomena can be derived. These statements can guide research into natural resource issues entailing a high degree of public involvement.

In summary, an identification of the behavior of actors and their strategies indicates that public participation through individual and group activities has drawn considerable public attention to recreation areas when they are threatened by development. The public participation identified has drawn together heretofore loosely related forces within the communities, including, among others, river runners, hikers, motel operators, and other members of the tourist industry, and it has galvanized them, based on their self-interests, into an effective force against development.

REFERENCES

Buchanan, J. M., & Tollison, R. D. (Eds.). (1984) *The theory of public choice II*. Ann Arbor: University of Michigan Press.

Cigler, A. J., & Loomis, B. A. (Eds.). (1983). *Interest group politics*. Washington, DC: Congressional Quarterly Press.

Gade, O., Stillwell, H. D., & Rex, A. (1986). *North Carolina: People and environments*. Boone, NC: GeoApp Publishing.

Lovrich, N. P., & Neiman, M. (1984). *Public choice theory in public administration— An annotated bibliography*. New York: Garland Publishing.

Mitchell, R. C. (1979). Natural environmental lobbies and the apparent illogic of collective action. In C. E. Russell (Ed.), *Collective decision making* (pp. 87–121). Baltimore: Johns Hopkins University Press.

Mueller, D. C.(1979). *Public choice*. New York: Cambridge University Press.

Soden, D. L. (1985). *Public choice in water resource management: Two case studies of the small-scale hydroelectric controversy*. Doctoral dissertation, Washington State University.

Soden, D. L. (1987a). *A conceptual formation of public participation and decision making in the natural resource and environmental policy issue area* (Occasional papers in Coastal Zone Studies). Pensacola: University of West Florida.

Soden, D. L. (1987b, March). *Ethical properties of politics: A research note on the application of public choice theory in natural resource and environmental politics*. Paper presented at the annual meeting of the Western Political Science Association, Annaheim, CA.

Sproule-Jones, M. (1982). Public choice theory and natural resources: Methodological explication and critique. *American Political Science Review, 76* (4), 790–804.

13.

Preservation or Use? Confronting Public Issues in Forest Planning and Decision Making

Dale J. Blahna and Susan Yonts-Shepard

The National Forest Management Act of 1976 (NFMA) required the U.S. Forest Service (USFS) to prepare land and resource management plans for each national forest. If possible, these plans were to be completed by 1985. NFMA mandated that public involvement be used in the development of the plans and that environmental impact statements (EIS) be prepared and made available for public comment according to the requirements of the National Environmental Policy Act (NEPA). As a result of the requirements of both NFMA and NEPA, the Forest Service developed an issue-driven planning model that is heavily dependent upon public input (36 C.F.R. 219.12; Jameson, Moore, & Case, 1982; Lee, 1983, p. 10).

Currently, the Forest Service is in the middle of the first round of planning. Draft plans for most forests have been issued for public review, but few have been able to advance to final plans. By the end of 1989, 892 administrative appeals had been filed against the 90 final plans that were released. Of these, only 56 have cleared the appeals process. Everette Towle, the national director of land management planning, expects that over 1,000 appeals will be lodged before the first round of planning is completed. Thus, despite the emphasis on public involvement and public issues, a great deal of controversy exists over the content of the forest plans.

In 1986, the Washington, D.C. office of the Forest Service conducted a national study of the use of public involvement in forest planning. One of the objectives of this study was to investigate how public input was used to identify public issues and how those issues were used in the development of forest plans.

Using this data base, approximately 80 percent of the contentious issues at the draft plan stage could be classified as conflicts over questions of preservation versus use. Every forest in our study was affected by several of these types of contentious issues.

The study data also suggest that while the Forest Service used formal issue identification procedures, often the issues as identified were not useful for developing the forest plans. One reason for this inefficiency was that the public issues were often described in terms of very broad statements or questions, such as: How much timber should be harvested from the national forest? How much dispersed recreation should the forest provide? or how much developed recreation should the forest provide? David Iverson, Region 4 (Intermountain Region) Forest Service economist, asserts that issue statements, such as the questions listed above, gave analysts little insight for developing the analysis models. He feels,

the [issue] statement should be couched as a question or series of questions to be answered by the analysis. . . . This is one of the most crucial steps in the analysis process. Failure to synthesize . . . [the issues] into workable analysis questions will render subsequent analysis meaningless. (Iverson, 1983, p. 1)

In fact, none of the forests in the study provided clear linkages between the public issues and how they were used in the development or analysis of planning alternatives. Furthermore, such crucial information as who was interested in different forest management prescriptions (or alternatives), the reasons for their stands on the issues, and what specific programs or resources were in question was overlooked. As a result, few issues were resolved during the planning process, and many issues intensified, especially when the draft plans were released—five or six years after the onset of planning. In short, many public issues were lost sight of in the planning process.

The objective identification of public issues and stakeholders is the first, and perhaps most critical, step for dealing successfully with the many preservation-versus-use conflicts facing resource agencies. The purposes of this chapter are to identify how issues were discounted during the forest planning process and to make recommendations for improving the way agencies identify public issues and use them in resource planning and decision making.

STUDY METHODS

This chapter is based on the results of the 1986 study conducted through the joint efforts of three units of the Forest Service: Land and Resource Management Planning, Public Affairs, and Environmental Coordination. The results represent summary data and case studies developed from a synthesis of four data sources: (1) a review of forest plans and environmental impact statements; (2) a survey sent to thirteen study forests; (3) documentation collected from the planning files of six site-visit forests; and (4) conversations with over sixty Forest Service staff members and administrators from eleven forests, two regional offices, and the Washington, D.C., office.

The thirteen forests included in the study were located in both eastern and western regions of the country; at least one forest was located in each of the eight Forest Service regions in the contiguous forty-eight states. The forests were also selected to ensure that a diversity of resource-use situations (from single-use emphasis to forests with many different types of uses) and distances from urban areas (from urban to remote locations) were represented.

From the original thirteen study forests, six that were representative of a typical national forest were identified. All of the site-visit forests had a high mixture of resource demands, with timber and recreation being the focus of the commodity uses of the forests. The six forests were located between three to eight hours by automobile from major metropolitan areas with a population of 500,000 or more. All the forests but one were located in areas that had experienced a moderate to high rate of population growth in recent years, and all of the forests contained designated wilderness and/or wilderness study areas. The major characteristic on which the site-visit forests differed was the level of conflict experienced during the planning process: four experienced a high degree of conflict over the draft or final plan, while two experienced very little conflict.

HOW PUBLIC ISSUES WERE LOST SIGHT OF IN THE PLANNING PROCESS

The formal identification and description of public issues is a relatively new activity for the Forest Service. However, experience has shown that an organized approach to issue management is critical for resource planning (Armour, 1986). Based on the study results, during the early stages of planning (i.e., before release of the draft plan), there were four barriers to the objective assessment and use of public issues in Forest Service planning: (1) a lack of input from many interested publics, (2) a vote-counting approach to the analysis of public input, (3) the grouping together of public issues and management concerns, and (4) the sanitizing effect of administrative review.

Lack of Interest Representation

The Forest Service planning direction states that one of the roles of public involvement is to "ensure that the Forest Service understands the needs, concerns and values of the public" (36 C.F.R. 219.1 [2]). An important, unanswered question on this subject is who is the public? The Council on Environmental Quality (CEQ), which wrote the regulations for implementing NEPA, suggests that "the public" refers to persons and agencies who may be interested in and affected by the forest plan (40 C.F.R. 1506.6 [b]). Armour (1986) takes this notion even further; she asserts that full participation is critical throughout the planning process:

Failure to achieve full involvement early enough in the planning process has often pro-duced serious problems and unnecessary delays. If well into the planning process, interests come forward who were somehow "overlooked" earlier on, the credibility of the planning exercise may be challenged and support for implementation of planning recommendations may be weakened. (p. 54)

Staff members from all the forests in our study attempted to solicit broad-based input by mailing informational brochures to persons on the forests' mailing lists. These brochures introduced interested citizens to the planning process and solicited written comments on a preliminary list of public issues, which had been compiled by the staff of the forest. The management of about two-thirds of the forests in our sample supplemented this written input by conducting meetings at which citizens could discuss the issues with staff members of the forest. These meetings were advertised by sending announcements to the persons on the mailing list and by issuing press releases to local and regional newspapers. The issue identification process was one of the first steps taken in the planning process.

Unfortunately, this effort resulted in very little input. Furthermore, the input that was received was heavily biased, often in favor of local residents and traditional users of the forests.[1] This resulted in a commodity-oriented bias in the early public input received on these forests.

This early information was especially misleading since little further input was solicited by most forests until after the release of the draft plan. Often, there was a period of five to six years in which the forest managers initiated few contacts with the public regarding the forest plans. Thus, interested citizens were never given the opportunity to comment on specific planning alternatives until after draft plans were released. As a matter of fact, most of the participants in the planning process did not become involved until after the draft planning documents were released. Therefore, the public issues and draft plans were developed after receiving only a few comments from a small subset of interested publics, and those comments were not directly related to Forest Service proposals for dealing with public issues.

For a few forests, however, input was received from a wide variety of both local and nonlocal publics. And, even though the input that was received during the development of the lists of public issues was biased, the study revealed that most forest staff members were aware of 72 percent of the contentious public issues before the drafts were released. Thus, there were yet other barriers to the identification of public issues.

Information Lost in Comment Analysis

Once comments were received on the draft list of issues, the individual comments had to be condensed into opinion statements that reflected common attitudes. In general, two different comment analysis methods were used for the site-visit forests. A formal content analysis was conducted on two forests, while on the other forests similar comments were summarized with neutral opinion statements. In both cases, much of the information useful for planning was lost in the analysis process because both methods essentially reflected a vote counting process.

For the forests in which formal content analysis was used, comments were coded as indicating support or opposition to a particular management action or program (e.g., for or against wilderness designation). The number of comments were then tallied to estimate the strength of opinion on different subjects. This method of analysis is dangerous because it implied that the vote of the people should dictate forest management, a practice against which several authors have cautioned (e.g., Hendee, Clark, & Stankey, 1974; Lee, 1983).

The analysts for the other forests believed they could escape this vote counting trap by eliminating the opinion tallying process and by wording the opinion statements in a neutral fashion. "A sizeable number of comments addressed the amount of wilderness on the forest," was a typical summary opinion statement. For the purpose of designing planning alternatives, however, the implicit assumption of these results was essentially the same as for the content analysis results, that is, some want more wilderness and some want less.

The major problem with both the comment analysis methods was that information important to planning was lost in the process. A common example of such loss occurred in the handling of input related to roading policies. The comments regarding forest transportation systems were typically coded as "pro-roading" (especially commercial logging interests and recreationists such as off-road vehicle enthusiasts, hunters, and fishermen) or "anti-roading" (especially the environmentalists). What was lost in this form of analysis was that the pro-roading recreationists were generally interested in retaining access to *existing* roads while the anti-roading interests were primarily opposed to the construction of *new* roads. When the Forest Service proposed to increase the number of new roads to enhance access for timber harvesting, they balanced the increase by closing or obliterating many miles of existing roads so that the total number of miles of forest roads appeared to decrease or stay relatively constant. On the surface, this gave the impression of appeasing both pro-roading (roads are being built) and anti-roading (no increase in the total miles of forest roads) advocates, when in fact, this action was contrary to the interests of all parties—except for the timber interests. In this way, the vote counting analysis masked the true characteristics of one of the major preservation-versus-use issues facing the national forests today.

In summary, these forms of comment analysis obscured some of the details of the real issues, giving the impression that the Forest Service was equitably addressing the issues. This illusion was temporary, however. The conflicts that emerged after the release of the draft plans demonstrated that the issues had merely been postponed from the early stages of planning until much later in the process—often up to six years after planning had begun.

Grouping Public Issues and Management Concerns

After tabulating the comments on the lists of public issues, the problem of reducing the large numbers of opinion statements to manageable numbers of "public issues" and "management concerns" (36 C.F.R. 219) remained. One of the most pervasive problems with the issue identification process for nearly all the forests was that opinion statements were combined into such broad categories of public issues that they became useless for planning purposes.

For instance, for one forest, an issue titled "How Should the Forest Respond to the Increasing Demand for Dispersed Recreation Opportunities?" was derived from grouping together comments related to the following topics: ability to meet demand for primitive recreation; overuse of camping facilities and related resource impacts; availability of support facilities (parking, trails, sanitary facilities, etc.); impacts of overuse on streams; roads and off-road vehicle use; and user conflicts (hikers vs. hunters, cross-country skiers vs. snowmobilers, and motorized recreationists vs. nonmotor recreationists). Because of its many facets, the Forest Service was not able to deal with any aspect of the issue in detail. For example, the draft environmental impact statement (DEIS) described the dispersed recreation issue as follows:

This issue was addressed by over 30% of the public who responded with the majority in favor of additional facilities and services. At the present time, dispersed use recreation activities account for approximately 75% of the total forest use. Many respondents to the forest's off-road vehicle (ORV) use policy mentioned facility needs and control of users. A need was identified to change the forest ORV policy from "open unless specifically closed" to "closed unless specifically open."

Obviously, this statement described only a small portion of the diversity of opinions from which the issue question was developed.[2] To reduce this tendency toward diluting the public issues, some comments should have been considered management concerns rather than public issues. The comments were not separated into these two categories for any study forest, however, because there was no clear distinction made between them in the definitions provided in the planning direction:

Public Issue. A subject or question of widespread public interest relating to management of the National Forest System.

Management Concern. An issue, problem, or condition which constrains the range of management practices identified by the Forest Service in the planning process. (36 C.F.R. 219.3)

These definitions were interpreted to mean that the major difference between a public issue and a management concern was that the former must originate from the public and the latter with the forest staff. When they found that the concerns of the public often overlapped with those of the forest's staff, it made sense to simply combine the two and call them public issues.

A much more functional description of an issue has been presented by Cobb and Elder (1983): "An issue is a conflict between two or more identifiable groups over procedural or substantive matters relating to the distribution of positions or resources" (p. 82). Based on this definition, the distinguishing characteristic of a public issue is that there should be two or more interested parties having contrasting opinions on the subject of concern. This critical distinction is also echoed by Armour (1986), who defined issues as "conflicting points of view about the value of the resources, how they should be used . . . " (p. 51). Conversely, when there is general agreement on a topic (e.g., facilities are overused or trail erosion must be stopped), it should be considered a management concern, not a public issue or issue subfacet, despite the fact that many citizens have voiced the concern or first identified the problem.

Using this distinction of opposing parties, it becomes obvious that most of the subfacets contained in the dispersed recreation example could have been considered management concerns. The public issues were roading and recreational conflicts between hikers and hunters and between motorized and non-motorized users. Since this distinction was not made, however, the broad and nebulous character of the issues kept these key public issues from becoming the focal points for designing planning alternatives.

Management concerns are also important for the development of the forest plan. But because of the contrasting opinions involved, the descriptions of public issues and the explanations of how they were used to develop planning alternatives must be more comprehensively detailed than management concerns. Furthermore, public issues require further public involvement. If the issues are not specific and described in detail, there is little guidance for meeting one of the primary goals of public involvement, that is, obtaining consensus on controversial issues.

The Sanitizing Effect of Administrative Review

A final factor inhibiting the use of public issues information was that staff and administrators at all levels of the agency were hesitant about highlighting certain controversial issues in the forest plans. This attitude influenced the official list of public issues for the forest and the extent to which the planning alternatives could address public issues.

The list of public issues had to filter through several layers of administrative review at both the forest and regional levels. First, the coding and analysis results (discussed above) were reviewed by the planning team. Next, the forest management team (forest supervisor and district rangers) reviewed the issues. Finally, the list of public issues was reviewed by administrators and resource specialists in the regional office. The issues or issue descriptions were revised at each step in the review process. On occasion, the issues were sanitized so that they did not directly discuss some contentious matters facing the forest or region.

For one western forest, for example, a memorandum signed by the planning staff officer was placed in the planning file. The purpose of the memorandum was to protest the forest supervisor's decision to deemphasize three important issues that had been identified by public input. The supervisor had told the planners to devalue each of the three (pesticide use, visual resource management, and range management) from full-fledged public issues to obscure subfacets under broader issue headings. For instance, he wanted the pesticide issue, which was a major controversy throughout the region, to be included as a subfacet under the broader designation of vegetation management. The memorandum read:

Pesticide use surfaced as a controversial subject that should be a separate issue. Its inclusion under Vegetation Management does not reflect many public concerns that relate to pesticides or herbicides, including . . . insecticides in campgrounds . . . Rotenone to kill fish . . . [and] herbicides for brush and trees [and for] . . . grass and weeds.

The pesticide issue escalated considerably in the years following the identification of public issues, and it remained one of the most contentious issues after the release of the proposed plan.

Decisions such as these often resulted from an attempt to meet the expectations of the regional office. In the case of the pesticide issue, the regional office was developing a region-wide vegetation management policy for pesticide use on all the forests in the region. The draft regional plan had supported past levels of pesticide use. This fact, however, does not warrant obscuring the issues identified by the public. Public issues should be objectively identified and then responded to, even if the forest management cannot meet the concerns of the public due to resource or policy constraints. Second, both NFMA and NEPA regulations state that alternatives requiring a change in policy can be considered if they address "a major public issue" (36 C.F.R. 219.12 [f] [5], 40 C.F.R. 1502.14 [c]). Finally, there may be creative ways to address an issue that do not require changes in existing policies. These potential measures can be lost if an issue is not addressed at the forest or regional level.[3]

Administrative review also affected the development of planning alternatives and the selection of the preferred alternative. Here the most pervasive influence was the review, or the impending review of the draft plan by the regional office. For example, Wilkinson and Anderson (1985) point out that the commodity production goals of the regional office often differed significantly from the alternatives generated by certain forests. To support this contention, they reprinted letters from two forest supervisors who criticized regional planning targets. One supervisor wrote:

In numerous public meetings within the past two years and extending back through the completion of all of our unit plans, we have assured our public that we will hear all sides and propose a course which reflects a reasonable balance between the issues and concerns expressed. The selection of Alternative L [in the regional plan] for the [Forest] will appear so illogical to our publics it will make a mockery of our issue identification and public involvement process. (p. 82)

While the forests were not required to meet regional production targets, plans had to be submitted for regional approval. According to Wilkinson and Anderson, two planners indicated that they felt informal pressure to meet certain regional targets. Although it was rare, this pressure was occasionally dictated by more formal means, such as the following memorandum received on one western forest in our study: "[I]n accordance with Reagan administration goals, as many planning alternatives as possible, *including the preferred alternative,* will increase grazing on the Forest by at least 43% (emphasis added)."

Thus, issue-related red flags were raised at every level of the agency.[4] Although these situations were rarely documented, it appears that these red flags hindered the planner's ability to be objective in designing alternatives that would address the public's concerns. It follows then that acknowledging public issues in resource agencies will require more than simply improving data collection and analysis techniques. Issue management must become institutionalized in the decision-making process of the agency.

MAKING BETTER USE OF PUBLIC ISSUES IN RESOURCE AGENCIES

The way in which public issues were used in the NFMA planning process reflects a common approach to decision making taken by resource agencies in general. William Freundenberg (1987) calls it the MAD approach: make the decision (M), announce the decision (A), and defend the decision (D). Resource agencies rarely identify public issues and then formulate a plan or decision around mitigation measures that address the issues.

As a result of NFMA planning, however, the Forest Service carried this MAD process one step further. Due to the debate generated by the proposed forest plans, the staff members on several forests met with opponents in an effort to reach resolutions on critical planning issues. For most forests, this was the first time the staff had discussed specific planning proposals with interested citizens. While some issues had already escalated to such an extent that resolution was impossible, many issues were resolved very effectively at this stage. From these eleventh-hour attempts at issue resolution, and from the experiences of those forest staffs that did not wait until after the release of draft plans to work on resolving public issues, several factors have been identified as crucial for effectively identifying and using public issues in both planning and on-going decision making.

Using Issues in Planning

Issue Identification. First, planners should focus on a small number of specific issues. To this end, it is important to incorporate the criteria of opposing parties in the formal operational definition of public issue. This will increase the specificity of the issues and make them more useful for designing management alternatives. It will also help reduce the number of public issues that must be addressed in planning.[5]

Even with the criterion of opposing parties, there will probably still be too many public issues to develop in detail in the forest plan. Therefore, other guidelines are needed to help further reduce issues to a manageable number. Since all public issues should be addressed in some manner, a classification and tracking system should be developed. This system should help identify how issues should be handled and monitor changes in the issues and actors, including those issues that are not addressed in detail in the forest plan.[6] Most forest plans should be able to focus on five to seven specific issues, and no more than ten to twelve issues for very contentious forest plans.

Issue Description. Only two forests in this study avoided the vote counting trap in the content analysis of early input. For one of the forests, all the issues for each district in the forest were described in a qualitative manner. In that way, they retained the information that was pertinent to planning. An analysis of their issue documentation suggests that issue statements should describe the components of the issues in detail, not just provide brief discussions of the issue topics. It is important to identify the interested parties, their positions on the issues, and the reasons for their stands. It is also important to tie the interests to specific forest resources or management policies, and to identify potential conflict resolution approaches. These resolution approaches should consider alternative public involvement strategies and alternative management prescriptions.

Most of the forests in this study eventually did develop issue statements as described above, but only after receiving comments on the proposed plan and DEIS. Some regional offices required that a critical issue report that summarized the comments on the draft plan be prepared for each forest. These reports were, in fact, excellent summaries of the issues and different approaches for addressing each issue.

It was unfortunate that the critical issue reports were not prepared until after the release of draft plans. Rather than being used to help design the basic plans, they were only used for reacting to public pressure at the eleventh hour. Furthermore, these reports were not available to the public. Even after the release of forest plans, there was still some agency resistance to discussing sensitive issues in a public forum. These bureaucratic barriers hindered the Forest Service's ability to consistently anticipate conflicts and to stay in command of the decision-making environment.

Use of Issues. A fundamental weakness in the forest plans was the lack of formal linkage between public issues and planning analyses and alternatives. Iverson (1983) has suggested that a broad issue question, such as "How much timber should be harvested from the forest?" should be converted into specific "analysis problem statements," such as the following:

1) If 175 MMBF/year is proposed as an average annual harvest in the first decade of the planning horizon (a 20% increase over recent historical cut levels):

    A. Over what period of time can we maintain the recent historical distribution of species/size class composition of the harvest? What is the composition throughout the planning horizon?

    B. Where in the forest will the cut originate? First decade? Later periods in the planning horizon?

2) Considering 1A and B, what impact will the 175 MMBF proposal have on wildlife habitat?

    A. Which management indicator species are significantly impacted? When? Where?

    B. Are there alternatives that would mitigate impacted habitat? At what cost?

    C. Can we direct investments into wildlife projects to mitigate significant impacts given? (pp. 1–2)

Resource agencies must also use the issues as a focus for planning public involvement activities. Without a focus, the number of potential meeting topics and participants can be infinite. On five of the six site-visit forests, meetings and workshops were held to address specific issues after the release of the draft plan.[7] One forest in the Great Lakes region, for example, held a two-day roundtable designed to bring together parties with conflicting interests on use and preservation-related issues (wilderness, timber harvest, roading, etc.). Following the meeting, the forest's public affairs officer was pleased with the success of the marathon workshop. The participants took less rigid stands than had been indicated by their written correspondence, and many areas of common interest were identified. As a result of personal contacts, the participants emerged with greater empathy for both the Forest Service staff and for other stakeholders on different sides of the issues.

A different approach was taken for a Colorado forest, where roading was the dominant concern of most plan opponents. Meetings were held with groups and individuals who held similar positions on the roading issues. This process required several iterations of meetings. The forest supervisor relayed the interests of groups on one side of the issue to the other groups so they could consider each other's concerns while formulating compromise roading proposals. In the end, while some participants stated that they were not totally satisfied with the final roading prescriptions, they expressed an understanding of the Forest Service position. There were no appeals of the forest plan.

Ideally, issue-directed public involvement should be obtained before draft plans are released. One low-conflict forest in this study, for example, conducted over sixty meetings during the development and selection of planning alternatives. These meetings were designed around specific public issues, and many citizens were invited to participate. By the time the draft was released, most of the issues were resolved, and the final plan was released without a major appeal.

This suggests that the Forest Service must redirect its notion of "issue driven" from the current lopsided approach to one that is an iterative process for designing and revising issues and alternatives based on public input. That is, the agency must remain flexible to changes in the issue agenda (Armour, 1986). To do this, the Forest Service must receive feedback on planning alternatives while they are being developed. The content of public input will differ drastically when a specific planning proposal (e.g., build 875 miles of new roads in the first ten years) is presented, as compared to a very general question such as, "What issues would you like to see us address in the forest plan?" Thus, feedback on various approaches to handling the issues is even more important than obtaining unfocused input before specific issues have been identified.

Using Issues in On-going Decision Making

There are many in the Forest Service who feel that as the formal planning process comes to an end, so does the need for issue identification and related public involvement. This attitude is unfortunate. Issues are not resolved simply because a legal document is in place that supports management decisions. Issues and actors change over time, and many management implications of a plan may not be apparent to interested citizens until implementation. The Forest Service should continue to identify and monitor public issues long after the adoption of final plans, for example, during plan implementation. Issue identification and management activities must be an on-going effort.

An excellent example of the use of interactive problem solving techniques during plan implementation was found for one low-conflict forest in the study. In the year following the approval of the final plan, the forest supervisor met periodically with a group of citizens that provided input on the most contentious issues raised during forest planning: roading and roadless area policies. The supervisor also met with other citizens on an issue-by-issue basis. For instance, when a sensitive area of the forest was due to be leased for oil and gas development, he met with representatives of state and local environmental interests. Together, they toured the sites and discussed potential impacts that could result from the development. Their concerns were used to identify the mitigation measures that became part of the lease agreement. The area was leased as scheduled without an appeal. This is the essence of using issue identification and public involvement as tools for proactive resource management.

As noted above, however, there is still considerable resistance by resource agency decision makers to identify and deal with controversial issues in public forums. Thus, issue management must become an institutionalized part of resource decision making. To this end, administrators need more experience and training in conflict resolution and integrative problem-solving skills. Furthermore, the ability to deal with public issues should be a primary criterion for hiring administrators and for their performance evaluations.

The psychological reaction against the discussion of controversial topics in public is natural, but it must be overcome. All too often, major, long-term conflicts emerge from small-scale, site-specific issues. This trend points to the need for increasing issue management efforts at the local level of decision making. Focusing on local-level decisions will reduce the potential for certain conflicts to escalate into symbolic issues that can be embraced by broader regional, state, or national interests.

CONCLUSION

Conflicts over forests have increased dramatically in recent years. Initially this was the result of increased activism by environmental groups. More recently, however, development interests have been active because they perceive that environmentalists have had an increased influence on Forest Service decision making.

This scenario has been reflected in forest planning. Originally, proposed plans were commodity oriented, resulting in a great deal of activism by environmental groups. Their activism led more recent plans to be more preservation oriented. As a result, several forest plans have been appealed by development interests and then counterappealed by preservation interests as a reaction to the initial appeal. At each step, forest managers have tended to react to the public issues rather than working proactively to obtain consensus before they escalated into full-fledged conflicts.[8] Thus, issue avoidance was practiced by most forests rather than openly addressing public issues in the early stages of planning. The end result, however, was merely to postpone issues.

This behavior is typical of resource agencies. Rarely will an agency identify controversial public issues and formulate a plan that is based on mitigation measures until it is forced to by public outcry. Resource planners and decision makers must focus more on specific public issues and use the issues to identify potentially interested publics and to evaluate management alternatives. Public involvement activities can then be designed around these issues. Several iterations of public involvement will be required to resolve the issues, especially for a complex decision-making activity such as forest planning. Resource agencies

Figure 13.1
Hypothetical Conflict Curves[1]

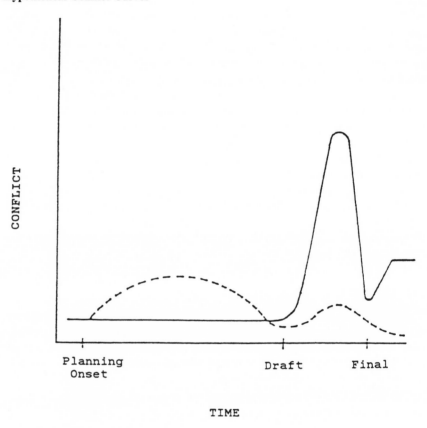

[1]The curves can represent the life history of an individual issue or cumulative effect of all issues encountered over a period of time. The area under the two curves may be about the same, but the distribution and intensity of conflicts varies.

[2]The recommended approach emphasizes continuous issue identification and cooperative problem solving.

should continue to identify and meet with interested publics until there is a consensus on the issues, or until the agency decision makers explain, in person, how and why decisions will differ from the concerns of specific, interested individuals or groups. This iterative approach should be taken during the development of alternatives, as well as after the release of the draft plan. This will require a much heavier investment in public involvement than has been allowed in the past.

This approach will not necessarily reduce the total number of conflicts faced by an agency. In fact, it may, as critics are likely to suggest, increase the number of conflicts. However, this approach will also dramatically affect the character of conflicts in a number of positive ways. For instance, planning issues will be spread out throughout the planning process, rather than being concentrated in a short period of time after the release of the proposed plan. And, on average, conflicts will be less intense (Figure 13.1).

With a smaller number of issues on the docket, and more time to deal with those issues, the potential for using the input of interested citizens in the planning or decision-making process increases. As a result of the continuing cooperation and personal contact between the resource agency and citizens over time, there will be less conflict in the long run, and planning and decision making will be more socially and politically proactive rather than reactive.

NOTES

1. For example, two of the forests in the study received written comments from fewer than sixteen persons from outside of the local areas.

2. This problem of grouping comments into very broad issue categories came about as the result of the misconception among staff members that all public input had to be used in the development of public issues. This misconception probably came about as a result of a misinterpretation of CEQ regulations that required that in the final EIS the planning agency must attach and respond to "all substantive comments received on the draft statement . . ." (40 C.F.R. 1503.4[a] [5a]). CEQ regulations do not, however, require that all input be reflected in construction of the planning issues. In fact, the planning directions define public issues as questions of "widespread" public interest (36 C.F.R. 219.3). Therefore, the process of continually broadening the public issues in an effort to absorb all substantive comments did not meet the intent of the planning legislation and only served to weaken the utility of the issues.

3. For example, in the pesticide issue cited above the supervisor's action eliminated from consideration those aspects of the current pesticide program that could have been changed without influencing the pattern of pesticide use for timber management, such as reducing pesticide use along roads and in visitor use areas.

4. It is not meant to be implied that it was just certain regional offices that, or forest supervisors who, wanted to dictate how or if certain issues were addressed. In fact, interviews suggested that red flags could be raised at any stage of the review process. These red flags, however, were rarely documented.

5. It is also important to note that the forests themselves can be considered an interest or party. If all the citizens who comment on a topic generally agree on a management action but that action is different from current policy or preferred practice, this topic can still qualify as a public issue. There are two reasons for this. First, the current management practice of the forest may represent the interests of unrepresented publics. Second, while public officials may act as neutral parties, they often have a vested interest in certain decisions (Cobb & Elder, 1983).

6. Some issues, for example, are site specific or will attract only local interest. These can be resolved best at the local (i.e., district) level outside the planning process. Other

issues may be handled differently, but only issues that are long term, forest wide, very contentious, or very broad in scope (interested parties beyond local area) need to be addressed in the forest plan.

7. Rather than formal negotiations or mediation processes, various forms of consensus group meetings designed to address specific issues were scheduled.

8. Susan Haywood (1988), policy analyst with the Washington, D.C., office of the Forest Service, stated that for several forests in the southeastern region, the process was the opposite: the early input was preservation oriented, and the commodity interests frequently entered the process only in the appeal stage. The outcome was similar, however, in that the Forest Service only reacted to the escalation of conflict after the fact, rather than actively soliciting input from all potentially interested parties and using that input during the development of the planning alternatives and the draft plan.

REFERENCES

Armour, A. (1986). Issue management in resource planning. In R. Lang (Ed.), *Integrated approaches to resource planning and management* (pp. 51–65). Calgary: University of Calgary Press.

Cobb, R. W., & Elder, C. D. (1983). *Participation in American politics: The dynamics of agenda-building.* Baltimore: Johns Hopkins University Press.

Freudenberg, W. R. (1987, August). *Sociological training for soil conservation.* Paper presented at the Rural Sociological Society Presymposium, Madison, WI.

Haywood, Susan. (1988, August). Telephone conversation with author.

Hendee, J. C., Clark, R. N., & Stankey, G. H. (1974). A framework for agency use of public input in resource decision making. *Journal of Soil and Water Conservation, 29* (2), 60–66.

Iverson, D. C. (1983). *Refining the decision space: Incorporating issues, concerns, and opportunities.* Ogden, UT: U.S. Department of Agriculture, Forest Service Region 4.

Jameson, D. A., Moore, M.A.D., & Case, P. J. (1982). *Principles of land and resource management planning.* Washington, DC: U.S. Department of Agriculture, Forest Service, Land and Resource Management Planning.

Lee, R. G. (1983). *Development of methods for using public participation as a data collection instrument for social impact assessment.* Seattle: University of Washington, College of Forest Resources.

Wilkinson, C. F., & Anderson, H. M. (1985). Land and resource planning in the national forests. *Oregon Law Review, 64* (1 and 2), 1–373.

Part V

Organizing Federal Outdoor Recreation Policies

14.

THE CHANGING FEDERAL ROLE IN THE PROVISION OF OUTDOOR RECREATION OPPORTUNITIES: A PERSPECTIVE FROM THE U.S. ARMY CORPS OF ENGINEERS

William J. Hansen

The U.S. Army Corps of Engineers is one of the nation's largest suppliers of outdoor recreation opportunities. Although known primarily for the recreation opportunities provided at multipurpose reservoir projects it constructs and manages, the corps is also involved in the planning, design, and construction of recreation developments at a wide variety of nonreservoir projects. Over 500 million recreation days[1] were reported at over 462 lake projects managed by the corps during 1986. Estimates of the additional amounts of use that occurred on the nonreservoir projects in which the corps participated in planning, design, and construction are unknown.

The corps has been officially involved in the provision of outdoor recreation opportunities for less than one quarter of its over 200-year history. During this period the corps' role as a recreation provider expanded from the simple accommodation of public use on project lands to the provision of highly developed recreation areas. In addition, its stewardship of resource responsibility expanded from a general laissez-faire posture to conscious and deliberate management of existing and potential project resources. Throughout this period, state and local governments, quasi-public, and private organizations have also played an important, but ever changing role in the provision of recreation opportunities at corps water resource development projects.

Many individuals unfamiliar with the corps often wonder how a military organization became involved in providing public recreation opportunities, or why the corps is sometimes limited in the types of recreation developments it can provide. The purpose of this chapter is to provide some insight into these issues by discussing the historical involvement of the corps in providing outdoor recreation opportunities at new water resource development projects. Significant changes in the legislative and administrative environment under which the corps has planned and developed recreation facilities are discussed. Factors influencing this political environment, such as increasing demand for recreation opportunities, public awareness of limitations on natural resources, and the nation's economic viability are identified. Also discussed are the changing information needs from social, behavioral, and natural sciences that occurred during these periods.

EVOLUTION OF CORPS INVOLVEMENT IN RECREATION

Early History

The corps was indirectly involved in recreation as far back as the 1870s, when it took part in the exploration, development, and maintenance of Yellowstone National Park (Verburg, 1975). Its first legislative involvement came with the Fletcher Act in 1932. This act broadened the scope of the federal interest in navigation to include as commerce the use of waterways by "seasonal passenger craft, motor boats, yachts, houseboats, fishing boats, motor boats, and other similar water craft, whether or not operated for hire" (47 Stat. 42, 33 U.S.C. 541). Although this act acknowledged recreation as a user of navigational facilities, it did not involve the corps in the provision of park-related recreation opportunities.

New Deal Era

The period from 1933 to 1943 has been described by Holmes (1972) as the New Deal era in water resource planning. An important initial consideration in New Deal planning was the need for immediate action in the form of public works projects to stimulate construction industries and provide jobs for the unemployed (Holmes, 1972). This was a period of severe unemployment, and public works projects were considered a means of creating jobs. As a result of severe floods in 1927 and the spring of 1936, Congress recognized the need for increased federal flood control assistance to include larger structures, such as dams and reservoirs. The Flood Control Act of 1936 addressed both of these national problems.

The Flood Control Act of 1936 authorized $320 million for the construction of 250 projects and a number of investigations and surveys. Section One of the act declared flood control to be a proper federal activity, and one in which the federal government should participate, "If the benefits to whomsoever they may accrue are in excess of the estimated costs, and if the lives and social security of people are otherwise adversely affected" (49 Stat. 1570, 33 U.S.C. 701a). Section Three further stipulated what became known as the "a-b-c" requirements of local cooperation for projects authorized therein, that is: (a) provide without cost to the United States all lands, easements, and rights-of-way required for project construction; (b) hold and save the United States free from damages due to the construction works; and (c) maintain and operate all the works after completion in accordance with regulations prescribed by the secretary of the army.

The Flood Control Act of 1936 was important in several ways. First, by declaring flood control to be a proper federal activity, it led to corps participation in a wide variety of water resource development projects with significant recreational development capabilities. The stipulation that the federal government should participate "if the benefits . . . are in excess of the estimated costs" established an evaluation standard that was subsequently applied to the incremental costs of recreation developments. Finally, the requirements for local operation delineated joint federal and local responsibilities that were also subsequently extended to provide for recreation developments. Although there have been changes through the years to the particulars of the a-b-c requirements, the joint federal and local cooperation continues to be an important integral part in the corps' participation in the provision of outdoor recreation opportunities.

Initial Authorization for Recreation

Following the enactment of the Flood Control Act of 1936, the corps became involved in the construction of dams for flood control purposes. The lakes created behind these dams proved immediately attractive for fishing and other recreational uses. Project lands were also leased to local governments on a short-term basis. In 1944, the state of Ohio, generated interest in long-term leases. The state wanted the long-term leases at two corps projects for recreation and wildlife management purposes. At that time, however, the corps did not have the authority to assist and sustain public outdoor recreation and was not prepared to enter long-term leasing arrangements (Lawyer, 1970). Congress eliminated these barriers with the first sentence of section four of the Flood Control Act of 1944, which authorized the chief of engineers to "construct, maintain, and operate public park and recreational facilities in reservoir areas . . . and to permit the construction, maintenance, and operation of such facilities . . . " (58 Stat. 889. 16 U.S.C. 460-b).

The 1944 act granted rather broad authority for the provision of recreation areas. Not only could the corps provide recreation developments, but leases could be granted to other federal or nonfederal government bodies, nonprofit organizations, or commercial enterprises for developing and maintaining such areas. Preference was to be given to local, state, and other federal governmental agencies, with monetary considerations waived when considered in the public interest. Any revenue received from leases was to be deposited in the United States Treasury as miscellaneous receipts (Verburg, 1975). The act also stipulated that the water areas of all reservoirs were to be open to public use generally without charge.

The Flood Control Act of 1946 contained similar provisions to the 1944 act, but it further clarified some issues concerning leases and their priorities. The act stipulated that local, state, or federal government agencies were to be given preference without monetary consideration, and nonprofit organizations were to be given leases at reduced rates. In addition, 75 percent of the lease rentals collected were to be returned to the state in which the reservoir was located (Verberg, 1975).

With the authority of the 1944 and 1946 acts and the pressing public demand for use of its lake areas, the corps faced an immediate need to provide basic facilities for public access, health, and safety. Early recreation planning efforts concentrated on the preparation of master plans, site plans, and facility designs to expedite construction. The primary concern was to provide access and sanitation facilities for health and safety; the behavioral and motivational aspects of recreation planning were not of major concern.

In the years immediately following the 1944 legislation, recreation development was treated as an incidental use of project resources, or in other words, a by-product of the project. Recreation facilities could be provided, but only if a project was justified for other purposes (e.g., flood control or navigation). Recreation developments were, therefore, not subject to the test of economic feasibility (i.e., benefits exceeding costs), nor were they considered in the project formulation process. As such there was little impetus to determine the underlying factors affecting recreation demand and benefits.

Full Project Status

The 1950s and 1960s were periods of tremendous growth in the demand for outdoor recreation opportunities. Study after study cited increases in leisure time, mobility, and income of the American public and their effects on the demand for leisure services. During this period, reported recreation use at corps' lakes increased from 16 million recreation days in 1950, to 109 million in 1960, to 250 million in 1970 (Lawyer, 1970). At the same time that recreation demand was increasing nationwide, the supply of outdoor recreation resources was sharply and visibly decreasing because of water pollution, highway construction, drainage of wetlands, improper uses of pesticides, and many other factors (Foss, 1971).

In response to the public need for additional recreation opportunities, the Flood Control Act of 1962, once again, importantly amended section four of the 1944 act. The words "at reservoir areas" were replaced by "at water resource development projects," broadening the corps' authority to include recreation in all types of water resources projects, not just reservoirs. Adoption of Senate Document 97, also in 1962, made recreation status equivalent to other project purposes in the determination of project benefits and provided a basis for estimating recreation values. This status was enacted into law in 1965 with the passage of the Federal Water Project Recreation Act (79 Stat. 213, 16 U.S.C. 460–1–12).

The 1965 act was important, not only for authorizing recreation as a project purpose, but also for further delineating the federal and nonfederal role in providing recreation opportunities. The act stipulated that recreational use of a project will be coordinated with other existing and planned federal, state, or local recreational developments. Nonfederal bodies were encouraged to operate and maintain the project's recreational and fish and wildlife enhancement facilities. The act further stipulated that such facilities will only be provided (and recreation and fish and wildlife benefits included in project benefits) if nonfederal bodies agreed, in writing, to administer the facilities at their expense and to pay one-half of the initial cost of the recreation facilities. If nonfederal bodies did not agree, facilities for recreation and fish and wildlife could not be provided, except those justified to serve other purposes or as needed for public health and safety.

The act contained additional provisions concerning types of projects affected, fee collection by nonfederal interests, methods for repayment of project costs, and options for purchasing land to preserve the recreation potential in the event that nonfederal bodies did not agree to provide the necessary cost sharing required by the act.

The implications of the 1965 act were widespread. Recreation and fish and wildlife were given a new status in the calculation of economic benefits and costs that was comparable to other project purposes. In addition, the joint federal and nonfederal role in providing recreation benefits was reaffirmed. The movement to absolve the federal government from a large portion of the financial responsibility, and especially the long-term commitment to operation and maintenance, was somewhat of a turnaround from the initial authorization of recreation in the 1944 act, but it was more consistent with the a-b-c of local participation contained in the original Flood Control Act of 1936.

Within the corps' organizational structure, recreation resources planning was now established as an integral part of multiple-purpose project planning. This meant that the full complement of planning concerns for determining demand, need, and supply, projecting use, and estimating economic costs and benefits was applicable. The need to advance the state of the art of recreation resources planning and develop an in-house capability was also apparent. District engineers responded by expanding their staffs to include landscape architects, biologists, architects, recreation resource planners, and foresters. In most districts, a recreation section was established within the existing planning branch.

Early efforts for projecting outdoor recreation demand, determining project use, and estimating benefits were highly judgmental and depended heavily upon information provided by the National Park Service Bureau of Outdoor Recreation. Projections for fishing and hunting use were provided by the U.S. Fish and Wildlife Service. These early visitation estimates proved later to be grossly understated (U.S. Army Corps of Engineers, 1978).

During this period, the corps acknowledged the need for improved information on visitors and visitor behavior for planning and managing its recreation resources. In 1965 the corps director of civil works authorized studies to be undertaken to develop theoretical models and methodologies to direct the corps' water-related outdoor recreation planning. There were four specific objectives: (1) to evaluate the recreation-use data collection procedures within the corps, (2) to develop methodology to predict recreation use of proposed lake projects, (3) to develop methodology to determine the number and type of recreation facilities needed to serve a given number of recreation days of use, and (4) to develop methodology to determine recreation benefits (Crane, Brown, & Kinsky, 1974). Thus, the corps initiated research efforts to support its recreation planning and management functions that continue today.

Increased Concern for Conservation

An increased awareness of the environment and conservation issues was observed in the nation during the 1960s and 1970s. Most notably, the National Environmental Policy Act (NEPA) of 1969 declared a national policy "to use all practicable means and measures . . . to create and maintain conditions under which man and nature can exist in productive harmony and fulfill the social, economic, and other requirements of present and future generations of Americans" (83 Stat. 852, 42 U.S.C. 4331).

Partially in response to NEPA, the corps, once again, broadened the types of social, biological, and economic issues that it addressed in the planning and management of its water resource development projects. The previous recreation sections were renamed environmental planning sections, and staffs were supplemented with increased expertise, especially in the biological and social sciences.

Also during this period, new multi-objective planning procedures were developed by the Water Resources Council (WRC) to guide the formulation and evaluation studies of the major federal water resources development agencies (WRC, 1983). These guidelines, initially referred to as the "Principles and Standards" and subsequently as the "Principles and Guidelines," established four accounts to facilitate the evaluation and display of the effects of alternative water resources development plans. The national economic development account displays changes in the economic value of the national output of goods and services and is required. Other information that is required by law or that will have a material bearing on the decision-making process should be included in the other accounts. The environmental quality account displays nonmonetary effects on significant natural and cultural resources. The regional economic development account registers changes in the distribution of regional economic activity that result from each alternative plan. The social effects account registers plan effects from perspectives that are relevant to the planning process but are not reflected in the other three accounts.

Although neither NEPA nor the WRC's "Principles and Guidelines" affected the types of recreational opportunities the corps could provide, they did affect the information required in their planning studies, especially in terms of the value of recreation to the social well-being of the American public.

Current Legislative and Administrative Policies

During the 1980s, domestic concerns have included inflation, deficit spending, and the roles of the federal and state governments in providing public services. Under Ronald Reagan's administration, there was a continued effort to reduce the role of the federal government in the economic and political life of the nation. This effort included reducing federal expenditures, as well as increasing the role of the states (and in some instances the private sector) in providing public services. With respect to the corps, this effort is reflected in the Omnibus, Water Resources Development Act of 1986 (WRDA) (PL99–662).

WRDA was the first major water project legislation passed in sixteen years and was, therefore, very important for revitalizing the corps' civil works program. An important component of WRDA is guidelines for, and congressional agreement to, an expansion of cost sharing required by nonfederal project sponsors for many of the water resource development outputs. In addition, WRDA requires nonfederal sponsors to pay for one-half of the cost of feasibility studies. Thus, nonfederal sponsors will not only be participating to a larger degree in the construction and maintenance of water resource development projects, but they will also be sharing in the cost of planning for these projects.

With the increased cost-sharing requirements of WRDA, nonfederal sponsors will be even more concerned about the impacts of projects on their constituents. Although national economic development will continue to be an important decision criterion, greater importance will likely be placed on delineating the incidence of project benefits (including negative benefits) and their impacts on local and regional economies. There will be a greater need for understanding the impacts of recreation-related expenditures on such factors as local and regional tax receipts, sales, and employment.

Increased nonfederal cost sharing is one approach to decreasing the federal role in the provision of water resource developments. Another, which may have an even greater impact on the corps' provision of future outdoor recreation opportunities at new water resource developments, is to limit the purposes that are considered to be appropriate for federal involvement.

One policy initiative of the Reagan administration was to reduce federal competition with private and nonfederal public sectors in providing recreation opportunities. This is reflected in the corps' present policy for planning new water resource development projects. This policy is that federal funds should only be used to support the development of recreational facilities when the recreation benefits are less than 50 percent of the total benefits and are produced jointly with other project benefits (i.e., recreation costs are not separable), or result from the development of recreation potential created by projects formulated and justified for other purposes. This means that future projects that depend on separable recreation benefits to be economically justified or for which recreation benefits are greater than 50 percent of the total benefits should not be part of the corps' civil works program.

Partially because of limited federal funds, recreation is once again considered a by-product of the other water resource development outputs. Separable recreation facilities can still be included in a new project if economically justified and a local interest is willing to provide the necessary cost sharing. The separable recreation benefits from such facilities are not, however, to be used to justify a project that is not economically feasible without the recreation features. There will be less participation by the corps in the provision of recreation opportunities at new water resource development projects under these conditions.

SUMMARY

The role of the U.S. Army Corps of Engineers in providing recreational opportunities is directed by legislative action and administrative policy, which in turn reflect the changing problems and needs of the nation. The corps' initial involvement in recreation resulted when the public works projects it built to provide needed flood protection and jobs also created lakes with substantial recreation potential. As the public began using these lakes, the corps was authorized to develop, or have developed by others, the facilities necessary to support this use. When the nation's economy improved and there was a tremendous increase in the demand for outdoor recreation opportunities, the corps' role in providing these opportunities was also expanded; recreation was authorized as a project purpose and allowed to be included in all water resource development projects. Economic evaluation and cost-sharing requirements became formalized. Following the dramatic increase in demand for recreation opportunities came a greater concern for conservation and an awareness of the limitations of our natural resources; the corps' planning and evaluation procedures were expanded to provide for greater consideration of environmental and social impacts in the development of recreation, as well as other project outputs. Today, the concern is with budget deficits and the role of the federal government in providing additional recreation opportunities at new water resource development projects. The corps will, however, continue to manage those recreation opportunities under its purview efficiently and effectively.

NOTE

1. A recreation day is defined in Supplement No. 1 to Senate Document 97 as a visit by one individual to a recreation development or area for recreation purposes during any reasonable portion or all of a twenty-four period.

REFERENCES

Crane, D. M., Brown, R. E., & Kinsky, A. M. (1974). *Plan formulation and evaluation studies—recreation, volume I. Evaluation of recreation use survey procedures.* Fort Belvoir, VA: U.S. Army Engineer, Institute for Water Resources.

Foss, P. O. (1971). *Conservation in the United States, "a documentary history, recreation."* New York: Chelsea House Publishers.

Holmes, B. H. (1972). *A history of federal water resources programs, 1800–1960.* Washington, DC: Department of Agriculture, Economic Research Service.

Lawyer, D. E. (1970). Recreation boom. *Water Spectrum, 1970* (Summer), 5–12.

Outdoor Recreation Resources Review Commission (1962a). *Federal agencies and outdoor recreation, ORRRC study report 13.* Washington, DC: U.S. Government Printing Office.

Outdoor Recreation Resources Review Commission. (1962b). *Land acquisition for outdoor recreation—Analysis of selected legal problems, ORRRC study report 16.* Washington, DC: U.S. Government Printing Office.

U.S. Army Corps of Engineers. (1978). *Information report on determination of recreation benefits, Corps of Engineers civil works water resources projects.* Unpublished manuscript.

Verburg, E. A. (1975). *The U.S. Army Corps of Engineers Recreation Development Program: A comparative perspective of equity related to policies and program outcomes.* Fort Belvoir, VA: U.S. Army Corps of Engineers, Institute for Water Resources.

Water Resources Council [WRC]. (1983). *Economic and environmental principles and guidelines for water and related land resources implementation studies.* Washington, DC: U.S. Government Printing Office.

15.

AGENCY VALUES AND WILDERNESS MANAGEMENT

Craig W. Allin

Wilderness management techniques are far from uniform. Although all formally designated federal wilderness areas are managed under the general terms of one statute, the Wilderness Act of 1964 (P.L. 88–577, 78 Stat. 890), the act lacks specifics and leaves many established distinctions in place. The relative absence of structured and uniform management direction allows wilderness managers and management agencies substantial administrative discretion. This chapter explores how the National Park Service and the U.S. Forest Service have exercised that discretion.

PRINCIPLES OF WILDERNESS MANAGEMENT

In the past decade a new generation of books dealing with public lands and the agencies that manage them has been published, but wilderness has received only modest attention, and wilderness management almost none. Most of the books and journal articles devoted to wilderness politics and policy have focused attention on battles over allocation in preference to issues of management. It is time to change that emphasis.

The Alaska National Interest Lands Conservation Act of 1980 (P.L. 96–487, 94 Stat. 2371) quadrupled the size of the National Wilderness Preservation System and permanently changed the focus of wilderness politics. Today the wilderness system embraces approximately 90 million acres, and the politics of wilderness allocation has nearly run its course. The future survival of wilderness

Table 15.1
Principles of Wilderness Management

Principle 1:	Wilderness is one extreme on the environmental modification spectrum.
Principle 2:	The management of wilderness must be viewed in relationship to the management of adjacent lands.
Principle 3:	Wilderness is a distinct, composite resource with inseparable parts.
Principle 4:	The purpose of wilderness is to produce human values and benefits.
Principle 5:	Wilderness preservation requires management of human use and its impact.
Principle 6:	Wilderness management should be guided by objectives set forth in area management plans.
Principle 7:	Wilderness preservation requires a carrying capacity constraint.
Principle 8:	Wilderness should strive to selectively reduce the physical and social-psychological impacts of use.
Principle 9:	Only minimum regulation necessary to achieve wilderness management objectives should be applied.
Principle 10:	The management of individual areas should be governed by a concept of nondegradation.
Principle 11:	In managing wilderness, wilderness-dependent activities should be favored.

Source: Hendee, Stankey, and Lucas (1978, p. 137).

resources in the United States depends increasingly on decisions regarding management rather than allocation.

If academics have been slow to take up issues of wilderness management, the same cannot be said for major land management agencies. The Wilderness Management Research Work Unit of the Forest Service's Intermountain Forest and Range Experiment Station has produced well over 100 published studies, and the cooperative park studies units, supported by the National Park Service at various universities, have contributed others. Although the bulk of this work has been technical and specific, surveying visitor attitudes or measuring campsite impacts, important policy issues have also been addressed.

The most important single work of this genre is the landmark text, *Wilderness Management,* by John Hendee, George Stankey, and Robert Lucas (1978). Its authors set forth the eleven principles presented in Table 15.1. These principles are significantly more specific than the general management direction provided by statute,[1] but there are important reasons why they cannot be accepted as the final word on wilderness management. First, it is doubtful that the principles are endorsed by all federal wilderness managers. Although a joint forward to *Wilderness Management* by cabinet secretaries Cecil Andrus and Bob Bergland seems to imply a general approval of the contents by the Interior and Agriculture departments, the authors were all associated with the Forest Service's Wilderness Research Unit, and the policy preferences expressed are more accurately viewed as those of the authors and the Wilderness Research Unit than those of land management line officers or the agencies generally. Second, even if the principles were written into law, they are insufficiently specific to provide much direction for the day-to-day decisions wilderness managers must make. They do not eliminate the need for professional judgment.

Wilderness bridge building is a case in point. Both the National Park Service and the Forest Service accept some recreational use of wilderness as appropriate. Each builds and maintains foot and stock trails to facilitate recreational access. Each recognizes some degree of responsibility for visitor safety in the use of such trails. As a result, wilderness managers in each agency are occasionally confronted with the necessity of building a bridge or of replacing one that has deteriorated. The task may be approached in two ways, and strong arguments can be made for each.

The first approach emphasizes native materials and wilderness-appropriate behaviors. A construction crew travels to the site on horseback or on foot and establishes a camp. Armed with hand tools and work animals, the crew digs footings, moves rock, and cuts timber, eventually constructing a relatively crude wilderness bridge from natural materials found in proximity to the site. The bridge itself presents a minimal intrusion in an otherwise largely undeveloped wilderness environment.

This advantage is offset by several disadvantages. The crew's camp, the grazing and trampling by pack and work stock, and the utilization of local materials degrade the wilderness environment. Furthermore, on-site construction, at a distance from civilization, using relatively primitive tools, is a time-consuming and expensive activity. In many wilderness climates, such work can only be undertaken during the summer season when the demand for labor is at its peak and when there is a maximum probability of interaction with wilderness users. Finally, if the resulting bridge is made of wood, its life expectancy, like that of other downed timber left in the forest, is likely to be relatively short.

The second approach emphasizes minimum permanent damage to the natural environment of the surrounding wilderness. A laminated or other high-technology bridge is fabricated in a factory remote from the wilderness. On a sunny day in the off-season a small crew picks up the bridge by helicopter and flies it to its new home in the wilderness. The factory-built bridge is in all probability lighter, cheaper, stronger, and more durable than the site-built alternative. Furthermore, off-site construction and air delivery virtually eliminate the ecological damage associated with extended camping, grazing, trampling, and timber cutting. Valuable labor is conserved and interaction with wilderness users is avoided. On the other hand, the resulting bridge is an intrusion on wilderness and a constant reminder of the overwhelming power of the technological civilization that surrounds and impinges on this remnant of a natural ecosystem.

No one could seriously doubt that this example raises important issues of wilderness management. For a conscientious manager the choice between these two approaches to wilderness bridge building is difficult, and the Hendee, Stankey, and Lucas principles do not provide much guidance. Principles four, five, and eight are compatible with building the bridge by either approach. Principles one, nine, and ten might raise second thoughts about building the bridge at all. None of the eleven principles suggests a clear preference for either method.

And what of the other choices that confront wilderness managers? Cat holes or chemical toilets? No trace camping or reservation-based camping at hardened sites? Laissez-faire in the wilderness or police and patrol cabins? The difficult issues of wilderness management remain matters of professional judgment. Yet there is evidence that park managers and forest managers exercise that judgment differently. Guidance must be coming from somewhere.

EXPLAINING AGENCY BEHAVIOR

The literature concerning agency-specific wilderness management differences is relatively limited. Schoenfeld (1976) characterized Forest Service wilderness management as decentralized, recreation oriented, and underfunded. Park Service wilderness management was described as being influenced by the tension between resource protection and mass recreation. Bury and Fish (1980; Fish & Bury, 1981) studied the management of wilderness recreation, concluding that Park Service managers were more focused on resource protection, more likely to take a regulatory approach to controlling recreational overuse, and more likely to adopt controls in anticipation of resource damage. Forest Service managers were more likely to focus on recreation, defer controls, and adopt strategies that were manipulative, for example, information dispersal, environmental education, and physical alterations, rather than regulatory. More recently Washburne and Cole (1983) surveyed managers in 308 areas that had been or probably would be designated as components of the National Wilderness Preservation System. The results of their study are discussed in some detail below.

The authors of other studies have paid less attention to the nature of interagency differences in wilderness management style and more to possible explanations for agency behavior. Foss (1960), Bernstein (1955), and McConnell (1966) have emphasized the impact of constituency or clientele groups. Gilligan (1960), Culhane (1981), Allin (1982; 1987), Twight (1983), and Foresta (1984) have all sought explanations in bureaucratic self-interest or interagency rivalry. Hendee and Stankey (1973) and Allin (1985) have examined agency values and norms. The central premise of these latter studies is that agency employees have accepted and internalized certain values, attitudes, assumptions, or systems of organization that predispose them toward different wilderness management strategies and practices. The further illumination of these attitudes and values and their possible influence on contemporary wilderness management is the primary purpose of this chapter.

THE CORE VALUES OF MANAGEMENT AGENCIES

The core values of the U.S. Forest Service arose from a marriage of Prussian and progressive ideals. The nineteenth-century German inventors of scientific forestry contributed their commitment to sustained-yield silviculture and philosophic utilitarianism. The doctrine of sustained yield declared that scientists could manage the forests for a perpetual flow of wood products. Philosophic utilitarianism viewed natural resource as worthless except in so far as they could be extracted and processed to meet human needs. To these views, twentieth-century American progressives added an optimistic view of government, science, and progress. With objective science as its guide, progressive government could manage the nation's forest resources, bringing progress and the promise of a prosperous posterity to an industrial sector characterized by profiteering, fraud, and corruption.

The public pronouncements of Gifford Pinchot and other members of the early leadership cadre in the Forest Service reflected the Prussian-progressive origins of the agency's ethos. Pinchot wrote that the goal of forestry was a "sane, strong people, living through the centuries in a land subdued and controlled for the service of the people, its rightful masters" (Pinchot, 1967, p. 27). The same day the national forests were transferred to the Department of Agriculture, Secretary James Wilson—in a letter drafted by Pinchot—explained that "all the resources of forest reserves are for use and this use must be brought about in a thoroughly prompt and businesslike manner." He continued, "Where conflicting interests must be reconciled, the question will be decided from the standpoint of the greatest good for the greatest number in the long run" (Cameron, 1928, pp. 239–240).

From its beginning, the core values of the U.S. Forest Service were utilitarian or anthropocentric rather than ecological or biocentric. And if Congress had decreed that the national forests were created "for the purpose of securing favorable conditions of water flow and to furnish a continuous supply of timber" (Act of June 4, 1897, 30 Stat. 34), there was nothing in the Forest Service's utilitarian tradition to preclude meeting other human needs as those needs were identified and articulated by the public. Thus, Pinchot was anxious to accommodate grazing, and subsequent Forest Service chiefs, Henry S. Graves (1917) and William B. Greeley (1927), were equally able to respond to the emerging demand for national forest recreation. In 1960, when Congress declared that the national forests "shall be administered for outdoor recreation, range, timber, watershed, and wildlife and fish purposes," it merely gave legislative sanction to the course the agency had always pursued (74 Stat. 215; 16 U.S.C. §528).

To this day, the mission interests of the Forest Service are expressed in terms of managing nature's bounty in the public interest.

From its creation in 1916, the core values of the National Park Service differed from those of the Forest Service. Park Service values were partially utilitarian, but they were also ecological and preservationist. In words that echo the principles of landscape architecture more than scientific forestry, the National Park Service Act called upon its creation "to conserve the scenery and the natural and historic objects and the wild life [in the parks], and to provide for the enjoyment of the same in such a manner and by such means as will leave them unimpaired for the enjoyment of future generations" (Act of August 25, 1916, Chapter 408, 39 Stat. 535).

The tension between preservation and use, inherent in the statute, is too well understood to require extended comment here. Less well understood is the degree to which the National Park Service was able to alleviate this tension by the adoption of values that had dominated the lives of the parks' military guardians prior to creation of the National Park Service.

Yellowstone, Yosemite, Sequoia, and General Grant national parks all predate the creation of the National Park Service, and military influence was apparent very early in their history. By 1883, hardly more than a decade after its creation, most of Yellowstone's modest appropriation was earmarked for roads and bridges and spent under the supervision of First Lieutenant Dan Kingman, United States Army, Corps of Engineers. In 1886, in response to a lack of Department of the Interior appropriations for park protection, administration of Yellowstone was handed over to M Troop, First U.S. Cavalry. Five years later, the newly created California parks were also given over to military administration (Hampton, 1971). The presence of both calvary and engineers in the parks resulted in unprecedented protection and unprecedented—though hardly unanticipated—development.

Under military administration important precedents were established for park management: a system of concessions by controlled monopoly, serious efforts to protect wildlife and prevent vandalism, a system of designated campgrounds, efforts to manage the fish population by stocking streams, early attempts at park interpretation and park research, and an ecologically sensitive system of roads and trails (Baldwin, 1976; Haines, 1977, Vol. 2; Hampton, 1971).

When the fledgling National Park Service took over management of the park system, the mutually supportive efforts of the cavalry and engineers provided a model for reconciling preservation and use. Aggressive law enforcement, in the tradition of the cavalry, would assure that visitors followed rules; good engineering would assure maximum visitation with minimum damage to the biophysical resource. In some parks the army provided the new Park Service with personnel as well as precedents. In Wyoming, "members of the Yellowstone Park Detachment who desired to remain in the park were discharged from the army and appointed as rangers in the Park Service" (Hampton, 1971, p. 179).

Seventy years have passed, but there can be little doubt that each agency continues to find continuity and direction in the attitudes and values that influenced its conception and guided its formative early years. Both the National Park Service and the Forest Service have been described as relatively closed and self-aware organizations, and this feature lends credibility to the notion that established norms and values would be effectively perpetuated through time (Everhart, 1983; Kaufman, 1967). Indeed, Paul Culhane (1981) recently concluded,

The Forest Service's . . . guiding principles are still almost identical to those of the progressive conservation movement, of which they are products: Multiple-use and sustained yield policies produce the "greatest good for the greatest number in the long run," and that outcome is best obtained by entrusting public lands to public agencies staffed by professional land managers. (p. 21)

In the case of the National Park Service, William Everhart (1983) asserts, "Even today there are clear reminders of army ways in the tradecraft of the rangers" (p. 18).

AGENCY VALUES AND WILDERNESS

The attitudes and values outlined above predate the National Wilderness Preservation System and the contemporary conception of wilderness as land "where the earth and its community of life are untrammeled by man" (Wilderness Act, 1964, Sec. 2[c]). Nevertheless, these attitudes and values do predispose each agency's response to the task of wilderness management. If this hypothesis is correct, what differences should researchers expect to find between wilderness management practiced by the Forest Service and that practiced by the Park Service?

The essential utilitarianism of the Forest Service is likely to be manifested as an effort to please the clientele. This commitment has placed the service in the unenviable position of having to balance the competing interests of opposing forces in many of its land management decisions, including decisions to recommend wilderness designations. Once designated, however, national forest wilderness is effectively withdrawn from the avaricious attentions of developers, and the service can be expected to reflect the desires of the recreation user.

Consequently, Forest Service wilderness managers should be more inclined than their National Park Service counterparts to take a laissez-faire approach to wilderness management as long as the recreational users are well pleased. Less aggressive management and a greater propensity to avoid or postpone management initiatives until serious problems arise should be anticipated. When problems become apparent, the Forest Service should stress voluntary solutions, like user education, in preference to outright regulation.

By comparison, the inherent tension between preservation and enjoyment and the Park Service's response to that tension through the adoption of army values should predispose its wilderness managers to a more aggressive management style. Park managers should be more inclined to act in anticipation of problems and more inclined to adopt strategies that focus on law enforcement and engineering. Law enforcement strategies would include rationing, party size or length of stay limits, camping and fire prohibitions, designated site camping, mandatory permit programs, and wilderness patrolling. Engineering strategies would include providing user facilities, such as toilets, shelters, fireplaces, and tables, and resource-hardening techniques such as the use of paving or soil cement on trails or nonnative turf grasses in campsites.

TESTING FOR AGENCY DIFFERENCES

A recent study by Randel F. Washburne and David N. Cole (1983) provided the opportunity for a test of hypotheses based on the core values of wilderness management agencies. Washburne and Cole surveyed managers of the 215 national park and national forest wilderness areas that had been formally designated or that had designation legislation pending before Congress in 1980. Complete responses were received from all but five areas. Data for the analysis that follows is drawn from the Washburne and Cole survey.

General Management Style

It is hypothesized that there is a more aggressive and more anticipatory management style within the national park wilderness. The degree to which the agencies have undertaken formal assessment of wilderness carrying capacity and the commitment of agency personnel to the wilderness resource provide possible measures of this general management style.

Carrying Capacity Assessment. Consistent with the hypothesis, the National Park Service has moved more rapidly than the Forest Service in assessing the carrying capacity of its wilderness domain. Carrying capacity limits have been formally established for the entire area in 21 percent of the park wildernesses but in only 9 percent of the forest wildernesses. This agency differential is further supported by an index measuring the degree of progress in completing a carrying capacity assessment. The index value is 37.6 for the Park Service and 26.2 for the Forest Service.[2]

Commitment of Personnel. Wilderness staffing appears to support the hypothesis as well, although it does not do so unambiguously. The Forest Service manages 17.7 million acres with a reported staff of 624. The Park Service manages 19.5 million acres with a staff of 450. The Forest Service has the larger ratio of staff to area, but wilderness management is largely user management. When user levels and the number of trail miles to be patrolled and maintained are considered, it is clear that the more intensive management is to be found in the national parks. An imaginary average backcountry ranger in the national parks is responsible for 16.5 miles of trail and 6,800 recreational visitor days

(RVDs) of use. His or her national forest counterpart is responsible for 34.3 miles of trail and 14,000 RVDs of use.

Law Enforcement Strategies

The Washburne and Cole (1983) data provide numerous measures of regulatory or law enforcement strategies. These strategies are almost always pursued to greater length by the Park Service than by the Forest Service. In some cases the differences are dramatic.

Rationing. Both agencies limit recreational use in some of their wilderness areas, but the National Park Service is much more aggressive in doing so. The Park Service's relatively high propensity to ration is reflected in a rationing index value of 32.5. Thirty-eight percent of park areas ration either all use or all overnight use. The index value of 7.4 for Forest Service areas reflects the fact that only 13 percent of its areas are rationed or even considered for rationing.

Party Size Limits. Contrary to our hypothesis, the relative frequency and restrictiveness of party size limits does not distinguish the two agencies' wilderness management practice. Index values based on party size are nearly identical, 42.7 for the Forest Service and 39.0 for the Park Service.

Length of Stay Limits. Length of stay limits are common in areas administered by both agencies, though it is doubtful that they restrict many users. Their relative frequency is consistent with the hypothesis that the National Park Service is more disposed to regulate. Under Park Service jurisdiction 63.8 percent of the management units impose such limits compared to 47.9 percent of the units under Forest Service management.

Regulation of Camping. The prohibition of camping except in designated sites is the most restrictive camping management strategy for which data is available. Designated site camping is imposed throughout the wilderness in 19.1 percent of national park areas but in only 3.1 percent of national forest areas. An additional 21.3 percent of national park areas require designated site camping in part of the wilderness. The comparable figure for the national forests is 2.5 percent.

In areas that are not entirely restricted to designated site camping, other prohibitions are sometimes promulgated. Typically these involve rules against camping within a specified distance of lakes, streams, trails, or other camps. A camping restrictions index based on six possible prohibitions produces values of 18.9 for the Park Service and 14.8 for the Forest Service.

Regulation of packstock. Few wilderness areas prohibit the use of pack animals, but the practice is common only in the Rocky Mountains and the Pacific Northwest. The degree of restraint imposed on stock users provides another test of the relative propensity to regulate. Table 15.2 depicts, by managing agency, the percentage of areas in which each of nine specific stock restrictions have been adopted. The Park Service adopts seven of the nine restrictions with greater frequency than the Forest Service. Total prohibition excepted, the Park Service

Table 15.2
Percentage of All Areas Adopting Specific Packstock Restrictions by Agency

Packstock Restriction	Park Service	Forest Service
User required to carry feed	57 (90)	22 (19)
Stock prohibited on some trails	46 (73)	18 (18)
Some methods of restraint prohibited	34 (57)	22 (24)
Stock prohibited in camp areas	28 (40)	12 (11)
Use of stock camps required	23 (37)	1 (0)
Permit required for grazing	11 (13)	10 (6)
Stock prohibited near bodies of water	9 (13)	36 (43)
Seasonal prohibitions applied	9 (13)	3 (3)
No restrictions applied	26 (10)	38 (31)
All stock prohibited	0	3

Note: The percentage of areas with regular stock use is indicated in parentheses.

Source: Washburne and Cole (1983). Calculated from Tables 22 and 33.

disproportionately embraces the most restrictive regulations, imposing area and trail closures and requiring the use of designated stock camps. When the discussion is limited to areas where stock use is frequent, the magnitude of the difference between Park Service and Forest Service management practices becomes more apparent.

A composite livestock restriction index yields a value of 23.9 for the Park Service and 14.8 for the Forest Service when all cases are included. When the index is limited to areas with regular stock use the disparity grows. Although the index value for the national forest areas grows to 16.1, the livestock restriction index of 30.7 for national park areas is nearly double that for the forests.

Regulation of Fires. The degree to which recreationists' use of fire is restricted provides dramatic evidence of the Park Service's greater proclivity to regulate. Many wilderness users would be hard pressed to imagine a wilderness experience without a campfire. For campers so inclined, the national parks may be a hostile environment. While the national forest wilderness areas rate a fire restriction index of only 11.8, the index value for national parks is 66.5. Indeed, 45 percent of national park areas prohibit all wood fires. Of the 163 national forest areas surveyed, only the Agua Tibia Wilderness in southern California reported prohibiting all fires.

Mandatory Permits. Permit requirements are another manifestation of an ag-

Table 15.3
Law Enforcement Strategies by Agency[a]

Wilderness Management Strategy	Park Service	Forest Service
Establish carrying capacity	37.6	26.2
Ration all use	43.3	9.8
Specificity of rationing	35.1	7.4
Breadth of mandatory permit requirement	22.7	37.8
Intrusiveness of registration	63.2	45.0
Limit group size	39.0	42.7
Limit length of stay	63.8	47.9
Specific camping prohibitions	17.0	14.7
Designated site camping	28.8	4.3
Recreational fire prohibitions	66.5	11.8
Law enforcement index[b]	41.7	24.8

[a]Agency means are expressed as a percentage of the most restrictive policy alternative.

[b]Index includes but is not limited to the above measures.

Source: Washburne and Cole (1983). Calculated from Tables 31 through 33.

gressive regulatory presence. The Forest Service is less likely to have a permit system, but more likely to require permits of all who enter an area. The National Park Service is more likely to require permits, but frequently only for overnight visits.

In principle the global permitting favored by the Forest Service is more intrusive than the selective permitting typically practiced by the National Park Service. It may not be so in fact. Permit systems in the national forests are more frequently implemented by self-registration at trailheads or wilderness boundaries. This practice is less common in the national parks. Forty-seven percent of the national forest areas where some form of registration is practiced rely exclusively on self-registration. Only 16 percent of national park areas do so.

In eight of the ten law enforcement strategies summarized in Table 15.3 the National Park Service has taken a more aggressive regulatory approach than has the Forest Service. A law enforcement index summarizing all the available measures suggests that the Park Service pursues law enforcement strategies with a frequency and intensity substantially greater than that of the Forest Service.

Table 15.4
Percentage of Areas Utilizing Specific Engineering Strategies by Agency

Wilderness Management Strategy	Park Service	Forest Service
Provide toilet facilities	45	29
Provide shelters	26	11
Provide fireplaces	19	9
Provide tables	15	7
Provide potable water	11	6
Harden trails (use soil cement, paving, or stairways)	11	6
Provide trash cans	2	0
Use non-native turf grass	2	1
Any of the above	57	41
Mean Reliance, 8 strategies	16.2	8.7

Source: Washburne and Cole (1983). Calculated from Table 32.

Engineering Strategies

Although each agency pursues engineering strategies less frequently than law enforcement strategies, the propensity to adopt engineering strategies is unquestionably greater in the Park Service than in the Forest Service. Engineering strategies are of two types, though no clear line can be drawn between them. The first type involves the construction of facilities for the benefit and convenience of wilderness users. Use tends to concentrate around facilities, leaving more remote areas relatively pristine. The second type involves development for the sake of resource protection, sometimes called site hardening. Many engineering strategies, like the provision of toilet facilities, may serve the aims of user concentration and resource protection simultaneously.

The relative reliance of the Park Service and the Forest Service on engineering solutions to resource management problems is summarized in Table 15.4. The pattern is remarkably consistent. On average the National Park Service relies on these engineering strategies at a rate nearly double that of the Forest Service.

Clearly, the pattern of administrative behavior revealed by the Washburne and Cole (1983) data supports the hypothesis that the Park Service is more aggressive in its general wilderness management and more disposed to adopt wilderness management strategies that emphasize law enforcement and engineering.

Nonregulatory, Educational Strategies

Based on the assessment of the Forest Service's core values, less aggressive management in national forest wilderness was anticipated. Decisions should be postponed until resource damage is apparent, and voluntary solutions should be preferred over regulatory ones. Two common management strategies use education to produce voluntary changes in user behavior. First, users or potential users can be taught minimum-impact camping techniques to reduce resource degradation. Second, the timely provision of information can result in visitors' making voluntary changes in travel plans to avoid areas and periods of peak congestion.

In spite of the fact that national forest wilderness areas are less aggressively managed and less well staffed, the Forest Service pursues educational strategies with a vigor that matches that of the Park Service. The Park Service reports efforts to communicate the minimum-impact camping message in 74.5 percent of its wilderness areas. More than 68 percent of national forest areas have similar programs. Educational efforts aimed at the voluntary dispersal of wilderness use are nearly as popular. They have been established in 60.1 percent of national forest and in 51.1 percent of national park wilderness areas.

In conclusion, the Washburne and Cole (1983) data demonstrate clear differences in the relative commitment of the park and forest services to various wilderness management techniques. Furthermore, although the differences demonstrated are consistent with hypotheses generated from an examination of the historical origins and core values of the agencies themselves, these patterns of management behavior are inconsistent with the differential use hypothesis frequently suggested by federal land managers in the field.

The Differential Use Hypothesis

The heart of the differential use argument is this: What differs from one wilderness to another is not philosophy or agency values but rather the nature and severity of management problems. Regardless of the agency that employs them, when wilderness managers confront the same circumstances, they react in generally the same way.

Managers point to two circumstances that they assert distinguish wilderness use in the national parks from that in the national forests and account for the differences in management strategies. National park wilderness users are said to be less experienced and more numerous than their counterparts in the national forests. Because they are less experienced, they both desire and require more regulation, more facilities, and a more active management presence in the wilderness. Several national park wilderness managers have told me: "We get the first-time users; people who want a real wilderness experience go to the national forests." The assertion that national park wilderness is more heavily used also serves to explain a more intrusive and regulatory management style.

Responses to the Washburne and Cole survey (1983) provide little support for the proposition that the national parks attract all the greenhorns. An overwhelming majority of the managers responding—two-thirds in the national parks and 73 percent in the national forests—described the typical experience level of users as average in their particular wilderness area. Typical users were described as beginners in 22 percent of the national forest areas and 24 percent of the national park areas. Experienced users were typical in 5 percent of the national forest areas and 10 percent of the national park areas.

The argument that national park wilderness is more heavily used appears equally destitute of support. In 1978, 8.49 million visitor days were recorded in national forest wilderness compared to only 3.07 million in national park wilderness. Thus, national forests received 73.5 percent of the total visitor use in spite of the fact that national forests account for only 47.6 percent of the acreage.

Even absent support for the propositions that national park wilderness users are less experienced and more numerous than their national forest counterparts, it is still possible that management strategy might be driven more by level of use than by the agency-specific predispositions of federal employees. In order to test the differential use hypothesis more fully, the comparisons between national park and national forest areas detailed above were reevaluated controlling for the level of reported use. Level of use was stated in terms of a congestion index based on recreational visitor days, area, trail miles, and use of pack animals, and the 208 areas for which complete data were available were divided into quartiles based on level of use.

General Management Style. If the differential use hypothesis were correct, the higher levels of use should be associated with greater progress in assessing carrying capacity and setting use limits. This expectation is dramatically confirmed in the case of the Forest Service, but it fails utterly where the Park Service is concerned (Table 15.5). For national forest areas the carrying capacity assessment index triples from 13.3 to 38.9 as one moves from the lowest to highest use quartiles. The positive relationship is consistent over all four quartiles. For the national parks the index ranges from 30.0 to 44.3, but the fluctuations are unrelated to the level of use.

While this data fails to support the alternative hypothesis, it is consistent with the original hypothesis based on the core values of the managing agencies. Managers of national park areas are more aggressive in assessing carrying capacity and setting limits regardless of the use level that prevails. Managers of national forest areas are generally less aggressive, but they do respond when challenged by high levels of use.

Law Enforcement and Engineering Strategies. As Table 15.5 demonstrates, distinguishing between high and low use areas fails to confirm the differential use hypothesis. The law enforcement index describes a pattern similar to that for the carrying capacity assessment described above. Management behavior is positively affected by increasing levels of use in the national forests, but it

Table 15.5
Measures of Management Behavior by Agency and Level of Use

Management Behavior	Park Service				Forest Service			
	1[a]	2	3	4	1	2	3	4
Carrying capacity assessment index	41.2	36.7	44.3	30.0	13.1	23.8	27.1	38.9
Law enforcement strategies index	28.6	25.6	31.5	26.4	10.7	14.0	15.5	20.4
Engineering strategies	14.4	22.2	19.8	16.7	9.8	9.8	6.7	9.3
Number of cases	17	10	9	10	35	42	43	42

Note: Level of use is indicated in quartiles from lowest to highest.

Source: Washburne and Cole (1983). Calculated from Tables 31 through 33.

remains low compared to the levels that prevail in the parks. The much higher levels in national park wilderness areas are unrelated to the amount of use. The index of engineering strategies is consistently higher for areas administered by the National Park Service. The prevalence of these strategies, however, is unrelated to level of use in either the national parks or the national forests. Level of use proves to be a poor predictor of management behavior overall.

CONCLUSION

The data presented here describe two federal agencies engaged in the task of wilderness management. The Forest Service is a reluctant wilderness manager. National forest areas get more wilderness recreational use, and national forest managers report higher levels of resource damage from that use. When levels of use and resource damage become very high, the Forest Service responds with regulation, but it would prefer not to interfere with the freedom and the fun of the user. When contrasted to the Forest Service, the National Park Service is an eager wilderness manager. Its areas receive less use, and its managers report less resource damage, yet it aggressively utilizes a wide variety of law enforcement and engineering strategies to prevent resource degradation.

This pattern of agency differences in wilderness management practices is consistent with hypotheses derived from an examination of the historical origins and core values of the respective agencies. It is inconsistent with the hypothesis that wilderness management decisions are driven by levels of wilderness use.

NOTES

1. The Wilderness Act of 1964 merely declares that wilderness areas "shall be administered for the use and enjoyment of the American people in such a manner as will leave them unimpaired for future use and enjoyment as wilderness, and so as to provide for the protection of these areas, [and] the preservation of their wilderness character" (Sec. 2[a]).

2. Each index attempts to measure the degree (in percent) to which an agency approaches total commitment to the most aggressive or restrictive policy alternative. The range of possible values is from zero to 100. Zero represents no regulation whatsoever. A score of 100, if it were ever achieved, would indicate every area included had adopted the most aggressive or restrictive policy alternative. Detailed descriptions are available from the author.

REFERENCES

Allin, C. W. (1982). *Politics of wilderness preservation*. Westport, CT: Greenwood Press.

Allin, C. W. (1985). Hidden agendas in wilderness management. *Parks and Recreation, 20*, 62–65.

Allin, C. W. (1987). Wilderness preservation as a bureaucratic tool. In Phillip O. Foss (Ed.), *Federal lands policy* (pp. 127–138). Westport, CT: Greenwood Press.

Baldwin, K. H. (1976). *Enchanted enclosure: The army engineers and Yellowstone National Park*. Washington, DC: United States Army, Office of the Chief of Engineers, Historical Division.

Bernstein, M. H. (1955). *Regulating business by independent commission*. Princeton, NJ: Princeton University Press.

Bury, R. L., & Fish, C. B. (1980). Controlling wilderness recreation: What managers think and do. *Journal of Soil and Water Conservation, 35*, 90–93.

Cameron, J. (1928). *The development of governmental forest control in the U.S.* Baltimore: Johns Hopkins Press.

Culhane, P. J. (1981). *Public lands politics*. Baltimore: Johns Hopkins University Press.

Everhart, W. C. (1983). *The National Park Service*. Boulder, CO: Westview Press.

Fish, C. B., & Bury, R. L. (1981). Wilderness visitor management: Diversity and agency politics. *Journal of Forestry, 79*, 608–612.

Foresta, R. A. (1984). *America's national parks and their keepers*. Baltimore: Johns Hopkins University Press.

Foss, P. O. (1960). *Politics and grass: The administration of grazing on the public domain*. Seattle: University of Washington Press.

Gilligan, J. P. (1960). *The development of policy and administration of Forest Service primitive and wilderness areas in the United States*. Doctoral dissertation, University of Michigan.

Graves, H. H. (1917). Recreational uses of the national forests. *American Forestry, 23*, 133–138.

Greeley, W. B. (1927). What shall we do with our mountains? *Sunset Magazine, 59*, 14–15.

Haines, A. L. (1977). *The Yellowstone story* (Vols. 1 and 2). Yellowstone National Park, WY: Yellowstone Library and Museum Association.

Hampton, H. D. (1971). *How the U.S. Cavalry saved our national parks*. Bloomington: Indiana University Press.

Hendee, J. C., & Stankey, G. H. (1973, September). Biocentricity in wilderness management. *BioScience, 23*, 535–538.

Hendee, J. C., Stankey, G. H., & Lucas, R. C. (1978). *Wilderness management* (Miscellaneous Publication No. 1365). Washington, DC: U.S. Department of Agriculture, Forest Service.

Kaufman, H. (1967). *The forest ranger: A study in administrative behavior*. Baltimore: Johns Hopkins University Press.

McConnell, G. (1966). *Private power and American democracy*. New York: Alfred A. Knopf.

Pinchot, G. (1910). *The fight for conservation*. Seattle: University of Washington Press.

Schoenfeld, C. (1976). Managing wildlife in forest wilderness. *American Forests, 82*, 38, 54–56.

Twight, B. W. (1983). *Organizational values and political power: The Forest Service versus the Olympic National Park*. University Park: Pennsylvania State University.

Washburne, R. F., & Cole, D. N. (1983). *Problems and practices in wilderness management: A survey of managers* (Res. Pap. INT–304). Washington, DC: U.S. Forest Service.

16.

FORESTRY AND OUTDOOR RECREATION POLICY: THE ORIGINS AND IMPACTS OF PROFESSIONAL CORE VALUES

J. Douglas Wellman

Foresters have pivotal roles in America's outdoor recreation service system. The National Forest System, comprised of 191 million acres of land distributed throughout the country, annually hosts the largest number of recreation visitors among the federal agencies. In 1985, for example, 228 million recreation visitor days were recorded in the national forests. By comparison, in that same year the National Park System—which many view as the leading federal recreation agency—received only 108 million visitor days of recreation use. Foresters' influence on outdoor recreation, however, extends far beyond the National Forest System. Individuals trained in forestry occupy important positions in other federal agencies that provide outdoor recreation, including the National Park Service, the Bureau of Land Management, the U.S. Army Corps of Engineers, the Bureau of Reclamation, the Tennessee Valley Authority, and the Fish and Wildlife Service. In addition, foresters manage 27 million acres of state forests and the 40 million acres of industrial forests open to public recreation (Knudson, 1984). Finally, extension foresters work with nonindustrial private forest landowners who together control nearly 300 million acres of land, much of which accommodates or could serve outdoor recreationists (Dana & Fairfax, 1980).

In few areas of domestic national concern has a federal agency played such a pivotal role in setting the tone for policy as the U.S. Forest Service has in forestry. Within the domain of forestry, issues relating to outdoor recreation have focused largely on the Forest Service. Therefore, this chapter concentrates on that agency, its history, and contemporary trends.

Legislative policy directives are often quite general, allowing wide latitude in managerial action. This certainly applies to public forest land management in the United States in general, and to the U.S. Forest Service in particular. Over twenty-five years ago, Charles Reich (1962) argued that the guiding policy of the Forest Service, the Multiple Use-Sustained Yield Act of 1960, was so broad and management under it involved so many values issues that it represented the transfer of legislative authority to the agency. In the years since Reich's analysis, legislation has constrained the service's autonomy somewhat, but the essential point still holds. Hundreds of thousands of managerial decisions bearing directly or indirectly on the outdoor recreation service system must and will be made by thousands of foresters. In the aggregate, these decisions will do much to shape the future of outdoor recreation in America. In effect, as W. H. Lambright stated, "public administration is public policy making" (Jenkins, 1978, p. 146).

Since management is as much an art as a science, professional forestry's core values may be expected to influence outdoor recreation management and, thereby, policy. Professional foresters have been deeply involved in the development of outdoor recreation policy. As our nation evolved from the early industrial period about the time of the Civil War to the postindustrial society of the 1980s, public demands on the forests changed. Professional forestry, grounded in utilitarianism, has found it difficult to accommodate rising demands for outdoor recreation and other amenity uses of the forests. A story from American forestry's distant past illustrates how professional core values can lead to problems when nonutilitarian interests in the forest are ascendent.

THE ADIRONDACK FORESTRY DEMONSTRATION
PROJECT

In 1898, following decades of rising alarm about the reckless exploitation of our forests, America's first professional forester set out to demonstrate the viability and value of scientific forestry (Thompson, 1963). The site of the demonstration was 30,000 acres of the Adirondack Forest Preserve in New York. The project was linked with America's first public forestry school, the New York State College of Forestry at Cornell University. For a variety of reasons, the experiment turned into a debacle for forestry. There was plenty of bad luck involved, but it was compounded by political ineptitude and an unbending adherence to the core values of utilitarian forestry. The forester in charge was Bernhard Fernow. In his many meetings with interested nonforesters, Fernow insisted that scientific forestry "is a technical art, wholly utilitarian, and not, except incidentally, concerned in the esthetic aspects of the woods: It is engaged in utilizing the soil for the production of wood crops, and thereby of the highest revenue obtainable" (Thompson, 1963, p. 18).

Fernow's position was correct in terms of the forestry tenets of the time, but it was out of touch with social and political reality. The experiment was situated in a forest that had been designated to remain "forever wild" by state constitutional amendment after years of abuse by loggers. The core of the political strength behind that policy was supplied by wealthy New Yorkers who had built summer homes in the area precisely because of the amenity values Fernow discounted. Fernow's insensitivity to their concerns and his professional rectitude in the face of their ignorance about scientific forestry turned adversity into disaster and led to the closing of the experiment, the dissolution of the Cornell School of Forestry, and a lasting distrust of foresters.

Fernow was a brilliant, energetic, purposeful man, in many ways an ideal public servant, unselfishly dedicated to advancing human welfare. Unfortunately, he failed to recognize the necessity of understanding the social context in which he was practicing his technical art. An important number of people who made up that social context were more concerned with the amenity values that could be derived from preserving nature than with the economic values that could be obtained from its use.

FORESTRY'S CORE VALUES

Foresters have always had difficulty with preservationists. By way of illustrating the philosophical chasm that separates them, consider the beliefs of John Muir, founder of the Sierra Club and archetypal preservationist, and Gifford Pinchot, founder of the Society of American Foresters and archetypal utilitarian forester. Muir believed that mankind was no more than a fellow traveler with the rest of creation, one certainly not intended to exercise dominion over the other passengers. Recovering from malaria while on a thousand-mile walk from Indiana to the Gulf of Mexico, Muir wrote:

The world we are told was made for man, a presumption that is totally unsupported by the facts. There is a very numerous class of men who are cast into painful fits of astonishment whenever they find anything, living or dead, in all God's universe, which they cannot eat or render in some way what they call useful to themselves. (Fox, 1981, p. 52)

In striking contrast, Pinchot believed that "the first duty of the human race is to control the earth it lives upon" (Pinchot, 1910, p. 42). Pinchot's vision of the proper relationship between mankind and nature was quite different from that of Muir:

The first great fact about conservation is that it stands for development. There has been a fundamental misconception that conservation means nothing but the husbanding of resources for future generations. There could be no more serious mistake. Conservation does mean provision for the future, but it means also and first of all the recognition of the right of the present generation to the fullest necessary use of all the resources of which this country is so abundantly blessed. Conservation demands the welfare of this generation first, and afterward the welfare of the generations to follow. (Pinchot, 1910, p. 42)

Pinchot built American forestry on the foundation developed by a group of intellectuals and civil servants historian Michael Lacey (1979) has called the Washington Seminary. This group of men, whose patriarch was anthropologist and Grand Canyon explorer John Wesley Powell, engaged in twenty-five years of "Spencer-smashing." They opposed English philosopher Herbert Spencer's social Darwinism, which rationalized the laissez-faire capitalism of the time so effectively. Powell and his colleagues sought to respond to the outrageous disparities of wealth and power that were the hallmark of the age. At the same time, they sought to avoid the individual stultification they feared would follow if those disparities, left unchecked, led to a communist revolution. To lead the nation between the Scylla of capitalistic abuse and the Charybdis of socialistic paralysis, the members of the Washington Seminary advocated an active government, working on behalf of the common citizen. Their chosen vehicle for restoring the common wealth they felt had been stolen from the public was state-regulated hydroelectric power development. The proceeds from this unending source of wealth would be used to support two national scientific centers in Washington, one to spearhead work on the earth and the other to lead initiatives concerned with people. These two great bureaus would be staffed by civil servants trained, at public expense, at a newly created national university that would recruit bright individuals from all levels of society. This public service would act as a powerful counterbalance to concentrated private-sector wealth, bringing science-based technical skill to bear on efficient resource use for the sustained benefit of all.

As it turned out, the dream of the Washington Seminary was most nearly realized not on the nation's rivers, but on its forests, since they had been reserved from disposal into private ownership. Gifford Pinchot brought the legacy of the Washington Seminary to American professional forestry. When Fernow began his odyssey in the Adirondacks, Pinchot replaced him in Washington as head of the Division of Forestry in the U.S. Department of Agriculture. After seven years of incessant effort, Pinchot gained control of the forest reserves, which at that time consisted of 33 million acres of mountainous land in the West, and the U.S. Forest Service as we know it today was born.

Pinchot was not motivated simply by empire building, but by a vision in which scientific forestry helped sustain democracy:

The imagination is staggered by the magnitude of the prize for which we work. If we succeed, there will exist upon the continent a sane, strong people, living through the centuries in a land subdued and controlled for the service of the people, its rightful masters, owned by the many and not by the few. If we fail, great interests, increasing their control of our natural resources, will thereby control the country more and more, and the rights of the people will fade into the privileges of concentrated wealth. (Pinchot, 1910, p. 27)

In particular, the national forests were to provide materials for the homebuilder. In Pinchot's words, "the nation that leads the world will be a nation of homes"

(p. 27). Like Thomas Jefferson's idealized yeoman farmers, Pinchot's home-owners had a stake in the country that would lead them to support and defend democracy:

The most valuable citizen of this or any other country is the man who owns the land from which he makes his living. No other man has such a stake in the country. No other man lends such steadiness and stability to our national life. Therefore no other question concerns us more intimately than the question of homes; permanent homes for ourselves, our children, and our Nation—this is a central problem. . . . The old saying, "Whoever heard of a man shouldering his gun to fight for his boarding house?" reflects this great truth, that no man is so ready to defend his country, not only with arms but with his vote and his contribution to public opinion, as the man with the permanent stake in it, as the man who owns the land from which he makes his living. (Pinchot, 1910, p. 21)

The progressive conservation core values Pinchot instituted in the Forest Service were supported and sustained by the professional organization he founded, the Society of American Foresters, and by professional education. Pinchot's family endowed the Yale School of Forestry to supply "American foresters trained by Americans for the work ahead in American forests" (Dana & Fairfax, 1980, p. 85). Under Pinchot, then, progressive and utilitarian core values were institutionally embedded in American forestry. The leading governmental agency, professional society, and educational institutions all reinforced the notion that expert foresters could apply their technical skills to produce economic benefits essential to the sustenance of American democracy (Clary, 1986; Hays, 1959). These interlocking institutional forces, combined with an elaborate bureaucratic control system, helped the far-flung Forest Service maintain a remarkable degree of uniformity in the actions and attitudes of its employees (Kaufman, 1960).

FORESTRY'S RESPONSE TO CHANGING AMERICAN ATTITUDES

American interest in nature preservation has blossomed as our seemingly inexhaustible legacy of wild lands has been brought under human control (Nash, 1973). Our urban culture has taught us to see worth in places once considered worthless (Hammond, 1977; Runte, 1979), while our economic system has provided the wealth, free time, and mobility to reach them in ever-increasing numbers (Clawson & Knetsch, 1966). One of the dominant themes in outdoor recreation in recent years is that Americans are "loving our parks to death."

Foresters have struggled against the desire, born of these changes, to allocate forest lands to economically nonproductive uses (Clary, 1986). In the years between 1902 and 1960, for example, 5 million acres of the National Forest system were transferred from the use-oriented Forest Service to the preservation-oriented National Park Service (Dana & Fairfax, 1980, p. 209). One of the major reasons for these transfers was that the foresters were unwilling to deviate from their mission of using natural resources to produce tangible, economic benefits (Twight, 1983).

Even more problematic for forestry than interest in parks has been interest in wilderness. In 1921, Aldo Leopold, then assistant supervisor of the Gila National Forest in New Mexico, proposed that large roadless areas be reserved from most economic uses and dedicated to wilderness recreation (Leopold, 1921). The Forest Service initially adopted Leopold's proposal in part as a way of staving off Park Service land raids. As interest in wilderness preservation gathered momentum, however, Forest Service efforts to respond administratively, while retaining the option to exploit natural resources when economic conditions were favorable, were seen as inadequate. It was distrust of the Forest Service to a large extent that led to the Wilderness Act of 1964, which designated 9.1 million acres of the National Forest System as wilderness and directed the agency to review other lands with wilderness potential. Through a series of amendments to the this act, by 1982 over 25 million acres of the National Forest System (13.5% of the total) had been set aside from logging and most other economic uses (Allin, 1982). Additional designations are currently being made in state-by-state wilderness acts.

The wilderness allocation process has found foresters in active opposition to a growing coalition of preservation interests. The factors that have governed Forest Service positions on wilderness allocation are of particular interest here. Although the agency has long prided itself on the application of science to land management, its second Roadless Area Review and Evaluation (RARE II) appears to have been influenced more by organizational and political factors than by objective analysis. In his analysis of the correlates of the service's wilderness recommendations in RARE II, Mohai (1987) concludes that the agency's long-standing utilitarianism led it to recommend most areas for nonwilderness. Recommendations favorable to wilderness were largely determined on the basis of public comment. The ten-step rational decision-making process the service designed to guide its review had little influence on wilderness recommendations.

The Forest Service's wilderness review process is but one instance of a larger pattern of beliefs and actions favoring traditional, economic uses of the national forests. Twight and Lyden (1988) examined the attitudes of Forest Service district rangers, the foundation of the agency's decision-making officer corps. The survey was based on forty-six items designed to measure attitudes concerning national forest policy issues and natural resource conservation values. Of the 629 district rangers in the Forest Service, 64 percent responded to the survey, and checks for nonresponse bias were negative. Under its multiple-use policy, the service should represent a variety of constituencies, and, according to the resource dependence theory of organizational behavior, one would expect ranger attitudes to reflect that variety of interests. Statistical analysis of the results, however, indicated a very high level of attitudinal homogeneity among the 400 district rangers in the survey. Twight and Lyden interpret their findings as showing a high degree of institutional coherence and commitment to the traditional core values of professional forestry. Years of challenges by nontraditional constitutional constituencies have apparently only further entrenched long-established beliefs and attitudes.

The U.S. Forest Service is an agency with a strong set of core values, a well-articulated core technology, and a powerful system of recruitment, socialization, and control that gives it great coherence of purpose. Supporting that agency culture are economically important traditional constituencies. Together, these elements have made it a "bureaucratic superstar" (Clarke & McCool, 1985). However, these particular institutional arrangements have lost much of their survival value as noncommodity interests in the National Forest System have emerged since the late 1960s.

EMERGING DIRECTIONS

In summary, American forestry emerged in the late nineteenth and early twentieth centuries, propelled by fear of an impending timber famine (Clary, 1986) and water supply problems. Professional foresters were to apply science-based technical expertise to problems and in solving them contribute to the success of the democratic experiment. The forestry profession was built around a strong federal agency, a supportive educational establishment, and a professional association that established the rules for training and entry into the profession. These institutional arrangements came to be aligned with economically influential constituencies to produce an exceptionally unified profession with limited interest in outdoor recreation and related amenities.

In light of these origins and the recent evidence of institutional inertia reported by Clary, Mohai, and Twight and Lyden, what are the prospects for the thousands of managerial decisions that will constitute much of the future policy making for the forest lands? The most likely prognosis must be for more of the same, with foresters clinging to traditional core values and resisting public demands for greater attention to amenity uses.

Optimists among those favoring the amenity uses, however, may find succor in certain recent events. New developments in forest planning, strategic thinking about the role of outdoor recreation in the National Forest System, and forestry education may be harbingers of a new era in which the multiple uses of the national forests are truly on an equal footing.

The national forest planning process mandated by the Forest and Rangelands Renewable Resources Planning Act of 1974 and the National Forest Management Act of 1976 is leading to changes favorable to amenity uses. Of the 123 national forest plans originally scheduled for completion by September of 1985, 107 were in draft form as of May 1987, and 64 of those were in final draft form (Coppleman, 1987). Most of the final draft plans have been appealed, and the disposition of these appeals may point the way toward a break with past directions on the national forests. For the Jefferson National Forest in Virginia, for example, conservationists and the Forest Service reached a negotiated settlement on the fifty-year plan that reduces the mileage of new forest roads from 400 to 200 miles, limits overall timber harvesting, shifts emphasis away from clearcutting, and improves protection of fish and wildlife habitat. Perhaps more significantly, the appeal and settlement have laid the foundation for a partnership approach to national forest planning and management that is setting a trend for the nation (Loesel, 1987). In January 1988, as required by the settlement, the Jefferson National Forest hosted the first of a series of annual meetings in which the agency will report its progress in implementing the plan to a full range of citizen interests. The meeting was a model of openness, and it was evident that the service was listening—and listening closely—to the public. It was also evident that those individuals and groups who had committed themselves to continuing self-education and involvement would have the greatest impact. Thus, the meeting represented a strong step in the direction of the transactive planning advocated earlier by Friedmann (1973).

A strategic planning process initiated by the chief of the Forest Service also may signal the start of a new era in forestry's relations with outdoor recreation. The goal of the National Recreation Strategy is to find new ways the National Forest System can contribute to meeting America's growing need for open space and outdoor recreation. As part of this effort, in 1986 six commissions were created within the Forest Service to explore new ideas about outdoor recreation visitor needs, management partnerships, settings, services, marketing, and technology. The commissions' findings were reviewed in a symposium in November 1986, and an official statement of intent was published by the Forest Service in 1988 (USDA Forest Service, n.d.). Early signs are that these proposals will represent a substantially improved position for outdoor recreation within the Forest Service.

Finally, changes are afoot in forestry education. The Society of American Foresters in 1986 revised its accreditation standards to deemphasize traditional forest biology and emphasize forest administration and policy. Increasingly, foresters are acknowledging the weaknesses of traditional forestry education in today's climate, with its strong demands for skill in working with people (Allen & Gould, 1986; Magill, 1983). Foresters speaking to other foresters are advocating a shift in emphasis from traditional biology-based technical training to management-oriented education (Duncan, 1986; Wisdom, 1985). Continuing education is changing as well. The Forest Service is encouraging current and prospective managers to pursue education in public administration, planning, and conflict resolution, and it offers two internally designed courses, each forty hours in length, "No Fault Public Administration and Media Relations" and "Interactive Management and Consensus Methodologies."

CONCLUSION

In these and other ways the forestry profession is beginning to move toward a new and more creative role in future wild land recreation management and policy. Forestry has a proud history, with a well-deserved reputation for competence and public service. The public good the profession has always sought to serve, however, is changing. If foresters fail to manage their areas with understanding of American society's evolving desires for outdoor recreation and related amenities, unfavorable public opinion will relieve them of their responsibilities. To the extent that this happens, many public benefits possible under multiple-use forest management will be lost, and the public good will be short-changed. If emerging events are to materialize into real changes within the profession, understanding is needed not only of the forest as a resource and the public demands on it, but also of the institutional framework that governs it.

REFERENCES

Allen, G., & Gould, E. (1986). Complexity, wickedness, and public forests. *Journal of Forestry, 84* (4), 20–23.

Allin, C. W. (1982). *The politics of wilderness preservation.* Westport, CT: Greenwood Press.

Clarke, J. N., & McCool, D. (1985). *Staking out the terrain: power differentials among natural resource management agencies.* Albany: State University of New York Press.

Clary, D. M. (1986). *Timber and the Forest Service.* Lawrence: University of Kansas Press.

Clawson, M., & Knetsch, J. L. (1966). *Economics of outdoor recreation.* Baltimore: Johns Hopkins University Press.

Coppelman, P. D. (1987). Crisis in forest planning. *Public Lands, 5* (2), 1–3.

Dana, S. T., & Fairfax, S. K. (1980). *Forest and range policy* (2nd ed.). New York: McGraw-Hill.

Duncan, D. P. (1986). What forestry is. *Journal of Forestry, 84* (8), 65.

Fox, S. (1981). *John Muir and his legacy.* Boston: Little, Brown.

Friedmann, J. (1973). *Retracking America: A theory of transactive planning.* Garden City, NY: Anchor Press/Doubleday.

Hammond, J. L. (1977). Wilderness and life in cities. *Sierra Club Bulletin, 62* (April), 12–14.

Hays, S. P. (1959). *Conservation and the gospel of efficiency: The progressive conservation movement, 1890–1920.* Cambridge, MA: Harvard University Press.

Jenkins, W. I. (1978). *Policy analysis: A political and organizational perspective.* New York: St. Martin's Press.

Kaufman, H. (1960). *The forest ranger: A study in administrative behavior.* Baltimore: Johns Hopkins University Press.

Knudson, D. M. (1984). *Outdoor recreation* (rev. ed.). New York: Macmillan.

Lacey, M. J. (1979). *The mysteries of earth-making dissolve: A study of Washington's intellectual community and the origins of environmentalism in the late nineteenth century.* Doctoral dissertation, George Washington University.

Leopold, A. (1921). The wilderness and its place in forest recreational policy. *Journal of Forestry, 19* (7), 718–721.

Loesel, J. E. (1987). Conservationists negotiate improvements in a forest plan. *Public Lands, 5* (2), 4–5.

Magill, A. W. (1983). The reluctant public servants. *Journal of Forestry, 81* (3), 201.

Mohai, P. (1987). Rational decision making in the planning process: Some empirical evidence from RARE II. *Environmental Law, 17* (3), 507–556.

Nash, R. (1973). *Wilderness and the American mind* (rev. ed.). New Haven, CT: Yale University Press.

Pinchot, G. (1910). *The fight for conservation.* Seattle: University of Washington Press.

Reich, C. A. (1962). *Bureaucracy and the forest.* Santa Barbara, CA: Center for the Study of Democratic Institutions.

Runte, A. (1979). *National parks: The American experience.* Lincoln: University of Nebraska Press.

Thompson, R. C. (1963). Politics in the Wilderness: New York's Adirondack forest preserve. *Forest History, 6,* 14–23.

Twight, B. W. (1983). *Organizational values and political power: The Forest Service versus the Olympic National Park.* University Park: Pennsylvania State University Press.

Twight, B. W., & Lyden, F. J. (1988). Multiple use vs. organizational commitment. *Forest Science, 34* (2), 474–486.

U.S. Forest Service. (n.d.). *America's great outdoors: The National Recreation Strategy.* Washington, DC: U.S. Department of Agriculture.

Wisdom, H. W. (1985, November). *What should the mix be between technical forestry and the social/managerial sciences: An academic point of view.* Paper presented at the Southern Forestry Symposium, Atlanta, GA.

Part VI

Management Techniques for Outdoor Recreation

17.

GOAL PROGRAMMING APPLICATIONS FOR OUTDOOR RECREATION POLICY

James L. Regens and Jackie Sellers

Recreation is a broad and diverse area of human activity. Public responsibility for providing services in this area has expanded dramatically over time. As a result, reflecting more than a century of national consensus, the United States has allocated a significant proportion of its federal, state, and municipal lands to support outdoor recreational activities. The last twenty years have witnessed rapid growth in demand for access to recreational services as well as expansion in available facilities for such popular uses as hiking, camping, hunting, sport fishing, and skiing, as well as organized team sports. For example, estimated visits to public land recreational areas in the National Park System (NPS) increased by 67 percent from 1964 to 1984, while the number of units increased by 34 percent (U.S. Council on Environmental Quality, 1985, p. 650). Because of such changes, the NPS has been transformed from a system characterized by large, scenic national parks such as Yellowstone and Yosemite in the West into one dominated numerically by sites in or near urban areas primarily east of the Mississippi River.

Moreover, the recreational opportunities available to an individual are limited by economic and social costs. These costs vary considerably among different activities. For many activities, the largest economic cost involves travel, both in terms of time and money. Noneconomic aspects largely involve perceptions of the availability and desirability of various activities. Social and cultural factors may also affect the utilization of outdoor recreational resources.

As a result, the process of formulating and implementing outdoor recreational policy by all levels of government has become increasingly complicated. This tends to increase the difficulty inherent in attempts to allocate specific physical resources for particular recreation activities among competing demands. Several sets of factors help to account for these changes. The first, relatively direct and most easily quantifiable are the input factors. These consist primarily of the financial and physical resources available to support recreational activity. The second set consists of factors more qualitative in nature, such as the relative desire for and valuation by the American public of recreational opportunities (i.e., preferences). These two sets of factors effectively function to establish constraints upon the ability of elected officials and public managers to maintain a recreational system responsive to a diverse set of user communities. Moreover, as the demand, desires, and wishes of the American public for outdoor recreational opportunities have grown—especially since the end of World War II—the environmental and physical resources available for those recreational uses have become increasingly more stressed (U.S. General Accounting Office, 1980). All indicators point to continued growth in total recreational demand. Thus, new approaches to foster more efficient management of existing facilities and more foresight in planning new acquisitions are needed. Goal programming to cope with multiple objectives in outdoor recreational administration holds substantial promise as one such policy analysis technique.

OVERVIEW OF GOAL PROGRAMMING

Regardless of what drives total demand for recreational opportunities, care must be taken by any public planning authority to be aware of the competition among the array of potential recreational uses for the natural and physical resources within its jurisdiction. Once these interrelationships have been estimated, the task confronting a recreation manager is to plan and provide for future interests as well as more short-term needs.

In theory, but not necessarily in practice, such planning and program implementation would be a relatively straightforward and simple task if there were homogeneity in demands and complementary relationships in usages. Decisions about the allocation and management of outdoor recreational resources could be reduced to a single function, a mathematical expression from which preferred solutions could be derived. For example, when decisions are assumed to be single criterion problems, they generally can be expressed as follows:

$$\text{Min (MAX) } \{f(x) = z\}$$
$$\text{S.T. } x \in S,$$

The decision mathematics for this equation, although complicated at times, are quite straightforward. However, very few policy decisions in the real world can be made that adequately conform to those relatively simple assumptions.

Moreover, the typical policy choice confronting outdoor recreational managers often involves the need to reconcile and satisfy two or more rival objectives within the context of a single decision. Thus, when multiple criteria problems must be handled, the problem changes conceptually and analytically. Mathematically, it involves solving a multiplicity of objective functions. As a system of equations, these functions generally take the following form:

$$\text{MAX } \{f_1(\chi) = z_1\}$$
$$\text{MAX } \{f_2(\chi) = z_2\}$$
$$\cdot$$
$$\cdot$$
$$\cdot$$
$$\text{MAX } \{f_k(\chi) = z_k\}$$
$$\text{S. T. } \chi \in S$$

Multiple Objective Analysis (MOA), particularly goal programming, offers an extremely powerful planning tool that assists in selecting from a possible group of outcomes that depend upon the same resource base. Multiple Objective Analysis is based upon the assumption of reliable data about such constraints on policy making as the availability of resources, the legality of proposed or on-going program activities, and good estimates of the different components that make up total model constraints. In the past, it tended to be difficult analytically to handle multiple objective–multiple criteria optimization. With upgraded information and computation processes, however, it now is not only possible to formally evaluate problems with more than one objective but also to make assessment of the affect of alternative courses of action on the attainment of various policy objectives (Steuer, 1986).

In the application of MOA to policy making, the decision maker must interact with most computational processes. This involves actively assisting in the identification of the various trade-offs that will generate a final solution that will be satisfactory under current assumptions. In fact, recognition of and active incorporation of subjective judgment through direct human intervention into the analytical process is one of the major characteristics of multiple-criteria optimization. This attribute is not commonly found in more traditional approaches to mathematical programming (Steuer, 1986, p. 4). This difference is reflected in the mathematics underlying both analytic approaches to decision making.

Solving Multiple Objective Problems

There are several computational algorithms that have been suggested to solve decision-making problems using the multiple-criteria optimization process (Steuer, 1986). How the goal programming (GP) method is applicable to recreational policy choices is demonstrated below. The GP method for MOA permits the policy analyst or resources manager to develop quantitative measures for multiple objectives, making it possible to evaluate varying levels of goal achievement for each of those recreation objectives. This is so because specific measures are constructed for each criterion considered in the decision analysis. This permits the development of a solution to the algorithm that identifies a potentially "satisfying'' option (Charnes & Cooper, 1961; Charnes, Cooper & Ferguson, 1965; Ignizio, 1976; Ijiri, 1965; Lee, 1972; Steuer, 1986).

Goal programming can be distinguished from standard, single objective linear programming by four key attributes. The first involves the conceptualization of objectives as goals. The second feature is the assignment of priorities and/or weights to the achievement of the goals. The third feature is the presence of the deviational variables d_i and d_i to measure overachievement and underachievement from target or goal levels of G_1. The fourth distinctive attribute of goal programming is the minimization of weighted sums of deviational variables to find solutions that best satisfy goals. In essence, GP involves vector maximization to identify the mix of program options that is likely to achieve recreational policy objectives. Two basic computational models, the Archimedean and preemptive, are available for solving goal-programming problems. In order to clarify their utility for recreation policy applications, both are summarized and demonstrated in the most general terms.

Archimedean Model

In the Archimedean model, candidate solutions for recreational policy problems are generated by computing points in the solution space whose criterion vectors are closest, in a weighted L_1- metric sense, to the utopian or ideal set in criterion space. The model for the goal program takes the following mathematical form:

$$\begin{aligned}
&\text{goal } \{c^1x = z_1\} \quad (z_1 \geq T_1) \\
&\text{goal } \{c^2x = z_2\} \quad (z_2 = t_2) \\
&\text{goal } \{c^3x = z_3\} \quad (z_3 \in [t_3^e, t_3^\mu]) \\
&\text{S.T. } x \in S
\end{aligned}$$

This model may be generalized as:

$$\begin{aligned}
\text{Min } &\{w_1^-d_1^- + w_2^+d^2 + w_2^-d_2^- + w_3^-d_3^- + w_3^+d_3^+\} \\
\text{S.T. } &c^1x + d_1^- \qquad\qquad\qquad\qquad \geq G_1 \\
&c^2x \qquad -d_2^+ + d_2^- \qquad\qquad = G_2 \\
&c^3x \qquad\qquad\qquad + d_3^- \qquad \geq G_3 \\
&c^3x \qquad\qquad\qquad\qquad - d_3^+ \leq G_4 \\
&\qquad x \in S \\
&\text{all d's} \geq 0
\end{aligned}$$

Where Ws are all positively weighted in objective function; G_1 = desired
goal levels; d^+ $(-)$ = deviations for desired goals; each goal giving rise
to at least one goal restraint; and only deviational variables associated with
undesirable deviations need to be employed in the formulation.

Archimedean models can be solved using adaptations of conventional linear
programming software. Such modifications have been applied since the early
1970s in studies ranging from examinations of water resources investment decisions (North, Neeley, & Carlton, 1976; Neely, North, & Fortson, 1971; Taylor
& North, 1975) to capital investment analysis (Wacht & Whitford, 1976).

One relevant illustration of this model's application provides an overview of
the model's usefulness to recreational policy analysis (North, Neely, & Carlton,
1976). In 1976, a reevaluation study was done for the then proposed Cross
Florida Barge Canal project. The major objectives of the study were to determine
the highest and best use of the study area, a typical challenge faced by natural
resource managers. That is, most sites under consideration for outdoor recreational activities already are being used for one or more public and/or private
purpose. Such a situation applied in this instance. For example, some elements
of the Cross Florida Barge Canal project already had been developed. Structures
had been built and portions of the canal had been excavated. As a result, the
basic intent of the reevaluation study was to determine if benefits similar to those
expected from completion of the canal could be produced from noncanal alternatives at a lower economic, environmental, and social cost.

The highest and best use application of goal programming focused on two
geographic areas. The first consisted of the free flowing Oklawaha River, its
forested valley, the Ocala National Forest, and adjacent areas. The second area
considered in the study was the region around Lake Rousseau. The intent of the
study was to develop an economic-environmental analysis that would aid decision
makers, including the general public, in reaching informed judgments respecting
the future uses of the Oklawaha River valley and the Lake Rousseau area.

A series of key substantive issues was examined in the study. First, an evaluation of the value of a preserved natural area was made. Second, it was also
necessary to identify and evaluate present and potential future land uses in the
corridor that would be impacted by the canal. The third task involved the enumeration and analysis of viable alternatives for the Oklawaha valley and Lake
Rousseau. Fourth, the study included an evaluation of the demands for recreational development in Florida, especially in the Oklawaha valley. The final task
involved the economic-environmental analysis of the Oklawaha River valley's
potential for development at various levels of intensity (North, Neely, & Carlton,
1976, pp. 6–8).

Basic data for the goal programming model used to generate solutions included
activity days, participation rates, habitat areas, productivity capabilities and
yield, goal statements, goal levels, and goal weights. Goal setting, alternative
outcomes, and preferences were obtained either from stated objectives of the

decision makers or from standard economic indexes. But one of the major problems associated with goal programming applications, the determination of weights to be assigned to deviations from the values in the objective function (i.e., the establishment of trade-offs), needed to be overcome. Goals, weights, and deviations were stated in dollars and estimated values were used where trade-offs had to be made between economic and environmental objectives (North, Neely, & Carlton, 1976).

It is difficult to precisely estimate future values of such variables as river miles, acres of habitat, visitor days, or fishing days. As a consequence, goal weighting is much more of a subjective rather than purely objective exercise. In order to deal with these limitations, probability distribution analysis was used to determine ranges and means for those values (Neely, Sellers, & North, 1980; North et al., 1984; Sellers, Neely, & North, 1981). The triangular distribution was chosen for both the probability analysis of the subjective estimates and to generate means and end points for resources and benefits that are valued at different rates under different conditions.

The Archimedean model yielded solutions that were agreeable to the various parties involved. Moreover, the development of the goal programming model, including data gathering, demonstrated another strength of this type of analysis, that is, a systematic and reasonable comprehensive search for alternative courses of action and desirable outcomes. This case demonstrated a method for integrating two seemingly dichotomous sets of variables, economic variables and environmental variables, into a common decision-making method. The specific programming algorithm used to solve the model was the IBM MPSX adaptation.

Preemptive Model

In the preemptive goal programming model, recreational goals are ranked according to established priorities. The goals with higher priority levels are said to be infinitely more important than goals with lower priority levels. For example, goal level one must be satisfied before goal level two can be considered. This leads to the following general model:

$$\partial \iota \upsilon \ \{P_1 \ (d_1^+) + P_2 \ (d_2^-) + P_3 \ (d_3^- + d_3^-)\}$$

$$\text{S.T.} \ c^1 x - d_1^+ \qquad\qquad \leq G_1$$

$$c^2 x \qquad + d_2^+ \qquad\qquad \geq G_2$$

$$c^3 x \qquad\qquad d_3^+ + d_3^- = G_3$$

$$X \ \epsilon \ S$$

$$\text{all d's} \geq = 0$$

Where P_i = priority level.

The possibility of goal exclusions is the major drawback with the preemptive model. When using the preemptive model to derive a solution, certain lower priority goals may not be considered in evaluating recreation policy options. This outcome potentially can occur because until higher-level goals are achieved, lower-level goals cannot be considered. In fact, the primary problems associated with the preemptive model are those relating to possible goal exclusion because of the requirement that one goal of highest priority must be solved before a lower goal can be considered. Nonetheless, if relatively clear goal hierarchies can be identified or are assumed to exist, the preemptive technique readily illuminates the underlying trade-offs. The usefulness of this procedure has been demonstrated for energy studies (Ruffner, Sieber, & Ahmadi, 1986) as well as in general production (Levin & Kirkpatrick, 1978; Taylor, 1982).

AN APPLICATION OF PREEMPTIVE GOAL PROGRAMMING TO RECREATION POLICY

Evaluating trade-offs that may commonly arise in the context of allocating public lands to either multiple-purpose parks or designated wilderness areas offers an excellent example of the type of problem for which the application of multi-objective analysis is clearly appropriate for outdoor recreational policy making. Conflict about the type and mixture of units to have in a recreation system can occur because of a variety of factors. Diversity in sports enthusiasts' and tourists' preferences for recreational opportunities and valuations of outdoor recreation benefits as well as the impact of use patterns on environmental quality, can affect allocation decisions (Pigram, 1983; Sax, 1978; Schechter & Lucas, 1978). The following example illustrates the use of goal programming to solve a hypothetical planning problem that involves designing a recreational system consisting of some units allocated to wilderness uses and others to multiple use.

The hypothetical outdoor recreational planner needs to assign units to either wilderness status or multi-purpose status since multiple use precludes an area being suitable for wilderness designation. In setting up a GP model to deal with this problem, X_1 symbolizes multi-purpose usage and X_2 symbolizes wilderness area. The desirability function can be set at $8X_1 + 6X_2$. The allocation of individual units to multi-purpose or wilderness use is subject to the constraints that outdoor recreational resources in 1,000 acre blocks equal $4X_1 + 2X_2 \leq 60$ with management and administrative requirements set at $2X_1 + 4X_2 \leq 48$. Finally, the satisfaction level desired is set at \$140. Given this information, a single goal model could be developed. Such a model designed to minimize underachievement of the satisfaction goal would take the following form:

$$\text{Min } Z = D_\mu$$
$$\text{S.T.} = 8X_1 + 6X_2 + D_\mu - DO = \$140.00$$
$$4X_1 + 2X_2 \leq 60 \text{ resource constraint}$$
$$2T + UC \leq 48 \text{ management constraint}$$

Solving the model reveals that $X_1 = 12$, $D_\mu = 8$, and $X_2 = 6$.

Our hypothetical planner, however, might confront the need to satisfy more than a single goal. What if providing general purpose outdoor recreation is of the utmost importance? This objective might be followed in importance by attaining the total satisfaction goal and then by meeting the opportunity for wilderness recreation goal. Note now that the notion of goal priorities has been introduced. This can be incorporated into the GP model by setting the goals and deviations as follows:

	Goal	Priority
1.	Multi-purpose goal of 13 units	P_1
2.	Total satisfaction goal of $135.00	P_2
3.	Wilderness area goal of 5 units	P_3

Where $D_{\mu s}$ = amount satisfaction goal is underachieved, D_{os} = amount satisfaction goal is overachieved, $D_{\mu g}$ = amount multi-purpose use is underachieved, D_{og} = amount multi-purpose use is overachieved, $D_{\mu w}$ = amount wilderness goal is underachieved, and D_{ow} = amount wilderness goal is overachieved.

The objective function then becomes:

$$\text{Min } Z = P_1 D_{\mu s} + P_2 D_{\mu w}$$
$$\begin{aligned}
\text{S.T.} = 8X_1 + 6X_2 + D_{\mu s} - D_{os} &= \$135.00 \text{ satisfaction goal} \\
X_1 \qquad\qquad + D_{\mu g} - D_{og} &= 13 \text{ units for multi-purpose goal} \\
X_2 + D_{\mu w} - D_{ow} &= 5 \text{ units for wilderness goal} \\
4X_1 + 2X_2 &\leq 60 \text{ units for resource requirements} \\
2X_1 + 4X_2 &\leq 48 \text{ units for management requirements}
\end{aligned}$$

This would lead to the tableau expressed in Table 17.1. The selection procedure for entering a variable is to go to P_1 and pick the most negative value of the $C_j - Z_j$ row. To determine the leaving variable, one uses the same procedure as the standard simplex procedure (e.g., select the smallest B_i / Y_{ik}). If during the selection procedure one finds a negative $C_j - Z_j$ value that has a positive $C_j - Z_j$ value in one of the "P" rows underneath it, that value is disregarded. Such a value means that deviation from the more important goal would be increased if that variable is brought into the solution set. The process is continued until all values in the $C_j - Z_j$ rows are positive, except in the case where one of the lower goal values ($C_j - Z_j$) is positive, until a final solution is indicated. That is, the values for $C_j - Z_j$ are positive or at least are equal to zero.

For this particular example, the final tableau would look like Table 17.2. The solution reveals that goal one to provide thirteen units of multi-purpose recreation was achieved. Goal two involving total satisfaction values at $135.00 was not

Table 17.1
Initial Tableau for Priority-Ranked Resource Allocation Problem

c_j			0	0	0	0	P_2	0	P_1	0	P_3	0
	Mix	Quantity	X_1	X_2	S_1	S_2	$D_{\mu s}$	D_{os}	$D_{\mu g}$	D_{og}	$D_{\mu w}$	D_{ow}
P_2	$D_{\mu s}$	135	8	6	0	0	1	-1	0	0	0	0
P_1	$D_{\mu g}$	13	1	0	0	0	0	0	1	-1	0	0
P_3	D_{ow}	5	0	1	0	0	0	0	0	0	1	-1
0	S_1	60	4	2	1	0	0	0	0	0	0	0
0	S_2	48	2	4	0	1	0	0	0	0	0	0
P_3	z_j		0	1	0	0	0	0	0	0	1	-1
	$c_j - z_j$		0	-1	0	0	0	0	0	0	0	1
P_2	z_j		8	6	0	0	1	-1	0	0	0	0
	$c_j - z_j$		-8	-6	0	0	0	1	0	0	0	0
P_1	z,		1	0	0	0	0	0	1	-1	0	0
	$c_j - z_j$		-1	0	0	0	0	0	0	1	0	0

attained. Only \$125.00 ($D_{\mu s} = 7$) was achieved. Goal three to achieve five units of wilderness was missed by one unit since $X_2 = 4$ and $D_{ow} = 1$. Notice also that there are six units of management not used.

This is a general illustration of GP using a relatively simple model. As illustrated by this example, if the model is increased in complexity, manually computed solutions become quite difficult. If properly used, however, the technique should generate acceptable solutions even using a noncomputer-generated result.

IMPLICATIONS FOR OUTDOOR RECREATION POLICY

With the information that is now becoming available about the attitudes of the public toward recreational opportunities and the cataloging of resources (Wollmuth, Schomaker & Merriam, 1985) as well as the economic importance of recreational use attributes for resource valuation and allocation (Ochs & Thorn, 1984), it is evident that the MOA models outlined in this chapter have direct application to the field of recreation policy. Rather than generating a quantitative solution per se, the greatest benefit of using MOA may be that the process of developing the models requires that the decision maker face head on the problem of multiple demands and limited resources. This enhances awareness of the fact

Table 17.2
Final Tableau for Priority-Ranked Resource Allocation Problem

c_j			0	0	0	0	P2	0	P1	0	P3	0
	Mix	Quantity	X_1	X_2	S_1	S_2	$D_{\mu s}$	D_{os}	$D_{\mu g}$	D_{og}	$D_{\mu w}$	D_{ow}
P2	$D_{\mu s}$	7	0	0	-3	0	1	-1	4	-4	0	0
0	X_1	13	1	0	0	0	0	0	1	-1	0	0
P3	D_{ow}	1	0	0	-.5	0	0	0	2	-2	1	-1
0	X_2	4	0	1	-.5	0	0	0	-2	2	0	0
0	S_2	6	0	0	-2	1	0	0	6	-6	0	0
P3	z_j		0	0	-.5	0	0	0	2	-2	1	-1
	$c_j - z_j$		0	0	-.5	0	0	0	-2	2	0	1
P2	z_j		0	0	-3	0	1	-1	4	-4	0	0
	$c_j - z_j$		0	0	3	0	0	1	-4	4	0	0
P1	z		0	0	0	0	0	0	0	0	0	0
	$c_j - z_j$		0	0	0	0	0	0	1	0	0	0

that all desires for recreational opportunities cannot be satisfied simultaneously. Thus, it tends to foster a deeper appreciation of the possibilities and limitations inherent in planning and implementing recreation policies.

Large-scale recreational policy decisions are multiple-objective problems. Quantifying analyses of what types, how much, present usages, future uses, and preservation of recreational resources logically requires that policy analysts and decision makers forego single function models. Moreover, enough research has been done so that goal solution and priority setting can be established for these problems, which have objectives that cannot be directly or indirectly expressed using market measures (Russell, Thor, & Elsner, 1979, pp. 67–68). As a result, the combination of goals and weights for a recreational policy analysis problem can be ascertained.

Using goal programming, MOA offers a powerful analytical technique for use in recreational policy analysis. Its principal advantage is the ability to handle multiple objectives (i.e., criteria) while weighing possible outcomes of various policy options. Moreover, it forces one to recognize and confront, rather than ignore, the problems of policy formulation and goal setting because "no matter how expertly the goal programming problem is formulated, in the end, goal weights and priorities must be explicitly established" (Russell, Thor, & Elsner, 1979, p. 67). As a result, if attention is paid to divergent preferences and underlying trade-offs in the problem formulation stage, the MOA process can foster an awareness of and more informed consideration of various alternative solutions and courses of action. Moreover, such sensitivity to the underlying values, possibilities, and limitations confronting recreational policy makers and recreation systems managers is enhanced by not having to reduce all objectives to a common metric.

Recent attempts have been made to combine the two models and have yielded considerable success (Steuer, 1986). In order to alleviate some of the problems associated with GP and incorporate the strengths of both the Archimedean and preemptive features, interactive GP models for MOA have been developed. Although there are now mathematical models for handling goal programming problems, problem formulation and the definition of variables still offer the most serious challenges to the use of GP in general (Lee, 1972; Russell, Thor, & Elsner, 1979; Steuer, 1986). Nevertheless, the superiority of a multiple-criterion optimization technique that is readily available for use on mainframe and microcomputers over simple functional analysis is obvious. Yet with that accessibility comes the possibility of model abuse or neglect on the part of the user. For example, Russell, Thor, and Elsner (1979) provide a very good assessment of the problems with and the benefits of goal programming. One point that needs to be highlighted is that the goal programming problem must truly involve multiple objectives. Otherwise, if all the goals could be reduced to a common denominator, a standard linear programming technique could be used.

REFERENCES

Charnes, A., & Cooper, W. W. (1961). *Management models and industrial application of linear programming* (Vol. 1). New York: Wiley.

Charnes, A., Cooper, W. W., & Ferguson, R. O. (1965). Optimal estimation of executive compensation by linear programming. *Management Science, 1* (2), 138–151.

Cohon, J. L., & Marks, D. H. (1973). A review and evaluation of multiobjective programming techniques. *Water Resources Research, 2* (2), 208–220.

Ignizio, J. P. (1976). *Goal programming and extensions.* Lexington, MA: D.C. Heath.

Ijiri, Y. (1965). *Management goals and accounting for control.* Chicago: Rand McNally.

Keeney, K. D., & Raiffa, H. (1976). *Decisions with multiple objectives: Performances and value tradeoffs.* New York: Wiley.

Klar, L. R., & Chirin, A. (1983). Recreation at drinking water reservoirs in Massachusetts: A survey of water managers. *Water Resources Bulletin, 19* (3), 477–481.

Lee, S. M. (1972). *Goal programming for decision analysis.* Philadelphia: Auerback.

Levin, R. I., & Kirkpatrick, C. A. (1978). *Quantitative approaches to management* (4th ed.). New York: McGraw-Hill.

Lindsay, B. E., & Dunn, D. L. (1982). An application of mathematical programming to water resources planning: An economic view. *Water Resources Bulletin, 18* (2), 289–296.

Neely, W. P., North, R. M., & Fortson, J. C. (1971). Planning and selecting multiobjective projects by goal programming. *Water Resources Bulletin, 12* (1), 14–25.

Neely, W. P., Sellers, J., & North, R. M. (1980). Goal programming priority sensitivity analysis: An application in natural resource decision making processes. *Interfaces, 10* (5), 83–89.

North, R. M., Neely, W. P., & Carlton, R. (1976). *The highest and best uses of the Oklawaha River basin and Lake Rousseau for the economy and the environment.* Jacksonville, FL: U.S. Department of the Army, Corps of Engineers, Jacksonville District.

North, R. M., Neely, W. P., Sellers, J., & Taylor, B. W. (1984). Goal programming applications in water project analysis. In Y. Y. Haines & D. Allee (Eds.), *Multiobjective analysis in water resources* (pp. 125–152). New York: American Society of Civil Engineers.

Ochs, J., & Thorn, R. S. (1984). Measuring the site-specific recreation benefits resulting from improved water quality: An upper bound approach. *Water Resources Bulletin, 20* (6), 923–927.

Pigram, J. J. (1983). *Outdoor recreation and resource management.* New York: St. Martin's Press.

Ruffner, E. R., Sieber, R. E., & Ahmadi, M. (1986, September). Assessing the potential of goal programming to improve the effectiveness of resource allocation among demand-side management programs. *Proceedings of the American Power Conference* (pp. 124–159). Orlando, FL.

Russell, R., Thor, E. C., & Elsner, G. H. (1979, June). GPLUS—A new program for multiple objective planning. *Proceedings of the U.S. Department of Agriculture and Farm Foundation Multiple Objective Planning Workshop* (pp. 1–149). Tucson, AZ.

Sax, J. L. (1978). *Recreation policy on the federal lands.* Berkeley: University of California Press.

Schechter, M., & Lucas, R. C. (1978). *Simulation of recreational use for park and wilderness management.* Baltimore: Johns Hopkins University Press.

Sellers, J., Neely, W. P., & North, R. M. (1981, March). Goal programming application in natural resource investment. *Proceedings of the conference of the southeastern region of the American Institute of Decision Sciences* (p. 144).

Steuer, R. E. (1986). *Multiple criteria optimization: Theory, computation, and application.* New York: John Wiley and Sons.

Taylor, B. W., III (1982). *Introduction to management science.* Dubuque, IA: William C. Brown Publishers.

Taylor, B. W., & North, R. M. (1975). Approaches to multiobjective planning in water resources projects. *Water Resources Bulletin, 2* (5), 999–1088.

U.S. Council on Environmental Quality. (1985). *Environmental quality: Fifteenth annual report of the Council on Environmental Quality.* Washington, DC: U.S. Government Printing Office.

U.S. General Accounting Office. (1980). *Facilities in many national parks and forests do not meet health and safety standards* (CED 80–115). Washington, DC: U.S. Government Printing Office.

Wacht, R. F., & Whitford, D. T. (1976). A goal programming model for capital investment analysis in nonprofit hospitals. *Financial Management, 5* (2), 37–47.

Wollmuth, D. C., Schomaker, J. H., & Merriam, L. C., Jr. (1985). River recreation experience opportunities in two recreation opportunities spectrum (ROS) classes. *Water Resources Bulletin, 21* (5), 851–858.

18.

Balancing Competing Interests to Achieve Policy Goals: A Conceptual Framework

Barbara A. Knuth

Outdoor recreation managers are increasingly faced with a multitude of responsibilities, some of which are contradictory or overlapping. Responsibilities to provide publicly available opportunities for outdoor recreation and enjoyment often become a balancing act in which the manager must juggle increasing, diverse, and vocal demands with an often limited supply of recreation opportunities. Drawing on lessons learned in public administration and program evaluation, a framework is presented for outdoor recreation managers to use as an aid in this juggling act, one that will assist in identifying conflicting demands and defining potential consequences that would result from different resource allocation approaches.

This chapter begins with a brief introduction to the contradictory nature of management responsibilities facing the public outdoor recreation provider. The main focus of the chapter, however, is on how this contradiction can begin to be addressed rationally. Potential management actions and consequences involved in using an outdoor recreation resources matrix are identified. The matrix is a heuristic device, one whose application is equally appropriate to outdoor recreation agency planning, evaluation, public outreach activities, or research.

RECREATION PROVIDERS AS BROKERS

Concerns for resource protection and conflicting demands for recreation opportunities are not new to outdoor recreation management. One outdoor recreation provider, the National Park Service, has been grappling with an inherently contradictory mandate, calling for both use and preservation, since 1916 (Foresta,

1984). As others have suggested, it is unlikely a single clear mission will ever be identified for that agency; yet there is a strong need for management approaches that help the agency function and make explicit choices within these given constraints. As Clarke and McCool (1985) illustrated, the National Park Service is not an organizational failure due to its contradictory mandate, but neither has it been able to capitalize greatly on its strengths, one of which is widespread support among the populace stemming from the diverse opportunities it does provide.

The dilemma faced by the Park Service, and by many outdoor recreation providers, is one that finds its roots in a pluralist conceptualization of government known as brokerism. According to Bozeman (1979), a brokerist view of public agencies maintains that these agencies are the force that holds society together by balancing interests. Pure brokerism, however, demands that all relevant interests be articulated clearly and explicitly, and that consideration of these relevant interests actually enters into policy and management dialogues. In practice, many interests are not well articulated or are not represented in an organized fashion and so are not considered in the brokering process. Without a conceptualization of the diverse interests encompassed by different recreation philosophies (e.g., use or preservation), outdoor recreation providers cannot be pure brokerists and cannot ensure an explicit consideration of all important interests and consequences of alternative management policies.

In the 1987 report of the PCAO (the President's Commission on Americans Outdoors), several trends were noted with regard to outdoor recreation in this country. Among these trends were increasing competition for access to available recreation sites, limited and decreasing resources for recreation development and management, growing gaps in coordination among recreation programs offered by different providers, and a pervasive lack of systematic monitoring of the conditions of recreation resources and the status of public needs. In that same report, several issues of concern for management were identified, including protection of natural resources and open space, conflicting uses of recreation lands and waters, and roles of recreation providers.

The challenge, then, is also multifaceted. The forces competing for access to recreation opportunities must be identified before resources can be allocated among them. Recreation opportunities must be defined in similar terminology before coordination among different recreation providers can be achieved. Characteristics of the outdoor recreation system that need monitoring must be identified before a systematic and comprehensive monitoring program can begin.

A COMPREHENSIVE APPROACH

Without a conceptual framework to identify relevant interests and relationships, the brokering of recreation opportunities often becomes an end in itself, with no regard to the ultimate consequences of those actions. Policy decisions cannot begin to address inputs needed to achieve delivery of particular recreation

Figure 18.1
Outdoor Recreation Management System Components

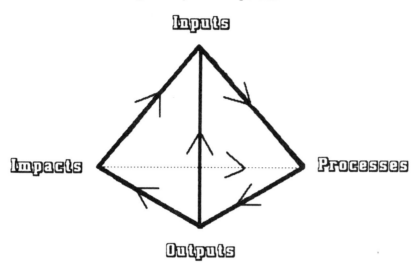

Arrows indicate interrelationships among components.

opportunities or assessment of the benefits to be generated from providing those opportunities.

A comprehensive approach to outdoor recreation policy recognizes that outdoor recreation management is a production process. Clear definition of the goods and services provided by outdoor recreation managers is necessary for setting good policy and for letting managers know what to provide and how.

The literature on program evaluation and systems analysis (Crowe, 1983; Giles, 1978) provides an approach to a holistic view of the outdoor recreation management system. Outdoor recreation can be viewed as being comprised of four basic, interrelated components: inputs, processes, outputs, and impacts (Figure 18.1). Inputs refer to the demands and resources with which an agency has to work, including factors within and outside of agency control. Processes refer to those management activities performed by recreation providers that use or rely on inputs. Process is an action-oriented concept. Outputs refer to the direct products of management actions, or the transformation of inputs through given processes. Impacts refer to the consequences of output production and use.

The relationships among these four components are dynamic. For example, one set of processes (management actions) may be applied to quite different sets of inputs, with the ultimate product or output being the same (Figure 18.2). Impacts, or consequences of producing this output, may be quite different in the two cases because of the inputs used in each situation.

It is important to recognize, however, that a comprehensive approach to outdoor recreation management clearly acknowledges all four components of the

Figure 18.2
Interaction of Outdoor Recreation Management Subsystems

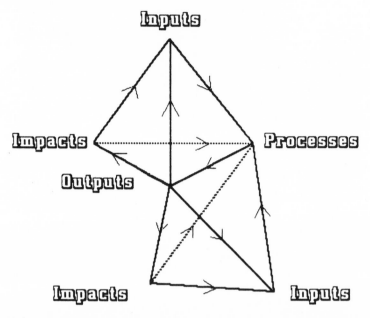

Note: Each outdoor recreation management subsystem (a unique combination of inputs, processes, outputs, and impacts) can interact with other subsystems by sharing one or more common components.

recreation system. It is not enough to focus only on easily measured processes (e.g., miles of access roads paved) or inputs (e.g., money available). Good policy and management asks the questions of what is the ultimate output achieved in paving those roads or what is the impact of increased access via paved roads.

THE OUTDOOR RECREATION RESOURCES MATRIX

Within the comprehensive systems approach discussed for outdoor recreation, subsystems can be identified that correspond to major responsibilities or program areas. Most recreation resource management can be described through some combination of four subsystems, discrete program areas that can and often do interact.

These subsystems are labeled social, biological, physical, and institutional. Social refers to the users or potential users of the recreation resource system, and the society to which those users belong. Biological refers to the animal and plant populations on the land and water base of that recreation system, sometimes enhancing and sometimes confounding recreation management. Physical refers to the actual land, water, and air in which those plant and animal populations

Figure 18.3
Framework for the Outdoor Recreation Resources Matrix

PROGRAM AREA

SYSTEM COMPONENT	SOCIAL	BIOLOGICAL	PHYSICAL	INSTITUTIONAL
INPUTS				
PROCESSES				
OUTPUTS				
IMPACTS				

Note: In practice, specific recreation system elements are classified into each of the sixteen matrix cells.

occur and on which recreation takes place. Institutional refers to the characteristics and internal concerns of the recreation providers.

Combining the four components with the four subsystem program areas produces a sixteen-cell conceptual matrix in which to classify all interests involved in outdoor recreation management (Figure 18.3). This is the first step toward meeting the challenges set forth earlier, the first step in identifying competing forces and defining recreation with a single terminology.

Methods used to develop the individual components within each cell of the matrix are described in detail by Knuth (1986). An extensive and methodological search of the literature in recreation, environmental, and resource administration, and social assessment disciplines was conducted to identify important aspects of outdoor recreation. Each characteristic identified was assigned to one of the sixteen cells of the recreation matrix. A select subset of those, four for each matrix cell, are presented in Tables 18.1 through 18.4 to provide an indication of the potential relationships and diversity among matrix elements. For example, matrix inputs and outputs may be identical, as the outputs produced during one management cycle become inputs for the next. In practice, specific recreation

Table 18.1
Selected Social Factors Identified for the Outdoor Recreation Resources Matrix

Component	Recreation Elements
Inputs	Public demands Market forces Existing sociological groups Regional population demographics
Processes	Law enforcement Providing facilities Interpretation activities Providing access

Outputs	Diversity of recreation
	    opportunities
	Quantity of recreation
	    opportunities
	Recreation proximity to users
	Participation frequency

Impacts	User knowledge/awareness Psychological benefits Societal benefits

elements for the matrix will be identified through consultation and discussion among recreation professionals and interest groups to determine those specific elements that are most relevant to a particular management situation.

USING THE MATRIX

While the sixteen cells of the matrix should be viewed as fixed, the elements within those cells should be viewed as dynamic and responsive to individual policy or management questions. The sixteen cells, representing the universe of concerns in recreation management, provide a concrete and comprehensive framework that can help identify and visualize potential conflicts faced by rec- reation providers. Tracing the interactions among the matrix cells can identify paths toward alleviating those conflicts.

For any one application of the matrix, recreation providers should seek out voices for, or represent themselves, each cell of the matrix. Under the brokerist philosophy of recreation management, all relevant interests must be clearly and explicitly articulated. For every management or policy issue, recreation providers can use the matrix as the framework for identifying how each program area and each system component may be affected by a particular alternative. In actual application, elements for the matrix should be pertinent to the policy or man- agement issue under consideration. Specific elements may be identified through

Table 18.2
Selected Biological Factors Identified for the Outdoor Recreation Resources Matrix

Component	Recreation Elements
Inputs	Historical ecological relationships Distribution of plant and animal populations General biological constraints Populations: quantity
Processes	Research on animal populations Species introductions/invasions Harvesting of biota Resource inventories
Outputs	Harvest: quantity Populations: quantity Ecological relationships Research results
Impacts	Endangered/threatened species status Future resource utilization Successional patterns Wildlife hazards to humans

a document review, brainstorming among managers and planners, open discussions with community leaders, or some combination of these methods. It is the recreation decision maker's responsibility, however, to ensure that recreation elements of concern are identified and discussed for each of the sixteen matrix cells.

For example, a recreation provider may be requested to increase the accessibility of a certain recreation site (e.g., a campground on publicly owned property) that is within close proximity to private landholdings. The recreation provider must then identify alternatives for addressing this issue.

Turning to the matrix, the recreation manager knows that there are four program areas that may be affected by or may influence the decision on access. After specific recreation elements are identified and listed in the matrix framework based on discussions among recreation planners or a review of documents associated with similar cases, the decision maker poses questions such as the following: What are the public demands for access to the site? What is the current distribution of campgrounds near the site? What wildlife populations exist in the area (e.g., bears) that may be affected by development of the campground? What are existing institutional policies regarding providing increased camping opportunities, especially where private lands may be affected? Once these input-level questions are posed, the manager can begin to address the interactions among

Table 18.3
Selected Physical Factors Identified for the Outdoor Recreation Resources Matrix

Component	Recreation Elements
Inputs	General physical/chemical constraints Geomorphological features Holdings: land, water Historical environmental quality
Processes	Land acquisitions Land use conversions Environmental monitoring Research on environmental quality
Outputs	Holdings accessible for recreation Research results Holdings by type Environmental quality
Impacts	Preservation potential Ecosystem values Availability for future uses Scientific study potential

program areas and system components: What are the likely outputs of increasing access? What are the likely impacts of producing those outputs?

Many managers will be in a situation in which they have no knowledge base from which to answer all these questions. The important point for improved policy and management decisions is that at least decision makers have a conceptual tool to use in helping them ask the right questions. Managers can then rely on other resource professionals or established interest groups to help answer the questions posed by examining the relationships among matrix elements.

Although not providing all the answers, the recreation matrix is useful for stimulating resolution of conflicts due to miscommunication and ignorance. If recreation managers have no knowledge about a particular cell, for example potential impacts on animal populations, they can seek out the appropriate expertise now that the need has been identified. All parties with some interest in a decision can study the recreation matrix, address recreation characteristics in common terminology, visualize the relationships among recreation characteristics, and explain their reasons for favoring one alternative over another by illustrating effects on other elements in the matrix. Public outreach efforts may be more successful because decision makers can articulate policy goals in terms of the matrix and explain allocation decisions to competing users based on the probable consequences for each matrix element arising from each alternative considered.

The matrix, therefore, can be applied to a variety of management responsi-

Table 18.4
Selected Institutional Factors Identified for the Outdoor Recreation Resources Matrix

Component	Recreation Elements
Inputs	Revenue Existing institutional policies/mandates Jurisdiction Personnel: quantity, quality
Processes	Planning activities Expenditures Personnel: training Interagency communications
Outputs	Documents and reports Interagency cooperation Personnel: productivity Agency focus
Impacts	Agency image among the public Use of agency reports Political influence of agency Coordination of recreation providers

bilities. It can assist planners and policy makers in articulating reasonable goals and objectives while recognizing interactions among the total recreation system. It can be used to target those system components most relevant to assessing whether goals and objectives have been met. It is rare that the process component of management is the true objective; yet, it is often the facet measured for evaluative purposes due to the relative ease in data collection, for example, measuring the number of miles of road paved. The matrix helps the evaluator develop measures directed toward the output and impact components of the recreation system that stem from management processes or actions. The matrix is also useful for research purposes. Gaps in the completeness of knowledge about any of the sixteen cells in the resource matrix indicate potential areas for future design to improve recreation management.

CONCLUSION

Inherent in outdoor recreation management are conflicts caused by competing interests, demands, and mandates. In many conflict situations, resolution is hampered by two factors: difficulty in identifying and involving all interested parties and disagreement or misunderstanding about the issues of concern (Bingham, 1986). The outdoor recreation resources matrix does not make the ultimate decision about how to resolve recreation conflicts; rather, it provides a tool through which conflicts can be articulated.

In many situations, the recreation manager will have an adequate knowledge base from past experience to identify concerns in each matrix cell. In this case, the recreation matrix is a heuristic device that assures the manager considered all relevant concerns and interactions. In other situations, a recreation manager will have incomplete or inadequate knowledge, in which case the recreation matrix will assist the manager in identifying the appropriate expert to consult before deciding on an alternative policy option.

The challenges posed in the report of the PCAO (1987) can be addressed using the recreation matrix. The matrix helps identify forces competing for recreation opportunities and examine the implications for the total recreation system of allocating recreation opportunities among those forces. Use of the matrix encourages common terminology among recreation providers and can help achieve coordination among different recreation providers by assigning various matrix elements and/or program areas as their primary responsibilities.

Finally, the matrix can be used as a monitoring tool by clarifying the relationships among different potential monitoring targets. Rather than instituting a monitoring program to track trends in process components, recreation providers have a device to help them focus also on output and impact monitoring, components which best represent the user-provider interface. With this approach, monitoring will become more relevant to policy goals focused on providing recreational opportunities for people.

REFERENCES

Bingham, G. (1986). *Resolving environmental disputes*. Washington, DC: The Conservation Foundation.

Bozeman, B. (1979). *Public management and policy analysis*. New York: St. Martin's Press.

Clarke, J. N., & McCool, D. (1985). *Staking out the terrain: Power differentials among natural resource management agencies*. Albany: State University of New York Press.

Crowe, D. M. (1983). *Comprehensive planning for wildlife resources*. Cheyenne: Wyoming Game and Fish Department.

Foresta, R. A. (1984). *America's national parks and their keepers*. Washington, DC: Resources for the Future.

Giles, R. H., Jr. (1978). *Wildlife management*. San Francisco: W. H. Freeman and Company.

Knuth, B. A. (1986). *A fisheries and wildlife indicator system for use in natural resource management*. Doctoral dissertation, Virginia Polytechnic Institute and State University.

President's Commission on Americans Outdoors [PCAO] (1987). *Americans outdoors: The legacy, the challenge*. Washington, DC: Island Press.

19.

Coping with Cutbacks in Park and Recreation Administration: Priorities, Innovation, and Mobilizing Interest Groups

Zachary A. Smith

For many state governments the 1980s has been a decade of fiscal constraint. From 1980 to 1985 funding for state park systems decreased nationwide by 17 percent (Myers & Reid, 1986). Overseeing what some policy makers consider a non-essential service, state park and recreation administrators in many state parks have been forced to make decisions and trade-offs about where to allocate scarce and/or diminishing resources. This is sometimes referred to as "cut-back management." As both state and national park systems have suffered budget cuts in recent years various adjustments have been necessary in the management of some parks. Park systems have been forced, for example, to close off parts of their recreational areas, and numerous state parks have cut maintenance costs by extending maintenance schedules, delaying improvements, laying off seasonal employees, and other means (Horstman, 1982; Tugman, 1985).

How park administrators have dealt with the changing budgetary environment is examined here. Particular attention is paid to the priorities of administrators when making budget reductions; innovations in park administration and management that have been used to mitigate the impact of budget reductions; and how budget officials within the state park organizations interact with interest groups, citizen organizations, or others outside the state park and recreation bureaucracy.

Previous studies have shown that in the 1980s decreased funding had been a major concern for state park and recreation administrators. This, of course, is not surprising given the overall reduction in state expenditures for park and recreation systems and the reductions in federal assistance through the Land and

Water Conservation Fund (WCF) since the beginning of the Reagan administration. (WCF state grants have, since 1981, dropped to one-third of the total appropriated in the previous five-year period [Myers & Reid, 1986, p. 4].) In a recent survey of state park administrators, 52 percent identified funding as the single greatest issue of importance to their state systems. This concern was raised by park administrators regardless of the size of the park system or the location of the state (Myers & Reid, 1986).

THE SURVEY

As part of the research undertaken for this chapter a survey was conducted of all 50 state park superintendents and/or directors and 300 ranger/managers responsible for one or a small cluster of state park recreation areas in six states of various sizes distributed around the country.[1] Surveys were sent out in November of 1986. At the end of December 1986, a follow-up survey was sent out to nonrespondents. (Both mailings contained a personalized cover letter to the park director and, when possible, the ranger/manager and a self-addressed stamped return envelope.) Forty-six of the fifty state park directors responded for a response rate of 92 percent. One hundred fifty-two of the park ranger/managers responded for a response rate of 51 percent.

PRIORITIES OF PARK AND RECREATION ADMINISTRATORS

In an effort to determine the priorities of park and recreation administrators when making budgetary cutbacks, the directors were asked to indicate on a list where they would or recently have reduced funding if forced to do so by budgetary cutbacks. The directors were asked to select their first three choices in where they would cut by indicating on the list a #1, #2, or #3 (#1 indicating the area where they would be most likely to cut). The list included building maintenance, grounds maintenance, trail maintenance, capital improvement, vehicles, other equipment, travel, utilities, staff, land acquisition, and public information. Of the forty-six state park directors that responded to the survey, twelve directors indicated that their first choice for making a cut would be in the capital improvement budget (26%). The second areas where park directors were most likely to reduce their budgets were in the areas of staff (15%) and land acquisition (15%). Ten percent of the directors chose vehicles as their first choice in budget cutting. By totaling the first, second, and third choice response areas, which are central to park system operations, areas most likely to suffer cutbacks in the event that they are necessary can be seen (Table 19.1).

It would appear from Table 19.1 that, to the extent a trend is evident, those functions and expenditures that are most likely to impact the public were the areas where state park directors were least willing to make funding reductions. Campground maintenance, trail maintenance, utilities, and public information

Table 19.1
First, Second, or Third Choice of Area Where Park and Recreation Directors Would Cut Budgets

Budget Category	Number of Responses
Capital improvement (construction)	23
Staff	21
Other equipment	16
Vehicles	15
Land acquisition	13
Travel	10
Building maintenance	6
Public information	6
Trail maintenance	4
Campground maintenance	2
Other	11

are all expenditures that to varying degrees have an impact on park and recreation clientele. In contrast, it might be argued that capital improvement, staff, and vehicles, as well as other equipment, and travel have less of a direct impact on users.

Although there are a number of similarities between the responses of the park directors and the rangers in the field, (Table 19.2) it is interesting to note the differences in attitudes toward land acquisition and travel. In both cases, there was much more willingness on the part of park rangers to cut in these categories than on the part of state park directors. This is not surprising, given the greater importance of travel to park directors (and the corresponding less likelihood of its need on the ranger level) and the greater role that land acquisition plays in the job of the park director vis-à-vis the job of a park ranger.

INNOVATIONS AND CHANGES USED TO DEAL WITH BUDGETARY CUTBACKS

A second section of the survey was designed to identify innovations and/or changes that had been made to deal with cutbacks in park budgets. Both the state park system directors and park ranger/managers in the field were asked the

Table 19.2
First, Second, or Third Choice of Area Where Park Rangers Would Cut Budgets

Budget Category	Number of Responses
Capital improvement (new construction)	58
Land acquisition	37
Travel	36
Staff	20
Vehicles	19
Other equipment	17
Trail maintenance	9
Utilities	6
Campground maintenance	5
Building maintenance	4
Public information	2
Other	3

open-ended question, "Can you suggest any innovations or do you have any suggestions on ways to avoid the impacts of budget cuts?" The response can be classified as roughly falling into one of three categories: (1) staff or personnel management, (2) revenue enhancement, and (3) public relations. Since there were more similarities than differences in the responses of park system directors when compared to the responses of the ranger/managers (and since the differences are more interesting) the responses of the park system directors are summarized below followed by a discussion of how the ranger/manager responses varied.

Staff Augmentation and/or Reduction

Within this category the suggestion made most often by directors (N = 7) was to increase the number of volunteers and the jobs performed by them. The second most often cited means of budget reduction that falls into this category was to close park units that receive the least number of visitors (N = 4). The remaining suggestions for budget reductions that had some impact on staffing were each mentioned by one director. They are as follows: staff reduction (by attrition, converting full-time staff and parks into seasonal operation, seeking assistance from other state or federal agencies, and using prison inmates to augment staff), turning parks over to resident volunteer managers, redefining job descriptions to allow greater flexibility of employee work schedules, and increased employee evaluations to improve efficiency.

Although park rangers/managers showed nearly identical support for the use of volunteers (approximately 16%) and a similar proportion suggested the use of prison inmates (or those assigned by the courts to do community service work—an important distinction not made by the state park director who made this suggestion), none of the other staff reduction/augmentation suggestions were made by the ranger/managers, which is not surprising given the greater impact such reductions would have on local managers.

Revenue Enhancement

By far and away the most often cited innovation by state park directors for dealing with budget cuts that might be classified as revenue enhancement was the suggestion to increase user fees (N = 11). Next a number of suggestions (N = 8) were made to increase park revenues through sales, marketing, or adding revenue producing attractions. Suggestions included taking over concession operations, producing a gift catalog, selling off surplus timber, land, or equipment, leasing buildings to groups with compatible missions, and renegotiating new contracts with concessionaires to increase income and/or require other contributions such as capital improvements.

Five directors suggested private donations be increased either through endowment plans or other efforts. Finally, although not a revenue enhancement measure per se, four state directors expressed a desire to have their budgets partially funded by some independent source (cigarette taxes and user fees were mentioned) and not out of general funds.

The revenue enhancement ideas of park ranger/managers in the field almost mirrored the responses from directors; however, the ranger/managers had a number of additional suggestions for savings in the field. Several (N = 6) ranger/managers suggested reducing mowing schedules and/or mowing less for aesthetic and more for practical reasons. Several others (N = 4) felt vehicles and equipment could be kept longer if more were spent on preventive maintenance, and two urged switching to wood heat and, when possible, using surplus park wood for heating.

Public Relations

Five park system directors and eight park rangers/managers suggested what might be termed public relations activities. These included developing relations with park users, communicating the economic and quality of life and other benefits of parks to the public and policy makers, increasing expenditures for marketing parks, and informing the public about the effects of budget reductions. As might be expected the responses of the directors and the field personnel differed primarily in the target audience. The ranger/managers were primarily concerned with developing relations with the users of their park units, while the directors were more concerned with the public as a whole.

In summary, although the trend is less clear in park director and ranger/manager attitudes toward innovations to mitigate the impact of budget reductions, there seems to be a general concern that budget cutbacks and changes made necessary by cutbacks should have a minimal impact on the public. Attention to the public might be more profitably directed (both for park administrators and those who use the parks) to cultivating public and outside organizations for their political and budgetary support.

INTEREST GROUPS AND PARK ADMINISTRATION

Unlike the previous discussion, the following survey results and analysis are made for state park and recreation system directors only. Although park rangers/ managers in the field reported similar rates of contact with outside organizations, they had less direct control over their budgets; hence, it was felt that the analysis was more appropriate for budgetary decision making on the director level.

The Role of Interest Groups

For a variety of reasons it might be anticipated that groups and other outside organizations using state park and recreation facilities would be involved with park and recreation administrators in their budgetary decision making. It is common in both the public administration and American politics literature to refer to "iron or policy triangles," "subgovernments," or "issue networks" to describe the mutually dependent relationships formed between legislators, administrators, and interest groups. Hugh Heclo, for example, has distinguished between iron triangles, subgovernments, and what he calls issue networks, finding that the former "presumes small circles of participants . . . coalesced to control fairly narrow public programs. . . . " In contrast, issue networks "comprise a large number of participants with quite variable degrees of mutual commitment" (Heclo, 1978, p. 102). Heclo goes on to say issue networks "operate at many levels, from the vocal minority who turn up at local planning commission hearings to the renowned professor who is quietly telephoned by the White House to give a quick 'reading' on some participant or policy" (p. 102). The analysis will use policy triangles to delineate the relationship between bureaucrats, elected officials, and outside organizations, usually interest groups.[2] The distinction that Heclo makes is an important one. It is quite likely that the relationships of major policy participants will vary as to size, complexity, commitment, as well as in other ways.

Regardless of the configuration or title given to the relationship between actors in a policy arena, there are some important similarities. On one side of the policy triangle, interest groups provide support for the programs bureaucrats administer through hearings, letters to legislators, and so forth. Interest groups, of course, also provide political and electoral support to elected representatives. On another side of the triangle, bureaucrats, in return for the support of interest groups, provide goods and services to group members and also provide elected officials with political credit (i.e., from association with a program) for the services they deliver to constituent groups. Finally, the elected officials provide bureaucrats with the support they need to run their organizations and provide interest groups with the programs that they support. Policy triangles then link the legislators, the clientele of interest groups, and administrators who have a stake in a particular program. Each participant in the policy triangle has an incentive to maintain the relationship, and thus the program or programs with which the actors are concerned, in order to maintain the benefits that are derived from the relationship: either electoral support, budgetary support, or the delivery of a program. These relationships have been well documented in case studies in a variety of policy contexts (Carter, 1964; Derthick, 1979; Freeman, 1965; Mazmanian & Nienaber, 1979; Walker, 1977).

Competent administrators are concerned with policy triangles on a continuous basis. Regardless of the label attached to the relationship, public administrators carefully monitor legislative events, try to develop good relations with legislators, and otherwise attempt to establish a feeling of mutual understanding with and respect for the appropriate members of the legislative branch. Capable administrators should also develop the other side of the policy triangle by cultivating supportive relations with interest group members and leadership. The development of relationships with interest groups has not, however, been seen by many public managers to be as crucial to agency health as has the development of relations with legislators (Mazmanian & Nienaber, 1979). Apparently that has also been the case with state park directors.

In an effort to identify the current role of outside organizations in state park and recreation budgetary decision making, park directors were first asked several questions to determine how much discretion they had within budgetary categories to make allocations in their operating budgets. None was found to lack budgetary discretion to the extent that he or she should be omitted from the survey. They were then asked to indicate which, if any, organizations they had contact with in making budgetary decisions (an open-ended question). Directors were also asked to characterize the utility of contacts with outside organizations (very useful, useful, neutral, not very useful, and disadvantageous) and to describe what, if any, benefit could be derived from consulting with outside organizations (another open-ended question). Finally, the directors were asked to identify the most important criteria they use in determining where to reduce funding for a program. "When deciding where to make necessary cutbacks in your program, what is the most important criteria you use, or, what factors are most likely to influence your decision on where to cut back a program? (1) public reaction; (2) lack of use; (3) visibility; (4) "other" (with space for a reply). Only seven directors reported having any contact with outside organizations (Table 19.3).[3]

Table 19.3
Outside Organizations Contacted Regarding Budgetary Decision Making

Type of Group	Number of States Reporting a Contact
User groups	6
Advisory groups	4
Park associations	4
Legislators	2
Other units of government	1
Civic groups	1
Chambers of commerce	1

Note: The user groups identified included recreational and environmental groups. Advisory groups were organizations created for the purpose of providing input into park decision making. The two directors who listed legislators referred to legislators representing an area where a park might be impacted by budget cuts.

Recall that only five directors mentioned some form of public relations as a way of mitigating damage from budget reductions.

Of those seven directors contacting outside organizations the groups contacted most frequently were, not surprisingly, those most likely to be using the parks (user groups) or organizations established by or for the parks (i.e., park associations and advisory groups). It is also not surprising that on the question of the utility of group contacts all seven directors found group contacts to be either very useful ($N = 3$) or useful ($N = 4$).

On the question of the criteria directors used for determining where to reduce funding, all seven directors indicated concern for public reaction or opinion either by selecting "lack of use" or "public reaction" as the most important criteria or by selecting "other" and providing an explanation that gave evidence of concern with impacts on the public.

In contrast, roughly half (51%) of those directors reporting no contact with outside organizations in making budgetary decisions selected "lack of use" or "public reaction." Two of the directors not contacting outside organizations selected "visibility" as the most important criteria and the remainder selected "other" and provided a wide variety of explanations, including three that noted all three criteria were important. There was one nonrespondent to the question.

Again there is nothing surprising about these findings. Directors who are in contact with outside organizations are likely to find such contacts important and more likely to identify the reactions of others outside the organization as the most important criteria to be used in determining where to make budgetary cuts.

Given what case studies have identified as the relationship between interest groups and administrators (i.e., policy triangles), one might have assumed prior to undertaking this survey that in making decisions as politically volatile and important to park and recreation administration that park directors would have been more likely to consult outside organizations prior to making their decisions as to where they should or should not make budgetary cuts. Of course it is possible that the influence of outside organizations is registered in other ways besides direct involvement. For example, influence and opinion can be registered through letters, complaints, and newspaper articles. Nevertheless, outside organizations apparently are not directly involved in the budgetary decisions of the overwhelming majority of the state park directors contacted in this survey.

One possible conclusion from these findings is that policy triangles exist on the state level in theory only. This, however, seems highly unlikely given the importance of interest groups to public administrators and elected officials (Smith, 1985). A more plausible explanation would seem to be that the influence of interest groups in state park and recreation budgetary decision making is more indirect and that state park and recreation directors and administrators anticipate interest group reaction to budgetary decisions and act accordingly. This conclusion is somewhat supported by the fact that when asked to list criteria they would use to determine areas for restricting their budgets "lack of use" was selected by a plurality of all directors (40%) and "lack of use" with "public reaction" was selected by a majority of respondents (51%). It is also possible, of course, that in some states individuals concerned with park and recreation management are not well organized.

Increase Participation?

It would seem that the lack of direct contact between outside organizations and park and recreation administrators in many states is a potential liability for park administrators. There are a number of practical political reasons, as well as practical management reasons, why decision making (and the options available to administrators) in state park and recreation administration could, in some cases, be greatly improved by increasing outside participation.

Advantages that may be derived for the public administrator by increased participation include the legitimizing of decisions (by allowing groups in on the decision-making process); co-opting possible opposition; identifying potential conflicts before they erupt; and improving the quality of policy analysis by introducing the decision maker to policy alternatives and/or problems with which he or she may not be familiar. Increased participation may also increase the likelihood that the result will be implementable (Gormley, 1981; Kamieniecki, 1981), is more likely to be viewed as credible (Hendee, et al., 1976), legitimate

(Collins, 1980), and it is likely to increase public confidence in administrative decision making (Aron, 1979).

There are a number of potential problems with or drawbacks to increased participation. These include the fact that participants are likely to be a nonrepresentative sample (particularly at hearings—a common form of participation); that demands of interest groups will pressure administrators into making bad or short-sighted decisions; and, relatedly, that the fear of citizen backlash will result in a reluctance to change policy (Cupps, 1977; Kamieniecki, 1981).

Should park administrators increase the participation of outside organizations in administrative decision making? For many state and federal administrators the issue is, in part, moot due to the existence of statutory requirements for participation.[4] In most cases, such as those types of budgetary decisions made by the state park directors in this study, the question of how much outside input and in what form that input will take is left to the administrator.

The argument for increased outside involvement may be best made by quoting the comments of some of the state park directors who use outside organizations. Park directors were asked, "What, if any, benefit can be derived from consulting with outside organizations?" Some of the comments were as follows: "Support for budget proposals in the General Assembly; support for new programs; . . . [provides a] . . . sounding board for expansions, new acquisitions, etc." "Development of public support and understanding. Strong public support and pressures placed on the legislature could eliminate the chance of budget reductions." "You get a feel where cuts would be accepted best." "Minimizes negative media reaction . . . generates support for budget increases in the legislature."

These are all positive benefits that would support a strong case for administrators to strengthen the interest group side of the policy triangle if they have been neglecting that potential asset. The best insurance against budgetary cutbacks is a strong, vocal, and well-organized constituency. The surest means of determining how cutbacks should be made to avoid adverse public (and legislative) reaction is to solicit the input of the affected publics.

It is possible that members of the public concerned with park and recreation administration in some states are not well organized or motivated to become involved in park management. However, virtually all states have organizations of user groups (e.g., "Good Sam" and similar clubs, youth organizations that engage in camping), environmental and/or wildlife groups, and others that could provide the basis for expanding the involvement of outside organizations.

Method of Involvement?

If the decision is made to increase the involvement of outside organizations in agency decision making, the question then becomes what means of involvement should be used. For purposes of analysis the types of involvement examined here are divided into formal and informal means of participation.

Formal means of participation include hearings, workshops, advisory committees, and survey research. Each method has its advantages and disadvantages. All, except for a scientific survey, provide a nonrepresentative sample of the public (but perhaps not, however, of one's primary constituency). Additional problems include the fact that hearings can get out of control (or otherwise become counterproductive); workshops are very time consuming and particularly nonrepresentative due to their usually small size (hence these naturally would be used with selected interest group elites); and surveys, when conducted properly, can be very expensive. On the positive side, hearings are relatively quick and easy to organize, can generate media attention, can be managed to maximize desirable outcomes, and can provide some sense of the sentiment of the motivated public. Workshops can generate high levels of participant interest and involvement, providing good opportunities for the discussion of alternatives, trade-offs, and other negotiations. Advisory committees, although they may not be representative of the public, do provide the opportunity for administrators to have regular input from a body representing the concerned public, which they can use to assess alternatives and gauge constituent opinion. An obvious drawback is the possibility of an advisory committee's becoming too powerful. Yet, this possibility can be somewhat reduced by the creation of several committees whose input is limited to specific subject areas.

Informal means of cultivating outside interests would include establishing contacts by responding to (and keeping a record of) constituent inquiries/complaints; developing a mailing list of members of the public concerned with agency operations (lists may be generated by field personnel from inquiries, visitor registrations, or acquired directly from group leadership); and making informal contacts with members of interest groups (e.g., a phone call for a suggestion). Other informal means might include subscribing to and reading interest group publications (newsletters, etc.) and communicating with group members through those publications. Administrators can monitor letters to the editor and respond to those dealing with the agency; write articles and press releases for newspapers and newsletters describing the agency, its mission, or problems (smaller daily papers and many weekly papers will publish press releases and articles with few, if any changes). The broadcast media is also a useful, sometimes neglected, means of communicating with constituents. Local radio and television stations often have interview and/or public affairs programs that can provide an opportunity to communicate the agency message and build public support.

Regardless of the means used, state park administrators, as well as other government managers, can benefit from increasing the interest group/constituency side of the policy triangle.

CONCLUSION

As survey results reported here have demonstrated, park and recreation administrators at both the director level and in the field are sensitive to the impact budget cuts will have on the public. When asked where budget cuts would be made, those activities having the most direct impact on the public are least often cited. Yet, in the case of park directors, this concern does not manifest itself in contacting outside organizations or cultivating the support of such organizations. Furthermore, although it was not part of the survey, many of the park ranger/managers in the field volunteered their displeasure at not being included in budgetary decision making on the state level. The comments of a park unit ranger in West Virginia were typical:

In West Virginia State Parks our budgets are set each year by a few misguided politicians without much input from field superintendents. The responses on the questionnaire are the ways I would make budget cuts. My views seldom ever correspond to the reduction policies set by our "leaders."

Such comments led this author to conclude that in addition to underutilizing outside organizations for building political support for park and recreation budgets, some park system directors may also be underutilizing intelligence within their own organizations.

This study suggests at least one important tool to prevent budgetary reductions in state park and recreation management. While it is wise to think in terms of which maintenance schedule can be adjusted, which recreation area closed, or which capital improvement postponed, some such decisions might be avoided and the impact of such decisions mitigated if administrators attempt to develop relations with outside organizations. Furthermore, to the extent that they are not currently now doing so (and this was not a measure included in the survey), volunteered comments of the park ranger/managers surveyed suggest that park directors might benefit from more field input.

NOTES

1. The states selected were California, Hawaii, Illinois, New Hampshire, North Carolina, and West Virginia.

2. Most, but not all, "outside organizations" examined in this study could be defined as "interest groups." Possible exceptions include advisory groups established by park administrators, legislators, and other units of government.

3. The directors were promised confidentiality and hence individual states will not be identified here.

4. For example, federal statutes that mandate some form of citizen participation include the Housing and Community Development Act of 1974, the National Environmental Policy Act of 1969, the 1972 amendments of the Federal Water Pollution Control Act, the Clean Air Act of 1970, the Older Americans Act of 1965, and the National Health Planning Resources Development Act of 1974 (Redburn, et al., 1980, p. 350).

REFERENCES

Aron, J. B. (1979). Citizen participation at government expense. *Public Administration Review, 39* (Sept./Oct.), 477–485.

Carter, D. (1964). *Power in Washington*. New York: Vintage.

Collins, W. P. (1980). Public participation in bureaucratic decision making: A reappraisal. *Public Administration, 58* (Winter), 465–477.

Cupps, D. S. (1977). Emerging problems of citizen participation. *Public Administration Review, 37* (Sept./Oct.), 478–487.

Derthick, M. (1979). *Policymaking for social security*. Washington, DC: The Brookings Institute.

Freeman, J. L. (1965). *The political process*. New York: Random House.

Gormley, W. T. (1981). Statewide remedies for public underrepresentation in regulatory proceedings. *Public Administration Review, 41* (July/Aug.), 454–462.

Heclo, H. (1978). Issue networks and the executive establishment. In A. King (Ed.), *The new American political system* (pp. 87–124). Washington, DC: American Enterprise Institute.

Hendee, J. C., Lucas, R. C., Tracy, R. H., Staed, T., Clark, R. N., Stankey, G. H., & Yarnell, R. A. (1976). Methods for acquiring public input. In J. C. Pierce and H. R. Doerksen (Eds.), *Water politics and public involvement* (pp. 125–144). Ann Arbor, MI: Ann Arbor Science.

Horstman, E. (Ed.). (1982). *National parks in crisis*. Silver Spring, MD: Information Dynamics.

Kamieniecki, S. (1981). Improving public representation. *The Bureaucrat, 10* (Fall), 50–55.

Mazmanian, D., & Nienaber, J. (1979). *Can organizations change? Environmentalism, participation, and the Corps of Engineers*. Washington, DC: The Brookings Institute.

Myers, P., & Reid, A. C. (1986). *State parks in a new era: A survey of issues and innovations*. Washington, DC: Conservation Foundation.

Redburn, S., Buss, T. F., Foster, S. K., & Binning, W. C. (1980). How representative are mandated citizen participation processes? *Urban Affairs Quarterly, 15* (March), 345–352.

Smith, Z. (1985). *Interest group interaction and groundwater policy formation in the Southwest*. Baltimore: University Press of America.

Tugman, S. J. (1985). Beyond fees and charges: The need for a pricing strategy. *Parks and Recreation, 20* (12), 50–53.

Walker, J. L. (1977). Setting the agenda in the U.S. Senate. *British Journal of Political Science, 7*, 432–445.

BIBLIOGRAPHY

Allen, G., & Gould, E. (1986). Complexity, wickedness, and public forests. *Journal of Forestry, 84* (4), 20–23.

Allin, C. W. (1982). *The politics of wilderness preservation.* Westport, CT: Greenwood Press.

Allin, C. W. (1985). Hidden agendas in wilderness management. *Parks and Recreation, 20,* 62–65.

Allin, C. W. (1987). Wilderness preservation as a bureaucratic tool. In Phillip O. Foss (Ed.), *Federal lands policy* (pp. 127–138). Westport, CT: Greenwood Press.

Almond, G. A., & Verba, S. (1963). *The civic culture.* Princeton, NJ: Princeton University Press.

Anderson, J. E. (1979). On the measurement of welfare cost under uncertainty. *Southern Economic Journal, 45* (April), 1160–1171.

Anderson, L. G. (1980). Estimating the benefits of recreation under conditions of congestion: Comments and extension. *Journal of Environmental Economics and Management, 7* (December), 401–406.

Andrews, K. (1984). *Recreation benefits and costs of the proposed Deer Creek Reservoir.* Cheyenne: Wyoming Recreation Commission.

Aristotle. (1975). *Nicomachean ethics.* Cambridge, MA: Harvard University Press.

Armour, A. (1986). Issue management in resource planning. In R. Lang (Ed.), *Integrated approaches to resource planning and management* (pp. 51–65). Calgary: University of Calgary Press.

Armstrong, S. (1987, June 11). Folks aplenty forecast in parks despite fee hike. *Christian Science Monitor,* p. 21.

Aron, J. B. (1979). Citizen participation at government expense. *Public Administration Review, 39* (Sept./Oct.), 477–485.

Athern, R. G. (1986). *The mythic western twentieth century America*. Lawrence: University of Kansas Press.

Baden, J., & Stroup, R. L. (1981). *Bureaucracy vs. environment: The environmental costs of bureaucratic governance*. Ann Arbor: University of Michigan Press.

Baldwin, K. H. (1976). *Enchanted enclosure: The Army engineers and Yellowstone National Park*. Washington, DC: United States Army, Office of the Chief of Engineers, Historical Division.

Bartik, T. J. (1987). The estimation of demand parameters in hedonic price functions. *Journal of Political Economy, 95* (February), 81–88.

Bartik, T. J. (1988). Measuring the benefits of amenity improvements in hedonic price models. *Land Economics, 64*, 172–183.

Baumol, W., & Bradford, D. (1970). Optimal departures from marginal costs pricing. *American Economic Review, 60*, 265–283.

Baumol, W. J., & Oates, W. E. (1975). *The theory of environmental policy*. Englewood Cliffs, NJ: Prentice-Hall.

Bernstein, M. H. (1955). *Regulating business by independent commission*. Princeton, NJ: Princeton University Press.

Bevins, M. I., & Wilcox, D. P. (1980). *Outdoor recreation participation: Analysis of national surveys, 1959–1978* (Bulletin 686). Burlington: Vermont Agricultural Experiment Station.

Bingham, G. (1986). *Resolving environmental disputes*. Washington, DC: The Conservation Foundation.

Boadway, R. (1979) *Public sector economics*. Boston: Little, Brown.

Bockstael, N. E., Hanemann, W. M., & Kling, C. L. (1987). Modeling recreational demand in a multiple site framework. *Water Resources Research, 23* (May), 951–960.

Bockstael, N. E., Hanemann, W. M., & Strand, I. E., Jr. (1986). *Measuring the benefits of water quality improvements using recreation demand models*. Unpublished manuscript.

Boulding, K. (1969). Economics as a moral science. *American Economic Review, 59* (March), 1–12.

Bozeman, B. (1979). *Public management and policy analysis*. New York: St. Martin's Press.

Brock, J. M., Larson, J. D., Huhs, W. F., Reilly, M. D., & Rogers, J. (1984). *Montana tourism marketing research project: Executive summary*. Helena: Montana Department of Commerce.

Brockman, C. F. (1973). *Recreational use of wild lands*. New York: McGraw-Hill.

Brown, G. M., & Mendelsohn, R. (1984). The hedonic travel cost method. *Review of Economics and Statistics, 59* (August), 272–268.

Brown, G. M., & Pollakowski, H. O. (1977). Economic valuation of shoreline. *Review of Economics and Statistics, 59* (August), 272–278.

Bryan, H. (1977). Leisure value systems and recreational specialization: The case of trout fishermen. *Journal of Leisure Research, 9* (3), 174–187.

Bryan, H. (1979). *Conflict in the great outdoors: Toward understanding and managing for diverse sportsmen's preferences*. Tuscaloosa: University of Alabama Press.

Bryan, H. (1982). A social science perspective for managing recreational conflict. In

R. H. Stroud (Ed.), *Marine recreational fisheries* (pp. 15–22). Washington, DC: Sport Fishing Institute.

Buchanan, J. M., & Tollison, R. D. (Eds.). (1984) *The theory of public choice II.* Ann Arbor: University of Michigan Press.

Burch, W. R., Jr. (1971). *Daydreams and nightmares: A sociological essay on the American environment.* New York: Harper and Row.

Burch, W. R., Jr., & DeLuca, D. R. (1984). *Measuring the social impact of natural resource policies.* Albuquerque: University of New Mexico Press.

Bury, R. L., & Fish, C. B. (1980). Controlling wilderness recreation: What managers think and do. *Journal of Soil and Water Conservation, 35,* 90–93.

Buttel, F. H., Geisler, C. C., & Wiswall, I. W. (1984). *Labor and the environment: An analysis of and annotated bibliography on work place environmental quality in the United States.* Westport, CT: Greenwood Press.

California Coastal Commission. (1986). Voters tackle offshore oil, approve control measures. *Coastal News, 1* (November), 3–4.

California Department of Commerce. (1986). *California's major commercial ports.* Sacramento: Author.

California State Coastal Conservancy. (1984). *Commercial fishing facilities in California.* Oakland: Author.

Cameron, J. (1928). *The development of governmental forest control in the U.S.* Baltimore: Johns Hopkins Press.

Cameron, T. A., & James, M. D. (1987). Efficient estimation methods for "closed-ended" contingent valuation surveys. *Review of Economics and Statistics, 69* (May), 269–276.

Carroll, P. N. (1969). *Puritanism and the wilderness.* New York: Columbia University Press.

Carson, R. T., Hanemann, W. M., & Mitchell, R. C. (1986). *The use of simulated political markets to value public goods.* Unpublished manuscript.

Carter, D. (1964). *Power in Washington.* New York: Vintage.

Cascade Holistic Economic Consultants. (1985). *Review of the Gallatin Forest plan and draft environmental impact statement.* Eugene, OR: Author.

Cascade Holistic Economic Consultants. (1987). *Economic database for greater Yellowstone forests.* Eugene OR: Author.

Catton, W. R., Jr. (1980). *Overshoot.* Urbana: University of Illinois Press.

Catton, W. R., Jr. (1982). *Social impact assessment in New Zealand—A practical approach.* Wellington, New Zealand: Ministry of Works and Development, Town and Country Planning Directorate.

Center for Continuing Study of the California Economy. (1982). *Recreation activity in California: 1980 with projections to 2000.* Palo Alto: Author.

Charnes, A., & Cooper, W. W. (1961). *Management models and industrial application of linear programming* (Vol. 1). New York: Wiley.

Charnes, A., Cooper, W. W., & Ferguson, R. O. (1965). Optimal estimation of executive compensation by linear programming. *Management Science, 1,* (2), 138–151.

Cheek, N. (1979). Visitor monitoring panel review. *National Park Service Report, Southeast Region, Atlanta, GA.* Atlanta: National Park Service.

Cicchetti, C. J., & Smith, V. K. (1973). Congestion, quality deterioration, and optimal use: Wilderness recreation in the Spanish Peaks Primitive Area. *Social Science Research, 2* (March), 15–30.

Cicchetti, C. J., & Smith, V. K. (1976). *The costs of congestion: An econometric analysis of wilderness recreation.* Cambridge, MA: Ballinger Publishing.

Cicin-Sain, B. (1986). Offshore oil development in California: Challenges to governments and to the public interest [Special issue]. *Public Affairs Report, 27* (2).

Cigler, A. J., & Loomis, B. A. (Eds.). (1983). *Interest group politics.* Washington, DC: Congressional Quarterly Press.

Cinchetti, C. J., Seneca, J. J., & Davidson, P. (1969). *The demand and supply of outdoor recreation.* New Brunswick, NJ: Rutgers University Press.

Ciriacy-Wantrup, S. V. (1947). Capital returns from soil conservation practices. *Journal of Farm Economics, 29* (November), 1181–1196.

Clarke, J. N., & McCool, D. (1985). *Staking out the terrain: Power differentials among natural resource management agencies.* Albany: State University of New York Press.

Clary, D. M. (1986). *Timber and the Forest Service.* Lawrence: University of Kansas Press.

Clawson, M. (1976). *The economics of national forest management.* New York: Resources of the Future.

Clawson, M. (1985, February). Trends in the use of public recreation areas. In *National Outdoor Recreation Trends Symposium II* (pp. 1–12). Myrtle Beach, SC.

Clawson, M., & Knetsch, J. L. (1966). *Economics of outdoor recreation.* Baltimore: Johns Hopkins University Press.

Cobb, R. W., & Elder, C. D. (1983). *Participation in American politics: The dynamics of agenda-building.* Baltimore: John Hopkins University Press.

Coffin, A. (1986). Economics of non-resident anglers. *Montana Troutline, 6* (May), 1, 11.

Cohon, J. L., & Marks, D. H. (1973). A review and evaluation of multiobjective programming techniques. *Water Resources Research, 2* (2), 208–220.

Cole, D. N. (1981). Vegetational changes associated with recreational use and fire suppression in the Eagle Cap Wilderness, Oregon: Some management implications. *Biological Conservation, 20,* 247–270.

Cole, D. N. (1982). Controlling the spread of campsites at popular wilderness destinations. *Journal of Soil and Water Conservation, 37,* 291–295.

Collins, W. P. (1980). Public participation in bureaucratic decision making: A reappraisal. *Public Administration, 58* (Winter), 465–477.

Conland, J. (1985). *Social impact assessment in New Zealand—A practical approach.* Wellington, New Zealand: Ministry of Works and Development, Town and Country Planning Directorate.

Coppleman, P. D. (1987). Crisis in forest planning. *Public Lands, 5* (2), 1–3.

Cordell, K., & Fesenmaier, D., & Leiber, S., & Hartman, L. (1985, February). Advancements in methodology for projecting future recreation participation. In *National Outdoor Recreation Trends Symposium II* (pp. 89–109). Myrtle Beach, SC.

Crandall, D. (1984). America's national forest: An essential link in recreation supply. In A. E. Gamache (Ed.), *Selling the federal forest* (pp. 212–221). New York: Institute of Forest Resources.

Crane, D. M., Brown, R. E., & Kinsky, A. M. (1974). *Plan formulation and evaluation studies—recreation, volume I. Evaluation of recreation use survey procedures.* Fort Belvoir, VA: U.S. Army Corps of Engineers, Institute for Water Resources.

Cropsey, J. (1980). Capitalist liberalism. In J. Cropsey (Ed.), *Political philosophy and the issues of politics* (pp. 53–75). Chicago: University of Chicago Press.

Cropsey, J. (1980). The invisible hand: Moral and political considerations. In J. Cropsey (Ed.), *Political philosophy and the issues of politics* (pp. 76–89). Chicago: University of Chicago Press.

Crowe, D. M. (1983). *Comprehensive planning for wildlife resources*. Cheyenne: Wyoming Game and Fish Department.

Culhane, P. J. (1981). *Public lands politics*. Baltimore: Johns Hopkins University Press.

Cummings, R. G., Brookshire, D., & Schulze, W. D. (1986). *Valuing environmental goods*. Totowa, NJ: Rowman and Allanheld.

Cupps, D. S. (1977). Emerging problems of citizen participation. *Public Administration Review, 37* (Sept./Oct.), 478–487.

Dailey, R. (1984). *The Montana travel industry, 1983*. Helena: Montana Department of Commerce.

Dana, S. T., & Fairfax, S. K. (1980). *Forest and range policy* (2nd ed.). New York: McGraw-Hill.

Daniels, S. E. (1986). *Efficient provision of recreational opportunities: The case of U.S. Forest Service campgrounds*. Doctoral dissertation, Duke University, Durham, NC.

Davis, R. K. (1963). *The value of outdoor recreation: An economic study of the Maine woods*. Unpublished doctoral dissertation, Harvard University.

Derthick, M. (1979). *Policymaking for social security*. Washington, DC: The Brookings Institute.

Devall, W., & Sessions, G. (Eds.). (1985). *Deep ecology*. Salt Lake City: Peregrine Smith.

Deyak, T., & Smith, V. K. (1978). Congestion and participation in outdoor recreation: A household production function approach. *Journal of Environmental Economics and Management, 5*, 63–80.

Diamond, M. (1979). Ethics and politics: The American way. In R. H. Horwitz (Ed.), *The moral foundations of the American republic* (2nd ed.) (pp. 39–72). Charlottesville: University of Virginia Press.

Dolan, E. G. (1969). *Tanstaafl: The economic strategy for environmental crisis*. New York: Holt, Rinehart, and Winston.

Dorfman, R. (1984). On optimal congestion. *Journal of Environmental Economics, 11* (June), 91–106.

Driver, B. L. (1987). Benefits of river and trail recreation: The limited state of knowledge and why it is limited. In S. Seguire (Ed.), *Proceedings of the first international congress on trail and river recreation*. Vancouver: Outdoor Recreation Council of British Columbia.

Dubos, R. (1968). *So human and animal*. New York: Scribners.

Dumas, L. J. (1986). *The overburdened economy*. Berkeley: University of California Press.

Duncan, D. P. (1986). What forestry is. *Journal of Forestry, 84* (8), 65.

Dunn, W. (1981). *Public policy analysis: An introduction*. Englewood Cliffs, NJ: Prentice-Hall.

Eckstein O. (1958). *Water resource development: The economics of project evaluation*. Cambridge: Harvard University Press.

Ellison, L. (1942). Trends of forest recreation in the United States. *Journal of Forestry*, *40* (8), 630–638.

Emerson, P. (1986). The below cost timber sale issue: Going against the grain? *Western Wildlands*, *4* (Spring), 16–21.

Everhart, W. C. (1983). *The National Park Service*. Boulder, CO: Westview Press.

The Federal Aid in Sport Fish Restoration Act. (1950). *U.S. Statutes at Large*, 81st Congress (2nd session), *64*, 430–434.

Fish, C. B., & Bury, R. L. (1981). Wilderness visitor management: Diversity and agency politics. *Journal of Forestry*, *79*, 608–612.

Fisher, A., & Krutilla, J. V. (1972). Determination of optimal capacity of resource-based recreation facilities. *Natural Resources Journal*, *12.*, 417–444.

Foresta, R. A. (1984). *America's national parks and their keepers*. Washington, DC: Resource for the Future.

Forest Service budget bureaucracy. (1987). *Wild Montana*, *4* (Summer), 7.

Foss, P. O. (1960). *Politics and grass: The administration of grazing on the public domain*. Seattle: University of Washington Press.

Foss, P. O. (1971). *Conservation in the United States, "a documentary history, recreation."* New York: Chelsea House Publishers.

Fox, S. (1981). *John Muir and his legacy*. Boston: Little, Brown.

Fraley, J. (1985). Should we manage it or leave it alone? *Montana Outdoors*, *16* (July/August), 34–37.

Fraley, J. (1986). The joy of backpacking. *Montana Outdoors*, *17* (July/August), 3–6, 24–25.

Freeman, A. M. (1985). Methods for assessing the benefits of environmental programs. In A. V. Kneese and J. L. Sweeney (Eds.), *Handbook of natural resource and energy economics* (pp. 223–270). Amsterdam: North Holland.

Freeman, A. M. III, & Haveman, R. H. (1977). Congestion, quality deterioration, and heterogeneous tastes. *Journal of Public Economics*, *8*, 225–232.

Freeman, J. L. (1965). *The political process*. New York: Random House.

Freudenberg, W. R. (1987, August). *Sociological training for soil conservation*. Paper presented at the Rural Sociological Society Presymposium, Madison, WI.

Frieden, B. J. (1979). The new regulation comes to suburbia. *The Public Interest*, *55* (Spring), 15–27.

Friedman, M. (1962). *Capitalism and freedom*. Chicago: University of Chicago Press.

Friedman, M. (1980). *Free to choose*. New York: Harcourt, Brace, Jovanovich.

Friedman, M., & Friedman, R. D. (1962). *Capitalism and freedom*. Chicago: University of Chicago Press.

Friedmann, J. (1973). *Retracking America: A theory of transactive planning*. Garden City, NY: Anchor Press/Doubleday.

Frost, J., & McCool, S. (1986). *The Montana outdoor recreation needs survey*. Helena: Montana Department of Fish, Wildlife, and Parks.

Gade, O., Stillwell, H. D., & Rex, A. (1986). *North Carolina: People and environments*. Boone, NC: GeoApp Publishing.

Gallup Organization. (1986, April 2). Consumer taste. *The Wall Street Journal*, Section 4, p. 13D.

Gamache, A. E. (Ed.). (1984). *Selling the federal forests*. New York: Institute of Forest Resources.

General Accounting Office. (1982). *Increasing entrance fees—National Park Service* (GAO/CED–82–84). Washington, DC: U.S. Government Printing Office.

Gibbs, D. (1983). *A comparison of travel cost models which estimate recreation demand for water resource development: Summary report*. Washington, DC: U.S. Bureau of Reclamation.

Gibbs, K. C., & Van Hees, W. S. (1981). Cost of operating public campgrounds. *Journal of Leisure Research, 13* (3), 243–253.

Gilder, G. (1981). *Wealth and poverty*. New York: Basic Books.

Giles, R. H., Jr. (1978). *Wildlife management*. San Francisco: W. H. Freeman and Company.

Gilligan, J. P. (1960). *The development of policy and administration of Forest Service primitive and wilderness areas in the United States*. Doctoral dissertation, University of Michigan.

Goldwin, R. A. (1979). Of men and angels: A search for morality in the Constitution. In R. H. Horwitz (Ed.), *The moral foundations of the American republic* (2nd ed.) (pp. 1–18). Charlottesville: University of Virginia Press.

Goldwin, R. A., & Scambra, W. A. (Eds.). (1980). *How democratic is the Constitution?* Washington, DC: American Enterprise Institute.

Goldwin, R. A., & Scambra, W. A. (Eds.). (1982). *How capitalistic is the Constitution?* Washington, DC: American Enterprise Institute.

Goodpaster, K., & Sayre, K. M. (Eds). (1979). *Ethics and problems of the 21st century*. Notre Dame: University of Notre Dame Press.

Gormley, W. T. (1981). Statewide remedies for public underrepresentation in regulatory proceedings. *Public Administration Reviews, 41* (July/Aug.), 454–462

Graham, P. (1986). A reflection of choices. *Montana Outdoors, 17* (April/June), 20–22, 26.

Graves, H. H. (1917). Recreational uses of the national forests. *American Forestry, 23*, 133–138.

Greeley, W. B. (1927). What shall we do with our mountains? *Sunset Magazine, 59*, 14–15.

Haines, A. L. (1977). *The Yellowstone story* (Vols. 1 and 2). Yellowstone National Park, WY: Yellowstone Library and Museum Association.

Hakim, C. (1982). *Secondary analysis in social research*. London: George Allen and Unwin.

Hamilton, A., Madison, J., & Jay, J. (1961). *The federalist papers* (No. 10). New York: American Library.

Hammitt, W. E., & Cole, D. N. (1987). *Wildland recreation: Ecology and management*. New York: John Wiley.

Hammond, J. L. (1977). Wilderness and life in cities. *Sierra Club Bulletin, 62* (April), 12–14.

Hampton, H. D. (1971). *How the U.S. Cavalry saved our national parks*. Bloomington: Indiana University Press.

Hanemann, W. M. (1984). Welfare evaluations in contingent valuation experiments with discrete responses. *American Journal of Agricultural Economics, 66* (August), 332–341.

Harrington, W. (1987). *Measuring recreation supply*. Baltimore: Johns Hopkins University Press.

Haveman, R. H. (1973). Common property, congestion, and environmental pollution. *Quarterly Journal of Economics, 87*, 278–287.

Hays, S. P. (1959). *Conservation and the gospel of efficiency: The progressive conservation movement, 1890–1920*. Cambridge, MA:Harvard University Press.

Heclo, H. (1978). Issue networks and the executive establishment. In A. King (Ed.), *The new American political system* (pp. 87–124). Washington, DC: American Enterprise Institute.

Heiman, M. (1986). *Coastal recreation in California: Policy, management, access*. Berkeley: University of California, Institute of Governmental Studies.

Heiman, M. (1988). *The quiet evolution: Power, planning, and profits*. New York: Praeger.

Held, V. (Ed.). (1980). *Property, profits, and economic justice*. Belmont, CA: Wadsworth.

Hendee, J. C. (1974). A multiple-satisfaction approach to game management. *Wildlife Society Bulletin, 2*, 104–113.

Hendee, J. C., Clark, R. N., & Stankey, G. H. (1974). A framework for agency use of public input in resource decision making. *Journal of Soil and Water Conservation, 29* (2), 60–66.

Hendee, J. C., Lucas, R. C. Tracy, R. H., Staed, T., Clark, R. N., Stankey, G. H., & Yarnell, R. A. (1976). Methods for acquiring public input. In J. C. Pierce and H. R. Doerksen (Eds.), *Water politics and public involvement* (pp. 125–144). Ann Arbor, MI: Ann Arbor Science.

Hendee, J. C., & Stankey, G. H. (1973, September). Biocentricity in wilderness management. *BioScience, 23*, 535–538.

Hendee, J. C., Stankey, G. H., & Lucas, R. C. (1978). *Wilderness management* (Miscellaneous publication No. 1365). Washington, DC: U.S. Department of Agriculture, Forest Service.

Hof, J. G., & Kaiser, H. F. (1983). *Projections for future forest recreation use* [Bulletin WO–2]. Washington, DC: U.S. Forest Service.

Hof, J. G., & Kaiser, H. F. (1983). Long-term outdoor recreation participation projections for public land management agencies. *Journal of Leisure Research, 15* (1), 1–14.

Hofstadter, R. (1979). The founding fathers: An age of realism. In R. H. Horwitz (Ed.), *The moral foundations of the American republic* (2nd ed.) (pp. 73–85). Charlottesville: University of Virginia Press.

Holmes, B. H. (1972). *A history of federal water resources programs, 1800–1960*. Washington, DC: Department of Agriculture, Economic Research Service.

Horstman, E. (Ed.). (1982). *National parks in crisis*. Silver Spring, MD: Information Dynamics.

Horwitz, R. H. (1979). John Locke and the preservation of liberty: A problem of civic education. In R. H. Horwitz (Ed.), *The moral foundations of the American republic* (2nd ed.) (pp. 129–156). Charlottesville: University of Virginia Press.

Humphrey, C. R., & Buttel, F. R. (1982). *Environment, energy, and society*. Belmont, CA: Wadsworth.

Ignizio, J. P. (1976). *Goal programming and extensions*. Lexington, MA: D. C. Heath.

Ijiri, Y. (1965). *Management goals and accounting for control.* Chicago: Rand McNally.

Irland, L. C. (1979). *Wilderness economics and policy.* Lexington, MA: Lexington Books.

Iverson, D. C. (1983). *Refining the decision space: Incorporating issues, concerns, and opportunities.* Ogden, UT: U.S. Department of Agriculture, Forest Service Region 4.

Jackson, D. H. (1986). Below cost sales: Causes and solutions. *Western Wildlands, 12* (Spring), 11–15.

Jameson, D. A., Moore, M.A.D., & Case, P. J. (1982). *Principles of land and resource management planning.* Washington, DC: U.S. Department of Agriculture, Forest Service, Land and Resources Management Planning.

Jenkins, W. I. (1978). *Policy analysis: A political and organizational perspective.* New York: St. Martin's Press.

Junkin, D. (1986, June 9). A commission looks at outdoor recreation. *High Country News,* p. 4.

Kalter, R., & Gosse, L. (1969). *Outdoor recreation in New York State* [Special Cornell Series No. 5]. Ithaca, NY: Cornell University.

Kamieniecki, S. (1981). Improving public representation. *The Bureaucrat, 10* (Fall), 50–55.

Kaplan, M. (1960). *Leisure in America: A social inquiry.* New York: John Wiley.

Kaufman, H. (1960). *The forest ranger: A study in administrative behavior.* Baltimore: Johns Hopkins University Press.

Keeney, K. D., & Raiffa, H. (1976). *Decisions with multiple objectives: Performances and value tradeoffs.* New York: Wiley.

Kelly, J. (1981). *Social benefits of outdoor recreation.* Washington, DC: U.S. Forest Service.

Kelly, J. (1983). Leisure styles: A hidden core. *Leisure Sciences, 5* (4), 321–338.

Kelman, S. (1981). *What price incentives?* Boston: Auburn House.

Kirschner Associates, Inc. (1975). *Interim report: Evaluation of five previous nationwide citizen surveys.* Washington, DC: Author.

Klar, L. R., & Chirin, A. (1983). Recreation at drinking water reservoirs in Massachusetts: A survey of water managers. *Water Resources Bulletin, 19* (3), 477–481.

Knott, J., & Wildavsky, A. (1980). If dissemination is the solution, what is the problem? *Knowledge: Creation, Diffusion, Utilization, 1* (4), 537–578.

Knudson, D. M. (1984). *Outdoor recreation* (rev. ed.). New York: Macmillan.

Knudson, D. M., & Curry, E. B. (1981). Camper's perceptions of site deterioration and crowding. *Journal of Forestry, 79,* 92–94.

Knuth, B. A. (1986). *A fisheries and wildlife indicator system for use in natural resource management.* Doctoral dissertation, Virginia Polytechnic Institute and State University.

Kronberg, C., & Tuholske, J. (1985). *Forest plans and fisheries: Threat or promise.* Missoula: National Wildlife Federation.

Krutilla, J. V. (1967). Conservation reconsidered. *American Economic Review, 57,* 777–786.

Krutilla, J. V., & Fisher, A. C. (1975). *The economics of natural environments.* Baltimore: Johns Hopkins University Press.

Lacey, M. J. (1979). *The mysteries of earth-making dissolve: A study of Washington's intellectual community and the origins of environmentalism in the late nineteenth century*. Doctoral dissertation, George Washington University.

La Page, W. (1971). Cultural fogweed and outdoor recreation research. *Proceedings of the recreation symposium, Northeast Forest Experiment Station* (186–193). Upper Darby, PA.

La Page, W. (1976, October). A plea for mediocrity in recreation research goals. *Proceedings of the research roundtable meeting of the Bureau of Outdoor Recreation*. Washington, DC.

Lareau, T., & Darmstadter, J. (1982). Energy and consumer expenditure patterns: Modeling approaches and projections. *Annual Review of Energy, 7,* 262–292.

Lawyer, D. E. (1970). Recreation boom. *Water Spectrum, 1970* (Summer), 5–12.

Layard, R. (1977). The distributional effects of congestion taxes. *Economica, 44,* 297–304.

Lee, R. G. (1975). *The management of human components in the Yosemite National Park ecosystem.* Yosemite National Park, CA: Yosemite Institute.

Lee, R. G. (1983). *Development of methods for using public participation as a data collection instrument for social impact assessment.* Seattle: University of Washington, College of Forest Resources.

Lee, S. M. (1972). *Goal programming for decision analysis.* Philadelphia: Auerback.

LeGuin, U. (1985). *Always coming home.* New York: Harper and Row.

Lenski, G., & Lenski, J. (1987). *Human societies* (5th ed.). New York: McGraw-Hill.

Leopold, A. (1921). The wilderness and its place in forest recreational policy. *Journal of Forestry, 19* (7), 718–721.

Leopold, A. (1949). *A Sand County almanac.* New York: Oxford University Press.

Levin, R. I., & Kirkpatrick, C. A. (1978). *Quantitative approaches to management* (4th ed.). New York: McGraw-Hill.

Lies, C. H. (1987). U.S. Crop and Livestock Report Service. Personal communication.

Light, S., & Groves, D. (1978). Policy issues in recreation and leisure: An overview. *Policy Studies Journal, 6* (8), 404–412.

Lindsay, B. E., & Dunn, D. L. (1982). An application of mathematical programming to water resources planning: An economic view. *Water Resources Bulletin, 18* (2), 289–296.

Loesel, J. E. (1987). Conservationists negotiate improvements in a forest plan. *Public Lands, 5* (2), 4–5.

Loomis, J., & Sorg, C. (1982). *A critical summary of empirical estimates of the value of wildlife, wilderness, and general recreation related to National Forest Regions.* Unpublished manuscript.

Lopach, J., McKinsey, L., Playne, T., Waldren, E., Calvert, J., & Brown, M. (1983). *We the people of Montana.* Missoula: Mountain Press Publishing.

Lovrich, N. P., & Neiman, M. (1984). *Public choice theory in public administration— An annotated bibliography.* New York: Garland Publishing.

Lucas, R. C. (1978, August). *Wilderness policy and management problems: Possible applications of psychology.* Paper presented at the meeting of the American Psychological Association. Toronto.

Lucas, R. C., Schreuder, H. T., & James, G. A. (1971). *Wilderness use estimation: A pilot test of sampling procedures on the Mission Mountains Primitive Area* (Research Paper INT–109). Washington, DC: U.S. Department of Agriculture, Forest Service.

MacRae, D., Jr., & Whittington, D. (1988). Assessing preferences in cost-benefit analysis: Reflections on rural water supply. *Journal of Policy Analysis and Management, 7*, 234–238.

Magill, A. W. (1983). The reluctant public servants. *Journal of Forestry, 81* (3), 201.

Manning, R. E. (1979). Strategies for managing recreational use of national parks. *Parks, 4*, 13–15.

Market Opinion Research. (1986). *Participation in outdoor recreation among American adults and the motivations which drive participation.* Washington, DC: President's Commission on Americans Outdoors.

Mazmanian, D., & Nienaber, J. (1979). *Can organizations change? Environmentalism, participation, and the Corps of Engineers.* Washington, DC: The Brookings Institute.

McConnell, G. (1966). *Private power and American democracy.* New York: Alfred A. Knopf.

McConnell, K. E. (1977). Congestion and willingness to pay: A study of beach use. *Land Economics, 53*, 185–195.

McConnell, K. E. (1980). Valuing congested recreation sites. *Journal of Environmental Economics and Management, 7*, 389–394.

McConnell, K. E. (1983). Existence and bequest values. In R. D. Rowe and L. G. Chestnut (Eds.), *Managing air quality and scenic resources at national parks and wilderness areas* (pp. 254–264). Boulder, CO: Westview Press.

McConnell, K. E. (1986). *The damages to recreational activities from PCBs in the New Bedford Harbor.* Unpublished manuscript.

McConnell, K. E., & Duff, V. A. (1976). Estimating net benefits of recreation under conditions of excess demand. *Journal of Environmental Economics and Management, 2*, 224–230.

McFadden, D. (1974). Conditional logit analysis of qualitative choice behavior. In P. Zarembka (Ed.), *Frontiers in econometrics* (pp. 172–187). New York: Academic Press.

McWilliams, W. C. (1979). On equality as the moral foundation for community. In R. H. Horwitz (Ed.), *The moral foundations of the American republic* (2nd ed.) (pp. 183–213). Charlottesville: University of Virginia Press.

Mendelsohn, R. (1987). Modeling the demand for outdoor recreation. *Water Resources Research, 23*, 961–967.

Merriam, L. C., Smith, C. K., Miller, D. E., Huang, C. T., Tappeiner II, J. C., Goeckerman, K., Bloemendal, J. A., & Costello, T. M. (1973). *Newly developed campsites in the Boundary Waters Canoe Area: A study of five years' use* (Bulletin 511). St. Paul: University of Minnesota Agricultural Experiment Station.

Mishan, E. J. (1976). *Cost benefit analysis.* New York: Praeger.

Mitchell, R. C. (1979). Natural environmental lobbies and the apparent illogic of collective action. In C. E. Russell (Ed.), *Collective decision making* (pp. 87–121). Baltimore: Johns Hopkins University Press.

Mitchell, R. C., & Carson, R. T. (1987). *How far along the learning curve is the contingent valuation method?* (Quality of Environment Division, Resources for the Future Paper 87–07). Unpublished manuscript.

Mitchell, R. C., & Carson, R. T. (1989). *Using surveys to value public goods: The contingent valuation method.* Washington, DC: Resources for the Future.

Mohai, P. (1987). Rational decision making in the planning process: Some empirical evidence from RARE II. *Environmental Law, 17* (3), 507–556.

Montana Department of Commerce. (1985). *Montana statistical abstract—1984.* Helena: Author.

Montana State University Statistical Research Center. (1982). *Survey of the economic impact of non-resident anglers in Montana—1982 season.* Bozeman: Trout Unlimited.

Morey, E. R. (1981). The demand for site-specific recreational activities: A characteristics approach. *Journal of Environmental Economics and Management, 8* (December), 345–361.

Morrison, D. E. (1978). Equity impacts of some major energy alternatives. In S. Warkov (Ed.), *Energy policy in the United States* (pp. 164–193). New York: Praeger.

Moulds, H. (1964). Private property in John Locke's state of nature. *The American Journal of Economics and Sociology, 23,* 179–188.

Mueller, D. C. (1979). *Public choice.* New York: Cambridge University Press.

Musgrave, R., & Musgrave, P. (1980). *Public finance in theory and practice.* New York: McGraw-Hill.

Mushkin, S. J., & Vehorn, C. L. (1980). User fees and charges. In C. H. Levine (Ed.), *Managing fiscal stress* (pp. 222–234). Chatham, NJ: Chatham House.

Myers, N. (1979). *The sinking ark.* Oxford: Pergamon Press.

Myers, P., & Reid, A. C. (1986). *State parks in a new era: A survey of issues and innovations.* Washington, DC: Conservation Foundation.

Nash, R. (1973). *Wilderness and the American mind* (rev. ed.). New Haven, CT: Yale University Press.

National Academy of Sciences. (1969). *A program for outdoor recreation research.* Washington, DC: Author.

National Recreation and Park Association. (1986). *Special revenue sources for parks and recreation: A survey of the states.* Alexandria, VA: Author.

Neely, W. P., North, R. M., & Fortson, J. C. (1971). Planning and selecting multiobjective projects by goal programming. *Water Resources Bulletin, 12* (1), 14–25.

Neely, W. P., Sellers, J., & North, R. M. (1980). Goal programming priority sensitivity analysis: An application in natural resource decision making processes. *Interfaces, 10* (5), 83–89.

1982 survey of purchases of 35 mm SLR cameras and accessories. (1982, March 13). *Newsweek,* p. 54.

Noe, F. P. (1974). Leisure life styles and social class: A trend analysis, 1900–1960. *Sociology and Social Research, 3* (58), 286–294.

North, R. M., Neely, W. P., & Carlton, R. (1976). *The highest and best uses of the Oklawaha River basin and Lake Rousseau for the economy and the environment.* Jacksonville, FL: U.S. Department of the Army, Corps of Engineers, Jacksonville District.

North, R. M., Neely, W. P., Sellers, J., & Taylor, B. W. (1984). Goal programming applications in water project analysis. In Y. Y. Haines & D. Allee (Eds.), *Multiobjective analysis in water resources* (pp. 125–152). New York: American Society of Civil Engineers.

Ochs, J., & Thorn, R. S. (1984). Measuring the site-specific recreation benefits resulting from improved water quality: An upper bound approach. *Water Resources Bulletin, 20* (6), 923–927.

O'Leary, J. T. (1985, February). Social trends in outdoor recreation. *Proceedings of the National Outdoor Recreation Trends Symposium II* (pp. 24–36). Myrtle Beach, SC.

O'Leary, J. T., Peine, J., & Blahna, D. (1980, February). Trends in selected day use activities. *Proceedings of the National Outdoor Recreation Trends Symposium I* (pp. 205–214). Durham, NH.

Oliveira, R. A., & Rausser, G. C. (1977). Daily fluctuations in campground use: An econometric analysis. *American Journal of Agricultural Economics, 59* (May), 283–293.

Outdoor Recreation Resources Review Commission. (1962). *Federal agencies and outdoor recreation, ORRRC study report 13.* Washington, DC: U.S. Government Printing Office.

Outdoor Recreation Resources Review Commission. (1962). *Land acquisition for outdoor recreation—analysis of selected legal problems, ORRRC study report 16.* Washington, DC: U.S. Government Printing Office.

Outdoor Recreation Resource Review Commission. (1962). *Outdoor recreation for America.* Washington, DC: U.S. Government Printing Office.

Parsons, J. E., Jr. (1969). Locke's doctrine of property. *Social Research, 36* (3), 289–411.

Patrick, R. H. (1989). Optimal cyclical congestion (Working Paper 89–7). Golden: Colorado School of Mines.

Pechman, J., & Okner, B. (1974). *Who bears the tax burden?* Washington, DC: The Brookings Institute.

Peterson, G. L., & Randall, A. (Eds.). (1984). *Valuation of wildland resource benefits.* Boulder, CO: Westview.

Pigram, J. J. (1983). *Outdoor recreation and resource management.* New York: St. Martin's Press.

Pinchot, G. (1910). *The fight for conservation.* Seattle: University of Washington Press.

Plato. (1968). *The republic.* New York: Basic Books.

Power, T. (1987). *The economic impact of wilderness classification for the Rocky Mountain front roadless areas in Montana.* Unpublished manuscript, University of Montana, Department of Economics.

President's Commission on Americans Outdoors. [PCAO] (1986, September 24). *Americans outdoors: A call to action.* Unpublished, manuscript.

President's Commission on Americans Outdoors [PCAO]. (1987). *Americans outdoors: The legacy, the challenge.* Washington, DC: Island Press.

President's Private Sector Survey on Cost Control. (1983). *Report of the task force on user charges, May 26, 1983.* Washington, DC: U.S. Government Printing Office.

Queenan, C. (1986). *Long Beach and Los Angeles: A tale of two ports.* Northridge, CA: Windsor.

Rambo, A. T., & Sajise, P. E. (1984). *An introduction to human ecology: Research on agricultural systems in Southeast Asia.* Los Banos: University of the Philippines.

Redburn, S., Buss, T. F., Foster, S. K., & Binning, W. C. (1980). How representative are mandated citizen participation processes? *Urban Affairs Quarterly, 15* (March), 345–352.

Regan, T. (1982). *All that dwell therein*. Berkeley: University of California Press.

Reich, C. A. (1962). *Bureaucracy and the forest*. Santa Barbara, CA: Center for the Study of Democratic Institutions.

Reid, R. T. (1987, February 12). From spuds to scenery: West shifts economic focus. *Washington Post*, pp. 20–21.

Reiger, J. F. (1975). *American sportsmen and the origins of conservatism*. New York: Winchester.

Ribaudo, M. O., & Epp, D. J. (1984). The importance of sample discrimination in using the travel cost method to estimate the benefits of improved water quality. *Land Economics, 60* (November), 397–403.

Rogers, E. M. (1983). *Diffusion of innovations*. New York: The Free Press.

Ruffner, E. R., Sieber, R. E., & Ahmadi, M. (1986, September). Assessing the potential of goal programming to improve the effectiveness of resource allocation among demand-side management programs. *Proceedings of the American Power Conference* (pp. 124–159). Orlando, FL.

Rules and regulations: National Forest System and resource management planning. (1979). *Federal Register, 44* (181).

Runte, A. (1979). *National parks: The American experience*. Lincoln: University of Nebraska Press.

Russell, R., Thor, E. C., & Elsner, G. H. (1979, June). GPLUS—A new program for multiple objective planning. *Proceedings of the U.S. Department of Agriculture and Farm Foundation Multiple Objective Planning Workshop* (pp. 1–149). Tucson, AZ.

Savas, E. S. (1982). *Privatizing the public sector*. Chatham, NJ: Chatham House.

Sax, J. L. (1978). *Recreation policy on the federal lands*. Berkeley: University of California Press.

Schaeffer, R. (1986). Lumbering into oblivion. *In These Times* (November), 19–25.

Schechter, M., & Lucas, R. C. (1978). *Simulation of recreational use for park and wilderness management*. Baltimore: Johns Hopkins University Press.

Schelling, T. (1968). The life you save may be your own. In S. B. Chase (Ed.), *Problems of public expenditure analysis* (pp. 127–162). Washington, DC: The Brookings Institute.

Scherer, D., & Attig, T. (1983). *Ethics and the environment*. Englewood Cliffs, NJ: Prentice-Hall.

Schmidt, J. C., & Boyer, J. (1983). An overview of coal leasing, mine development, and future production in the Powder River coal basin, Montana and Wyoming. *Coal Development VI*. Billings, MT: Bureau of Land Management.

Schmookler, A. B. (1984). *The parable of the tribes*. Berkeley: University of California Press.

Schnaiberg, A. (1980). *The environment: From surplus to scarcity*. New York: Oxford University Press.

Schoenfeld, C. (1976). Managing wildlife in forest wilderness. *American Forests, 82,* 38, 54–56.

Schwartz, W. (Ed.). (1969). *Voices for the wilderness*. New York: Ballantyne.

Scitovsky, T. (1978). *The joyless economy: An inquiry into human satisfaction and consumer dissatisfaction*. Oxford: Oxford University Press.

Scott, R., & Gartner, W. C. (1987). An economic feasibility analysis for concessionaire management of campgrounds in the Siuslaw National Forest. *Western Journal of Applied Forestry, 2* (3), 91–94.

Sellers, J., Neeley, W. P., & North, R. M. (1981, March). Goal programming application in natural resource investment. *Proceedings of the conference of the southeastern region of the American Institute of Decision Sciences* (p. 144).

Shaw, W., & Mangun, W. (1984). *Nonconsumptive use of wildlife in the United States* [Service Resource Publication No. 154]. Washington, DC: U.S. Fish and Wildlife Service.

Shelby, B. B., & Nielsen, J. M. (1975). *Use levels and user satisfaction in the Grand Canyon.* Boulder, CO: Human Ecological Research, Inc.

Siehl, G. (1985). *Outdoor recreation: A new commission is created.* Washington, DC: Congressional Research Service.

Singer, P. (1981). *The expanding circle.* New York: Farrar, Strauss, and Giroux.

Smith, A. (1904). *The wealth of nations.* New York: G. P. Putnam's Sons.

Smith, V. K. (1981). Congestion, travel cost recreational demand models and benefit evaluation. *Journal of Environmental Economics and Management, 8,* 92–96.

Smith, V. K. (1987). Nonuse values in benefit cost analysis. *Southern Economic Journal, 54,* (July), 19–26.

Smith, V. K., & Desvousges, W. H. (1985). The generalized travel cost model and water quality benefits: A reconsideration. *Southern Economic Journal, 52* (October), 371–381.

Smith, V. K., & Desvousges, W. H. (1986). *Measuring water quality benefits.* Boston: Kluwer-Nijhoff.

Smith, V. K., & Desvousges, W. H. (1986). The value of avoiding a LULU: Hazardous waste disposal sites. *Review of Economics and Statistics, 68* (May), 293–299.

Smith, V. K., & Kaoru, Y. (1986). Modeling recreation demand within a random utility framework. *Economic Letters, 22* (December), 395–399.

Smith, V. K., & Kaoru, Y. (1987). The hedonic travel cost model: A view from the trenches. *Land Economics, 63* (May), 179–192.

Smith, V. K., & Kaoru, Y. (1990). "Signals or noise? Explaining the variation in recreation benefit estimates." *American Journal of Agricultural Economics, 72* (May), 419–433.

Smith, V. K., & Kopp, R. J. (1980). The spatial limits of the travel cost recreation demand model. *Land Economics, 56,* 64–72.

Smith, Z. (1985). *Interest group interaction and groundwater policy formation in the Southwest.* Baltimore: University Press of America.

Social Science Research Council. (1973, March-July). *Social Indicators Newsletter.* Washington, DC.

Soden, D. L. (1985). *Public choice in water resource management: Two case studies of the small-scale hydroelectric controversy.* Doctoral dissertation, Washington State University.

Soden, D. L. (1987). *A conceptual formation of public participation and decision making in the natural resource and environmental policy issue area.* (Occasional papers in Coastal Zone Studies). Pensacola: University of West Florida.

Soden, D. L. (1987, March). *Ethical properties of politics: A research note on the application of public choice theory in natural resource and environmental politics.* Paper presented at the annual meeting of the Western Political Science Association, Anaheim, CA.

Solan, D. (1982, October). A macro value-determined model of outdoor recreation behavior. *Proceedings of the NRPA/SPRE Leisure Research Symposium*. Louisville, KY.

Sorg, C. F., & Loomis, J. B. (1985). *Empirical estimates of amenity forest values: A comparative review* (General Technology Report RM–107). Fort Collins, CO: U.S. Forest Service, Rocky Mountain Forest and Range Experiment Station.

Sowell, T. (1981). *Markets and minorities*. London: Basil Blackwell.

Sproule-Jones, M. (1982). Public choice theory and natural resources: Methodological explication and critique. *American Political Science Review, 76* (4), 790–804.

Stamps, S., & Stamps, M. (1985). Race, class, and leisure activities of urban residents. *Journal of Leisure Research, 17* (1), 40–56.

Stankey, G. H., Cole, D. N., Lucas, R. C., Petersen, M. E., & Frissell, S. S. (1985). *The limits of acceptable change (LAC) system for wilderness planning* (Research Paper INT-176). Washington, DC: U.S. Department of Agriculture, Forest Service.

Stanley, G., & Lucas, R. (1986, May). *Shifting trends in backcountry and wilderness use*. Paper presented at the National Symposium in Social Science Resource Management, Corvallis, OR.

Steuer, R. E. (1986). *Multiple criteria optimization: Theory, computation, and application*. New York: John Wiley and Sons.

Stevens, T. H., & Allen, P. G. (1980). Estimating the benefits of recreation under conditions of congestion. *Journal of Environmental Economics and Management, 7*, 395–400.

Stockman, D. (1986). *The triumph of politics*. New York: Harper and Row.

Suits, D. (1977). Measurement of tax progressivity. *American Economic Review, 67*, 747–752.

Taylor, B. W., III (1982). *Introduction to management science*. Dubuque, IA: William C. Brown Publishers.

Taylor, B. W., III, & North, R. M. (1975). Approaches to multiobjective planning in water resources projects. *Water Resources Bulletin, 2* (5), 999–1088.

Taylor, R. (1988, February 24). Panel approves final O.K. of 3 offshore Exxon rigs. *Los Angeles Times* (Section I), pp. 3, 18.

Taylor, S. V., & Reilly, M. D. (1986). *Economic impact of the outfitting industry on the state of Montana*. Bozeman: Montana State University School of Business.

Thompson, R. C. (1963). Politics in the wilderness: New York's Adirondack forest preserve. *Forest History, 6*, 14–23.

Tocqueville, A. de (1969). *Democracy in America*. Garden City, NY: Doubleday.

Toole, K. R. (1959). *Montana: An uncommon land*. Norman: University of Oklahoma Press.

Travis, W. (1985). Must oil development be ugly? *California Waterfront Age, 1* (Winter), 25–37.

Treiman, D. (1977). *Occupational prestige in comparative perspective*. New York: Academic Press.

Tugman, S. J. (1985). Beyond fees and charges: The need for a pricing strategy. *Parks and Recreation, 20* (12), 50–53.

Twight, B. W. (1983). *Organizational values and political power: The Forest Service versus the Olympic National Park*. University Park: Pennsylvania State University Press.

Twight, B. W., & Lyden F. J. (1988). Multiple use vs. organizational commitment. *Forest Science, 34* (2), 474–486.

U.S. Army Corps of Engineers. (1978). *Information report on determination of recreation benefits, Corps of Engineers civil works water resources projects.* Unpublished manuscript.

U.S. Army Corps of Engineers. (1985). *Final programmatic environmental impact report/ environmental impact statement for landfill development and channel improvements Los Angeles–Long Beach harbors* (Vol.1). Los Angeles: Author.

U.S. Council on Environmental Quality. (1985). *Environmental quality: 15th annual report of the Council on Environmental Quality.* Washington, DC: U.S. Government Printing Office.

U.S. Department of Agriculture. (1983). *Principle laws relating to Forest Service activities* (Agriculture Handbook #453). Washington, DC: U.S. Government Printing Office.

U.S. Department of Agriculture. (1985). *Forest Service manual.* Washington, DC: U.S. Government Printing Office.

U.S. Department of Agriculture. (1985). *Land areas of the national forest system* (Forest Service Publication FS–3F3). Washington, DC: Author.

U.S. Department of the Interior. (1982). *National survey of fishing, hunting, and wildlife-associated recreation: National summary.* Washington, DC: U.S. Government Printing Office.

U.S. Department of the Interior. (1984). *Preliminary findings of the 1982–83 nationwide recreation survey.* Washington, DC: National Park Service.

U.S. Department of the Interior, Bureau of Outdoor Recreation. (1974). *Proceedings of the outdoor recreation research needs workshop.* Washington, DC: U.S. Government Printing Office.

U.S. Department of the Interior, Bureau of Outdoor Recreation and School of Natural Resources, University of Michigan. (1963). *Proceedings: National conference on outdoor recreation research.* Ann Arbor, MI: Ann Arbor Publishers.

U.S. Department of the Interior, Heritage Conservation and Recreation Service. (1978). *National urban recreation study: Executive report.* Washington, DC: U.S. Government Printing Office.

U.S. Department of Labor. (1978). *Consumer expenditures survey, 1972–1973.* Washington, DC: U.S. Government Printing Office.

U.S. Fish and Wildlife Service. (1985). *Potential funding resources to implement the Fish and Wildlife Conservation Act of 1980.* Washington, DC: U.S. Department of the Interior.

U.S. Forest Service. (n.d.). *America's great outdoors: The National Recreation Strategy.* Washington, DC: U.S. Department of Agriculture.

U.S. General Accounting Office. (1980). *Facilities in many national parks and forests do not meet health and safety standards* (CED 80–115). Washington, DC: U.S. Government Printing Office.

U.S. House Committee on Interior and Insular Affairs. (1986). *Greater Yellowstone ecosystem.* Washington DC: U.S. Government Printing Office.

U.S. International Trade Commission. (1981). *Photographic cameras: Summary of trade and tariff information.* Washington, DC: Author.

U.S. International Trade Commission. (1981). *Sporting goods: Summary of trade and tariff information.* Washington, DC: Author.

U.S. International Trade Commission. (1983). *The U.S. auto industry: U.S. factory sales, retail sales, imports, exports, apparent consumption and suggested retail prices, 1964–1984*. Washington, DC: Author.

U.S. National Park Service. (1982). *Federal recreation fee report—1982*. Washington, DC: U.S. Department of the Interior.

U.S. Senate, Committee on Energy and Natural Resources. (1985, June 27). *Hearings before the subcommittee on public lands, reserved water, and resource conservation: Recreation user fees*. Washington, DC: U.S. Government Printing Office.

U.S. Senate, Committee on Interior and Insular Affairs. (1974). *The recreation imperative*. Washington, DC: U.S. Government Printing Office.

U.S. Water Resources Council. (1983). *Economic and environmental principles and guidelines for water and related land resource implementation studies*. Washington, DC: U.S. Government Printing Office.

Van DeVeer, D., & Pierce, C. (1986). *People, penguins, and plastic trees*. Belmont, CA: Wadsworth.

Vaughan, W. J., & Russell, C. S. (1982). Valuing a fishing day: An application of a systematic varying parameter model. *Land Economics, 58* (November), 450–463.

Verberg, K. (1975). *The carrying capacity of recreational lands: A review* (Occasional paper No. 1). Ottawa: Parks Canada Planning Division (Prairie Regional Office).

Verburg, E. A. (1975). *The U.S. Army Corps of Engineers Recreation Development Program: A comparative perspective of equity related to policies and program outcomes*. Fort Belvoir, VA: U.S. Army Corps of Engineers, Institute for Water Resources.

Wacht, R. F., & Whitford, D. T. (1976). A goal programming model for capital investment analysis in nonprofit hospitals. *Financial Management, 5* (2), 37–47.

Wagar, A. (1966). Quality of outdoor recreation. *Trends, 3* (3), 9–12.

Wagar, J. A. (1975). Recreation insights from Europe. *Journal of Forestry, 73*, 353–357.

Walker, J. L. (1977). Setting the agenda in the U.S. Senate. *British Journal of Political Science, 7*, 432–445.

Wallerstein, I. (1975). *The modern world system*. New York: Academic Press.

Wallwork, S., Lenihaw, M. L., & Polzin, P. E. (1980). *Montana outdoor recreation survey*. Helena: Montana Department of Fish, Wildlife, and Parks.

Walsh, R. G., Gillman, R. A., & Loomis, J. B. (1982). *Wilderness resource economics*. Denver: American Wilderness Alliance.

Walsh, R. G., & Loomis, J. B. (1987). "The contribution of recreation to national economic development." In *Literature Review*. Washington, DC: President's Commission on Americans Outdoors.

Walsh, R. G., Loomis, J. B., & Gillman, R. A. (1986). Value option, existence and bequest demands for wilderness. *Land Economics, 60*, 14–29.

Ward, F., & Loomis, J. B. (1986). *The travel cost demand model as an environmental policy assessment tool: a review of the literature*. Unpublished manuscript, New Mexico State University.

Washburne R. F., & Cole, D. N. (1983). *Problems and practices in wilderness management: A survey of managers* (Research paper INT-304). Washington, DC: U.S. Forest Service.

Water Resources Council (WRC). (1983). *Economic and environmental principles and guidelines for water and related land resources implementation studies*. Washington, DC: U.S. Government Printing Office.

Wilderness Society. (1987). *Forests of the future? An assessment of the national forest planning process*. Washington, DC: Author.

Wilderness Society. (1987). *Management directions for the national forests of the greater Yellowstone ecosystem*. Bozeman: Author.

Wilkinson, C. F., & Anderson, H. M. (1985). Land and resource planning in the national forests. *Oregon Law Review, 64* (1, 2), 1–373.

Williamson, L. (1985, May). Doing the budget two-step. *Outdoor Life*, p. 56.

Wilson, J. (1983). *Direct expenditures for hunting and fishing in Montana—1983*. Unpublished manuscript.

Wisdom, H. W. (1985, November). *What should the mix be between technical forestry and the social/managerial sciences: An academic point of view*. Paper presented at the Southern Forestry Symposium. Atlanta, GA.

Wollmuth, D. C., Schomaker, J. H., & Merriam, L. C., Jr. (1985). River recreation experience opportunities in two recreation opportunities spectrum (ROS) classes. *Water Resources Bulletin, 21* (5), 851–858.

Wyoming Game and Fish Department (1987). *Proceedings of the privatization of wildlife and public lands access symposium*. Cheyenne: Author

Yu, J. (1985). The congruence of recreation activity dimensions among urban, suburban, and rural residents, *Journal of Leisure Research, 17* (2), 107–120.

INDEX

About the Editors and Contributors

JOHN D. HUTCHESON, Jr. is a professor of urban studies and public administration at Georgia State University. His research interests include the politics of land use planning and regulation, and citizen involvement in public decision making.

FRANCIS P. NOE is a research sociologist with the National Park Service and adjunct professor at a number of southeastern universities. His research has focused on national, regional, and park-specific issues and appears in sociological, environmental, leisure-recreation journals and textbooks.

ROBERT E. SNOW administers the database for Georgia's statewide comprehensive planning program and has taught at Georgia State University, West Georgia College, and Emory University. His research interests involve methodological problems using survey research in the policy analysis process.

CRAIG W. ALLIN is a professor of political science and chair of the Department of Politics at Cornell College in Mt. Vernon, Iowa. He earned his B.A. degree at Grennell College and his M.A. and Ph.D. in political science at Princeton University. He is the author of *The Politics of Wilderness Preservation* (Greenwood Press, 1982) as well as articles on wilderness preservation and public lands management.

DALE J. BLAHNA is an assistant professor in the Department of Geography and Environmental Studies at Northeastern Illinois University. At the time of this research he was a postdoctoral research fellow with the University of Michigan School of Natural Resources and a consulting sociologist for the U.S. Forest Service. He received his Ph.D. in environment and behavior from the University of Michigan in 1985.

HOBSON BRYAN is professor and Chair of the Department of Sociology at the University of Alabama. His research interests include social implications of natural resource issues and environment/resource policy. He worked with the U.S. Forest Service in developing their social impact assessment program and was awarded a Fulbright Senior Research Fellowship to study natural resource and social impact assessment issues in New Zealand in 1984.

JERRY W. CALVERT is the chairman and professor of the Department of Political Science at Montana State University.

JAMES CARROLL has viewed the natural resource activities of four Department of the Interior agencies. In 1979 he served on detail to the White House Domestic Policy Staff, where his duties involved President Carter's energy initiatives. Prior to joining the federal government, he was a journalist in New Mexico.

STEVEN E. DANIELS is an assistant professor in the Department of Forest Resources at Oregon State University. Previous academic positions include assistant professor in the Department of Forest Resources at Utah State University and lecturer in the School of Forestry and Environmental Studies at Duke University. He received his B.A. degree in economics from Whitman College and his M.S. degree in forestry and his Ph.D. in natural resource economics from Duke University. His research interests involve the efficient public management of natural resources, with special interest in forestry and outdoor recreation.

F. D. DOTTAVIO is the regional chief scientist in the southeastern region of the National Park Service. He is responsible for all science programs in the region and has been actively involved with the President's Commission on Americans Outdoors.

WILLIAM E. HAMMITT is a professor of forest recreation in the Department of Forestry, Wildlife, and Fisheries at the University of Tennessee, Knoxville. He received his Ph.D. in forestry from the University of Michigan. Current research interests involve visitor perceptions of outdoor recreation environments and wilderness solitude studies. He is the co-author of *Wildland Recreation: Ecology and Management* (1987).

GARY HAMPE is an assistant professor of sociology at the University of Wyoming. His research focuses on problems of aesthetic appreciation and management in parks. Family and aging are also areas of specialization.

WILLIAM J. HANSEN received both his B.S. and M.S. from the University of California at Davis in agricultural economics. He has worked for the U.S. Army Corps of Engineers in the areas of natural resource economics and recreations economics for over eighteen years. He was a primary author of the recreation section of the Water Resource Council's *Economic and Environmental Principles and Guidelines for Water and Related Land Resources Implementation Studies* (1983).

MICHAEL K. HEIMAN is an assistant professor of environmental studies and geography at Dickinson College. His latest book, *The Quiet Evolution: Power, Planning, and Profits in New York State* (Praeger, 1988), addresses the political economy of capitalist regional planning. Current research projects include a study of state/local relations on the location of hazardous waste management facilities and implications for the genesis of community-based environmental movements.

PATRICK JOBES is a professor of sociology and a professor in the Agricultural Experiment Station at Montana State University. He is also the current treasurer of the Rural Sociological Society.

BARBARA A. KNUTH is an assistant professor of natural resource policy and management at Cornell University. Her research focuses on evaluation of planned resource management systems, analysis of fisheries and wildlife policy at state and regional levels, and social science applications in recreation and resource management. She has received fellowships from the National Wildlife Federation and Resources for the Future and is a member of numerous professional and honorary societies, including Phi Beta Kappa, Policy Studies Organization, Human Dimensions of Wildlife Study Group, the American Fisheries Society, and the American Society for Public Administration.

JOHN B. LOOMIS is an assistant professor of environmental studies and agricultural economics at the University of California at Davis. He has published articles in the area of resource economics in *Land Economics, Journal of Environmental Management*, and *Journal of Leisure Research*. He has served as a resource economist with the U.S. Fish and Wildlife Service in Ft. Collins, Colorado.

STEPHEN B. LOVEJOY is an associate professor of agricultural economics at Purdue University. He received his Ph.D. in environmental sociology and political economy of natural resources from Utah State University. He has published over fifty journal articles, book chapters, and research bulletins. He specializes in interdisciplinary research especially in the area of public policy of natural resources.

WILLIAM R. MANGUN is the director of the public administration program and associate professor of political science at East Carolina University. He has written papers, articles, book chapters, and books on environmental management-related topics, including financing wildlife and outdoor recreation programs. He is the author of *The Public Administration of Environmental Policy* and the co-author of *Managing the Environmental Crisis: Incorporating Competing Values in Natural Resource Administration* (1989). He was previously employed by the U.S. Fish and Wildlife Service as the project manager for policy analysis and national surveys.

FRANCIS A. McGUIRE is an associate professor at Clemson University. His research deals with aging and leisure activity changes across the life cycle.

LLOYD G. NIGRO is a professor of political science and public administration at Georgia State University. He is the author of several texts and articles in public administration.

JOSEPH T. O'LEARY is an associate professor of forest recreation at Purdue University. His research focuses on the analysis of nationwide recreation surveys, recreation specialization, and life cycle development.

ROBERT H. PATRICK is an assistant professor of mineral economics at the Colorado School of Mines. He received his Ph.D. from the University of New Mexico in 1985. He specializes in natural resource, environmental, and energy regulation and pricing policy and has published several articles in these areas.

JAMES L. REGENS is a professor of political science and the associate director of the Institute of Natural Resources at the University of Georgia. He specializes in policy analysis, environmental regulation, and energy policy. He is the author of numerous publications, including *The Acid Rain Controversy* (1985).

WILLIAM D. RICHARDSON is an associate professor of political science at Georgia State University who has published numerous articles and a book in the area of American political thought.

JACKIE SELLERS is the associate director of the Institute of Natural Resources of the University of Georgia. Research interests include resource management and energy policy.

V. KERRY SMITH is a university distinguished professor of North Carolina State University and a university fellow at Resources for the Future. His research focuses on valuing recreation resources and other issues in resource and environmental economics. His recent works include *Measuring Water Quality Benefits* (1986), co-authored with W. H. Desvousges, and *Environmental Resources and Applied Welfare Economics* (1988), an edited volume honoring John Krutilla.

ZACHARY A. SMITH is an associate professor of political science and public administration at Northern Arizona University, where he is the director of the Masters of Public Administration Program. He has taught courses in public administration, public policy, and American politics at the University of California at Santa Barbara, Ohio University, and the University of Hawaii at Hilo. He has interests in a wide variety of natural resource and environmental problems. His work has appeared in a variety of journals, including the *Natural Resources Journal, Journal of Political Science, Publius: The Journal of Federalism, Journal of Land Use and Environmental Law* and various other law reviews. He has also authored *Groundwater Policy in the Southwest, Interest Group Interaction and Groundwater Policy Formation in the Southwest* (1985), and *Groundwater in the West* (1989).

DENNIS L. SODEN is a professor of political science at the University of Nevada, La Vegas. He earned his Ph.D. in Political Science from Washington State University. His research interests include a broad range of natural resource and environmental topics with particular interest in the public's role in the decision-making processes. He is the author of several articles on public decision making.

NICHOLAS TAYLOR is an independent consultant affiliated with Dynamics Consulting Network and a visiting research fellow in the Department of Sociology, Canterbury University, New Zealand. His research in rural sociology, rural development, and social impact assessment focuses on the social effects of New Zealand agricultural aid projects in the South Pacific and coal development and the sociology of resource communities. He is a former research officer at the Centre for Resource Management, Lincoln College, Illinois.

J. DOUGLAS WELLMAN is an associate dean in the College of Forestry, North Carolina State University. His research focuses on public administration in forest recreation and park management. He is the author of *Wildland Recreation Policy: An Introduction* (1987).

SUSAN YONTS-SHEPARD is the branch chief for congressional liaison for the U.S. Forest Service. At the time of this research, she was the national inform and involve coordinator for public affairs officer for the Idaho Panhandle National Forest.

Policy Studies Organization publications issued with Greenwood Press/Quorum Books

Federal Lands Policy
Phillip O. Foss, editor

Policy Evaluation for Local Government
Terry Busson and Philip Coulter, editors

Comparable Worth, Pay Equity, and Public Policy
Rita Mae Kelly and Jane Bayes, editors

Dimensions of Hazardous Waste Politics and Policy
Charles E. Davis and James P. Lester, editors

Small Business in a Regulated Economy: Issues and Policy Implications
Richard J. Judd, William T. Greenwood, and Fred W. Becker, editors

Rural Poverty: Special Causes and Policy Reforms
Harrell R. Rodgers, Jr., and Gregory Weiher, editors

Fundamentals of the Economic Role of Government
Warren J. Samuels, editor

Policy Through Impact Assessment: Institutionalized Analysis as a Policy Strategy
Robert V. Bartlett, editor

Biomedical Technology and Public Policy
Robert H. Blank and Miriam K. Mills, editors

Implementation and the Policy Process: Opening up the Black Box
Dennis J. Palumbo and Donald J. Calista, editors

Policy Theory and Policy Evaluation: Concepts, Knowledge, Causes, and Norms
Stuart S. Nagel, editor

Biotechnology: Assessing Social Impacts and Policy Implications
David J. Webber, editor

Public Administration and Decision-Aiding Software: Improving Procedure and Substance
Stuart S. Nagel, editor